The Gifted Child, the Family, and the Community

The American Association for Gifted Children

Edited by
Bernard S. Miller *and* Merle Price

Walker and Company
New York

The Gifted Child, the Family
and the Community
Bernard S. Miller and Merle Price, eds.

The editors wish to thank the following for permission to reprint previously published material:

Sunshine Press, for "Recognizing the Gifted Child," by Willard Abraham, one of a continuing series of articles for parents of young children.

The Council for Exceptional Children for "Recognizing Creative Behavior," by Felice Kaufmann, from pp. 11-20 of her book *Your Gifted Child and You.*

"The Underachieving Gifted Child," by Willard Abraham, is taken from *Focus on Guidance* (now *Counseling and Human Development*) 9 (1). September 1976. Reprinted by permission of Love Publishing Company, Denver.

First published in the United States of America
in 1981 by the Walker Publishing Company, Inc.

Published simultaneously in Canada
by Beaverbooks, Limited, Don Mills, Ontario.

ISBN: 0-8027-0673-8

Library of Congress Cataloging in Publication Data
Main entry under title:

The Gifted child, the family, and the community.

Bibliography: p.
Includes index.
1. Gifted children—Addresses, essays, lectures.
2. Gifted children—Family relationships—Addresses,
essays, lectures.   3. Gifted children—Education—
Addresses, essays, lectures.   I. Miller, Bernard S.
II. Price, Merle E.   III. American Association for
Gifted Children.
HQ773.5.G54   1981   371.95   80-54485
ISBN 0-8027-0673-8   AACR2

The American Association for Gifted Children
15 Gramercy Park
New York, N.Y. 10003

Printed in the United States of America

10   9   8   7   6   5   4   3   2

Contents

Acknowledgments

All of us associated with the preparation of this book dedicate it to gifted children the world over and to the adults who nurture their gifts.

While it is impossible to acknowledge all the good people whose efforts are responsible for this project, several individuals warrant special mention. I have had the great benefit of having Merle Price as co-editor, the astute guidance of Marjorie Craig, vice-president and executive director of the American Association for Gifted Children, and the collaborative assistance of Gail Robinson in lightening burdens for everyone. Phyllis Harris rendered valuable service with the initial outline of the book. Richard Winslow and Ruth Cavin of Walker and Company were most helpful in offering suggestions that kept us on our major focus — a book for adults who live and work with gifted children. I am also indebted to Anna Galschjodt, Rosanne Fimiani, and Lillian Caprara at the Hunter College Campus Schools for helping type material long after working hours, as well as Stacey Riddell of the American Association for Gifted Children.

Continuing the pattern of partnership in our happily married lives, my wife, Betty Cottin Miller, gave me unending support and encouragement on the basis of her professional skills as an educator and her special understanding of my wants and needs. Her own essay in this book is particularly appreciated, as is the joy of being together for more than three decades.

Finally, a long, deep bow to all the generous contributors who gave gladly of their time and talents and accepted the editors' cuts so that the book could meet publishing requirements. If their contributions do not provide all the answers for parents and educators who are living and working with gifted youngsters, they do raise and answer most of the right questions. To all these kind people, my warmest expression of thanks.

Bernard S. Miller

Note: The authors' and editors' affiliations are listed as of the time of preparation of this work.

Preface

"Of course my child is special," you declare. And you add, after a brief hesitation, "But then I suppose we all think our children are unique in some way or other. But gifted? I mean, I couldn't recognize a gifted child if I saw one. Sure, I've heard of gifted children, but do you really think one of mine might be? How would I know?"

There are many signs. For example, does your child seem more curious and demanding than other children? Does he learn more rapidly? Is she unusually creative and imaginative? Does he become more totally absorbed in what he is doing? Does she display a greater readiness with words or numbers or musical phrases? Does he have a particular facility with his hands? His body? If the child manifests any or all of these symptoms, it may well be that he or she is gifted and/or talented.

"Well," you respond, frowning slightly, "it seems to me that children with abilities like the ones you mention can probably take care of themselves. I don't see where I could do much good."

Such an attitude goes some distance toward explaining why gifted and talented children are our most neglected minority. It should never be forgotten that though children may be gifted, they are still *children.* They need love and understanding if they are to be well adjusted and fully realized human beings. First and foremost, of course, they must have the love, understanding, and support of their parents and families. Then they need the encouragement of their teachers and the community. But because the gifted and talented are such truly special people, they require special recognition and appreciation. Their needs must be answered with enlightened responses and sustained caring from those to whom they turn for guidance. To deny them such attention is to turn our backs on our greatest natural resource, for from the ranks of the gifted and talented should emerge, it is to be hoped, our future leaders in the arts, the sciences, in business, industry, and government.

Because so many parents have appealed for advice in dealing with their gifted and talented children, the American Association for Gifted Children has developed this book. It is written, however, not for parents alone, but for teachers and librarians and community leaders and

vii

for all those who can in various ways offer nourishment to these children. The nurture we provide them now can be our important contribution to the fulfillment of their promise. Through our commitment to these exceptional children we prepare the way for a richer tomorrow.

Foreword
Who Are the Gifted?

Nicholas Hobbs

How does one recognize a gifted child?

It is not easy, for gifted kids come in all sizes and colors. They come from ghettos and suburbs, from all the neighborhoods of America. Giftedness is not all endowment in talent; drive is important too, as well as opportunity for the expression of one's talent.

As a general guide, good things tend to go together. Contrary to popular opinion, the gifted child is not typically frail, delicate, bespectacled, or bowed with books and burdensome thoughts, although he or she may be, for there is no set pattern, only general trends. Generally, gifted children, boys or girls, may be taller, heavier, and healthier than average children. They may have a wider range of interests, and their moral and ethical values may be on a different level from those of an unselected group of children. Often they are voracious readers.

But it is really not as simple as all that. Although positive traits tend to go together, there are always great individual differences. There are gifted kids who are scrawny, myopic, and mean. People who are gifted are nonetheless capable of inflicting harm and pain on themselves and on society.

All the more reason why as a society we cannot afford to overlook giftedness wherever it may occur, among children of all backgrounds and circumstances.

If young people are both gifted and productive, solid and zestful achievers, they are likely to have come from a family that communicates, that shares enthusiastic commitments to shared enterprises. Such young people are often remarkably well organized and goal directed.

Nicholas Hobbs, Ph.D., is director of the Center for the Study of Families and Children at Vanderbilt University, Nashville, Tenn.

Their commitment to some pursuit is thorough, and they husband their time for their own private purposes. They are passionate about learning, about filmmaking, intellectual games, Mozart, Chinese history, lasers, and ferns of the region. The adults' pleasant task is to identify and to provide sources of information to further well-defined, self-designed projects. Such gifted young people are a joy, though often regarded by their peers as somewhat unusual because of the range and depth of their engagements.

Considerably less fortunate and even more challenging are the potentially gifted and productive young people who grow up in economically impoverished environments. Early deprivation of opportunity to learn may be irreversible. Many a potentially gifted person fails to develop for lack of stimulation, lack of people to emulate, lack of opportunity to acquire motivations essential to success: love of books, persistence, the ability to delay gratification. The most promising means of reaching deprived children early is through their parents. Parents from deprived circumstances generally wish to help their children succeed but are unaware of how to do it.

Gifted children can create problems for themselves and often do. It is not easy to manage knowing twice as much math as one's ninth-grade teacher or to have read more than the librarian who earnestly wishes to help. A special grace is required of both children and adults. Gifted children can be extraordinarily difficult, stretching the patience and the skill of us all. Meeting the challenge of raising and teaching gifted children can be frightening, but it can also be enormously rewarding.

1 THE GIFTED CHILD

Bright Child—Laura Tuchman

A brightening sight before the age of seven,
A mind but turning in a swifter cycle,
Which rises as its own ideas' disciple;
What strange unbidden gift are the gifted given?

A sharpening sight, potential depth of vision;
Acceptance of a thought, of quick reacting
To problems' challenge; questions are for asking;
Thinking, expands enough for each revision.

Juxtaposing unlined mind and wisdom,
And promising a scholar's future brilliance;
How difficult to describe the thoughts' resilience,
And name a gift defying definition.

Age 17
Hunter College High School
New York

1

Gifted Children and Their Families

Bernard S. Miller

"Our three-year-old daughter has already learned to read without any encouragement from us. Friends say she is extremely bright and needs special attention or she will not have a normal, happy childhood. Please help . . ."

"What can we do with a precocious nine-year-old son who drives me crazy with endless questions about everything under, on, and over the sun?"

"Our teenager seems to have no friends in school. He is teased and called a 'brain' by his classmates. His teachers tell me that he alternately shows off by shouting out answers and refuses to pay attention."

"She is bold, self-willed, and her curiosity knows no bounds. I sometimes feel she is raising me. From daybreak to bedtime she is superactive. Our first child seems to have been spun from angel cloth and is rather ethereal. This little minx seems to have sprung from the loins of a desert Gypsy. How can I be a super mom to an intellectually super child and the same time be a normal mom to our intellectually normal daughter?"

These and related questions come daily to my office at Hunter College and to the schools of colleagues across the country where special

Bernard S. Miller is a professor at Hunter College, City University of New York, and director of the Hunter College Campus Schools for Gifted and Talented Children in New York City. He has served as associate director of the John Hay Fellows Program in the Humanities, sponsored by the Ford and Whitney Foundations and, with his wife, Betty Cottin Miller, has conducted a series of summer institutes in the humanities at Bennington College, Colorado College, and the University of Oregon. Dr. Miller has also been executive associate of Harvard president James B. Conant in his Study of American Education.

attention is paid to gifted and talented children. The parents are anxious to understand how to help their youngsters. In recent years the number of such requests has multiplied both from parents and from educators faced with a gifted child in a classroom with average-ability classmates.

TO BE GIFTED AND TALENTED— SOME DEFINITIONS

What do we mean when we say that a child is gifted? Standard dictionary definitions leave much to be desired. We are told in Webster's New World Dictionary that the gifted are those "having a natural ability or aptitude; talented."[1] Such an explanation could imply that giftedness cannot be acquired, that giftedness is a divine endowment gracing select individuals. Indeed, as will be detailed in subsequent chapters, we have no foolproof evidence to substantiate any hypothesis as to why some children are born with special gifts and talents. From the great dialogues of Plato on the teaching of wisdom and virtue to the current controversy on genetic versus environmental influences on "intelligence," we have failed to document definitively why giftedness and talent are hallmarks of some people and not others.

Whatever is dimly understood is often ignored. As we shall see, few groups in our society have received shorter shrift than gifted and talented children. Although the question of why we have gifted and talented people cannot be fully reconciled, we can reach some agreement as to their identification. In 1972 the U.S. Office of Education formulated the following broadly based working definition to identify the gifted and talented:

> Gifted and talented children are those identified by professionally qualified persons who by nature of outstanding abilities, are capable of high performance. These are the children who require differentiated educational programs and/or services beyond those normally provided by the regular school program in order to realize their contributions to self and society.
>
> Children capable of high performance include those with demonstrated achievement and/or potential ability in any of the following areas, singly or in combination:
>
> 1. general intellectual ability
> 2. specific academic aptitude
> 3. leadership ability
> 4. visual and performing arts
> 5. creative or productive thinking
> 6. psychomotor ability.[2]

Several organizations seriously question the USOE's definition of the gifted and talented. The Council for Basic Education, for example, objects to the inclusion of physical skills and leadership, preferring instead to emphasize academic mastery.[3]

A number of agencies representing minority populations fear that differentiated educational programs for the gifted and talented may serve to resegregate previously integrated classes. On the other hand, psychologist Jacob Getzels prefers that the concept of giftedness be broadened even more than the USOE's definition. Getzels wishes to add "talent for mechanical achievement, talent for expressive achievement, talent for social achievement, talent for altruistic achievement . . ."[4] For the sake of clarity and brevity, we have accepted the definition of gifted and talented as set forth by Dr. Paul Witty, one of the early members of the American Association for Gifted Children. To Dr. Witty *a gifted and talented child is "one whose performance in a potentially valuable line of human activity is consistently remarkable."*

THE IQ PANACEA

Some educators cling to the administration of intelligence or aptitude tests as the single determinator of talent. A child's intelligence quotient, alas, is all too simplistic a measure of talent. The IQ is neither a totally consistent nor a totally sound indicator of intelligence. Think of the fantastic apprehension four-, five- and six-year-old children must face when they are taken to an unfamiliar center to determine their intelligence rating. The parent or parents may try to mask their own concern by making light of the experience, in which case the child may be so relaxed that he or she will refuse to try very hard to solve the test problems. When a child comes to the test all fired with resolve and seriousness by their parents, errors in judgment caused by tension frequently occur, which lower the test scores. Sometimes the youngster is ill or has had a bad sleep or a disagreement with a sibling or feels cold or hot or just out of sorts at the moment. All these feelings could be reflected in the eventual IQ score that is placed on a child. The examiner may seem too harsh, too old, too young, too much like an unfavored relative, too aloof, or too folksy to the child, and again the test score could change considerably. And if the child has trouble hearing, has eye problems, or is guarded because the examiner speaks with a different accent or has different coloration, a true test score will not occur. And beyond the human dimensions and limitations are the questions one must raise concerning the soundness and dependability of the test itself. Furthermore, there are a countless number of young people whose talents for excellence and creativity in music, dance, the arts, and creative writing, to mention but four areas, are not discovered by test scores but by performance.

One need not be a testing expert to recognize that something is ridiculous when one hour of testing for an IQ can determine a child's whole future in terms of school admission! We have witnessed IQ scores of 155 at age three drop to 120 when the same child was retested at age four. The reverse progression is also possible. Giftedness encompasses far more than a numerical score. A wise counselor has suggested that a child's GQ, the gumption quotient, is a more reliable indicator of functional ability and future success than the IQ.

The wisdom of this suggestion has been documented by Stanford University Professor Lewis Terman's monumental study of three hundred intellectually gifted students whose careers were followed long after they graduated from high school. Here is Professor Terman's explanation for the success of some gifted adults and the lesser achievement of others who were equally gifted:

> personality factors are extremely important determiners of achievement. . . . The four traits on which (they) differed most widely were persistence in the accomplishment of ends, integration toward goals, self-confidence, and freedom from inferiority feelings. In the total picture the greatest contrast between the two groups was in all-round emotional and social adjustment and in drive to achieve.[5]

We have had many revolutions in technology and in governments since Terman made his studies of the gifted youth back in 1920. But his finding that "the drive to achieve" explains in large measure the success of some bright people and the relative failure of others is as true for the 1980s as it was more than a half century ago.

THE UNIDENTIFIED AND NEGLECTED GIFTED

With good reason, some parents will dispute the contention of the U.S. Office of Education that a "professionally qualified person" determine whether their children are gifted and talented. The list of universally recognized talented people whose gifts were not identified by the professionals in their youth is distressingly long. Winston Churchill, Thomas Edison, Albert Einstein, Emily Dickinson, Lincoln Steffens, and Edward Gibbon, to name but a few examples, were considered undistinguished students by the professionals of their time. "Late bloomer" is the term used to describe these and other gifted people whose forward propulsion and talents were acknowledged relatively late in life. Unfortunately, for every such gifted late bloomer, there are hundreds of gifted "early wilters," who give up because they find the fight for recognition too offensive or too frustrating. As a result, they are forced to settle for a life of mediocrity.

The U.S. Office of Education estimates that out of a total elementary and secondary school population of 52 million, the gifted and talented constitute approximately 5 percent, or 2.6 million. Unfortunately, the overwhelming majority of these children are presently neither adequately identified nor nurtured in their homes, their communities, or their schools. Most parents of gifted children are totally unaware that their youngsters have the potential to perform outstandingly in an area important to human endeavor.

Fortunately pressures from several advocacy groups promise to make the 1980s a decade in which the U.S. Congress will provide more adequate funding for bright youngsters. But as recently as 1972, U.S. Commissioner of Education Sidney Marland, Jr., reported that the gifted and talented were of no great concern to the federal, state, and most local education agencies. As a result, he informed Congress that the gifted and talented "are, in fact, deprived and suffer psychological damage and permanent impairment of their abilities to function" because of this neglect.[6] Indeed, when gifted children did dare to assert their talents, they often suffered hostility or apathy and were afflicted with the same kinds of self-doubts that are recognized in other mistreated minority children. When classmates treated talented youngsters with teasing, ridicule, and social ostracism, the intellectually gifted students learned early in life how to keep their intelligence firmly in check. Intellectual potential, however, is like a delicate flower; it cannot survive neglect.

Why have our gifted and talented people been served so poorly in our American society? One explanation will be found by noting the conscious restrictions we place on the gifted in the name of democracy. To too many people democracy means that if you see a person's head above the rest, you knock it down. When special provisions are suggested to meet the special needs and opportunities of our gifted and talented pupils, such ideas are attacked by those favoring equal education for everyone as being in violation of our fundamental egalitarian traditions. Yet it is interesting to note that Thomas Jefferson felt no conflict with his concept of democracy when he advocated "the selection of the youths of genius from among the classes of the poor," for a free, special education. Said Jefferson, "We hope to avail the State of those talents which nature has sown as liberally among the poor as the rich, but which *perish without use, if not sought for and cultivated.*"[7]

MYTHS ABOUT THE GIFTED

Often, too often, we hear parents with a gifted child lament that they would have preferred a "normal" youngster. Such parents have been led to believe terrible tales about gifted and talented children — that they are unhappy, difficult people who do not or cannot communicate with others, who are physically weak, socially inept, read too many books, and wear glasses. In fact, research studies indicate that the opposite is true. Gifted and talented children tend to be more physically active; they are socially better adjusted and less nervous than their intellectually average counterparts. Another popular myth that does not square with reality is that gifted children "ripen early and rot early." When properly identified and nurtured, gifted children lead adult lives of tremendous consequence both for themselves and for society. Actually, in most areas of life, gifted children are indistinguishable from their "normal" peers. But in some crucially important dimensions of growth there are differences. Gifted children do ask more complex questions, do demonstrate a creative drive; they are curious, they enjoy associating with adults, they love to learn.

Problems can and do occur when parents and educators, out of ignorance or stubbornness, restrict gifted children within a straitjacket pattern of conduct and a traditional curriculum. As a nation and as a people we talk a great deal about individual rights. We mouth the Jeffersonian ideal of "calling from every condition of our people the natural aristocracy of talents and virtue and of preparing it by education at the public expense for the care of the public concerns."[8] But practice does not conform to theory, no matter how elegantly stated by honored people. We cater far more to the bandwagon approach in schooling and in life. We join the crowd and march in community and educational lockstep with those around us.

Of course it is simpler to follow a uniform model when dealing with children. And so we prefer to establish the same rules for everyone. In this atmosphere, recognizing and teaching youngsters based on individual differences becomes a noble concept to be obeyed as long as the individuals conform to the mores of the mass. When gifted and talented individuals face the inevitable frustrations of patterned uniformity, the alternatives they take sometimes do cause parents and educators to wish they could deal with more tractable, more manageable children.

The sad fact of life is that most gifted and talented youngsters, in their understandable desire to associate with their age peers and not be isolated, do settle for social acceptance over intellectual independence. They learn to wear a protective blinder on their thoughts and to keep the probing questions within themselves. Only the rare parent or the rare teacher will challenge the child to be better than average. Lorraine Hansberry described such a teacher in her Pulitzer Prize-winning play *To Be Young, Gifted, and Black:*

> *Teacher* (with an Irish brogue: severely but pungently) 'Tis true the English have done little enough with the tongue, but being the English I expect it was the best that they could do. In any case, I'll

have it learned properly before a living one of y'll pass out of this class! That I will! As for you — surely you will recognize the third letter of the alphabet when y' have seen it?'

1st Actress (terrified) "C"

Teacher Aye, a "C" it 'tis! And now, my brilliance — would you also be informing us as to what a grade signifies when it is thus put upon the page?

1st Actress Average.

Teacher "Average." Yes, yes — and what else in your case, iridescence? Well then, I'll be tellin' you in fine order. It stands for cheat, my luminous one! For them that will do *half* when *all* is called for. For them that will slip and slide through life at the edge of their minds, never once pushing into the interior to see what wonders are hiding there! Content to drift along with whatever gets them by, *cheating* themselves, *cheating* the world, *cheating* Nature.[9]

Most talented children learn "to drift along" and hide their abilities because their parents and teachers have accepted such procedures as proper. Furthermore, there is no need to pressure the gifted or to spend time and money on them, so goes the fiction, because these people can take care of themselves. By the very nature of their abilities, they will eventually excel in whatever profession they enter. Those who favor this position compare the gifted to a drop of oil in a bucket of water. No matter how we mix the ingredients, the oil will always rise to the top.

Sociologist Bruno Bettelheim has voiced a similar view by citing the way the cream in a container of unhomogenized milk will move to the highest level no matter how the contents are turned. But a young gifted student, after hearing Bettelheim's argument, replied that if the cream is left without care, it will soon turn sour. The potentialities of a gifted child if left without care can also turn sour. Potentialities that are not identified, respected, and nurtured will atrophy. Parents who ask where the wonder went in their gifted children will find a partial answer in society's failure to inspire and encourage thinking. As a result many young people with talent are destined to settle for a life of mediocrity. Those few who survive the fear, indifference, hostility, envy, and sarcasm of society toward their giftedness are sometimes able to triumph as adult leaders in their fields. But to do so involves a constant struggle against the status quo, a struggle the majority of gifted youngsters generally find not worth the battle.

Thanks to the growing awareness on the part of parents and educators that the gifted require attention, the prevailing atmosphere in our homes and in our schools is moving away from the hidebound view that everyone must be treated exactly alike. On the national, state, and local educational levels, attention in the early 1980s is beginning to focus on the identification and nurture of our gifted and talented children. Support for these children will take many forms, because giftedness is not one-dimensional. Abstract reasoning; depth perception; physical stamina; special talent in music, art, or dance; leadership ability; empathy skills; creativity; and constructive divergent thinking are all areas in which one can perform outstandingly and be recognized as gifted. As parents and as educators we must become more sensitized to the special needs and opportunities for our gifted and talented children, or the prospective financial and moral support from federal and local sources will prove illusory.

THE GIFTED—FROM GESTATION TO FORMAL EDUCATION

Although many parents and educators claim they can intuitively identify the sparks of giftedness in a child, research efforts in this regard have been sporadic and spotty. All sorts of lists have been published in popular and educational magazines, and in this book we have also presented, in chapter 2, a collection of characteristics which help identify the gifted and talented. But we would be naïve to claim that any list or combination of traits is guaranteed to pinpoint any and/or all gifted youngsters. At best these lists serve as initial guidelines, as benchmarks to alert people that further exploration and attention to the child is in order.

Of course there are always people who thrive on superstition and claim special forecasting ability. Some pregnant mothers believe that their frequent attendance at an art museum or music concert will motivate their child to favor an artistic or musical career. We do know that the fetal brain can be damaged by drugs and other stimuli taken by pregnant mothers. One can also understand why in homes where the parents love and play music as a way of life, the child may become interested in music at an early age. But by no means do all children automatically reflect their home environments! Some children of doctors become farmers; some children of farmers become doctors. We are still many, many years away from the realization of the prediction that desirable hereditary traits can be transmitted to offspring by either some form of genetic engineering or by environmental exposure.

Giftedness is a monopoly neither of heredity nor of the environment. Nor do we find the gifted exclusively in any race, religion, sex, or national or regional grouping. Being born to a wealthy family does not guarantee wisdom in the sciences, in art, in history, in leadership ability, or in anything else. Giftedness comes individually wrapped in a variety of packages to diverse human beings. Gifted children, as defined in this book, occur in about the same numbers in all socioeconomic groups. While it is undoubtedly true that far more gifted youngsters have been identified from upper-income professional families than from the families of the economically poor, the discrepancy has far more to do with the comparative effort made by both groups of parents to seek such information about their children and the kinds of schools attended than with inherited differences. At the Hunter College Elementary and Secondary schools, for example, nearly 40 percent of the more than 1,600 students in these academically demanding laboratory schools for the gifted are minority youngsters who live in disadvantaged environments. More than 75 percent of these special-admission students are able to master the school's demanding program of studies. When these students graduate, they are eagerly sought by the most prestigious colleges and universities in the nation. Affirmative action programs in schools and colleges across the country have led to the discovery of thousands of potentially gifted students from poverty backgrounds. Giftedness is not a monopoly of the rich and the well born.

We do know that preciously few children or adults have ever developed their talents to their full genetic potential. We know, too, that the child of a recognized genius can be mentally retarded and that an intellectually superior child can be born to intellectually average or retarded parents. We know most of all that far too little is done to discover and develop our gifted children from all backgrounds. The urgency for scholarly studies to provide more precise knowledge in determining how much a person's giftedness and talents come from heredity and how much can be attributed to environmental factors – and then to act on such findings – is all too obvious.

Research has shown that once a child is born, the subsequent psychological and motor development in the first months and years of growth is influenced considerably by the way the parents feel and act toward their child. Dr. T. Berry Brazelton, a pediatrician affiliated with the Harvard Medical School, is convinced that a baby's self-image is affected at a very young age by the parents' confidence in themselves. In one study Dr. Brazelton explained to a group of parents how they might cater to the normal needs of their newborn children and encouraged the parents to spend time watching and playing with them. He then compared the results with a control group of parents who saw and fed their infants with no encouragement to think of them as needing any special attention. After two years his research revealed that the children in the first group ``knew more words and used them more inventively, in sentences, than the control babies. They also explored their environment more, pointed out more objects, and played with toys in more complex ways, talking all the while."[10]

Similar studies have confirmed the belief that cognitive development during a child's earliest years can be accelerated by stimulating a desire and curiosity to learn. The Educational Testing Service, in a significant study on the growth of intellect among infants, concludes that "infants who are provided with more home environmental stimulation (i.e., reading, talking, playing) habituate faster to test stimuli. They appear to be more intellectually alive."[11]

Children wish to please those responsible for their food and comfort. Parents, or others in charge of a child's nurturing, should capitalize on the child's urge to show appreciation. Children can be encouraged and supported when they grope for new words to express themselves, new toys to examine, new sights and relationships to comprehend. For a child, such changes are a struggle. But the struggle is worthwhile when a child's favored adults reinforce such learning with a demonstration of love and approval. One would be naïve today to believe that the habits, fears, and prejudices of adults are not transmitted to children. To restate an old cliché, the fruit does not fall far from the tree. Rodgers and Hammerstein captured the power of adults over children in the award-winning Broadway show *South Pacific* in which the American explains to his Asiatic sweetheart why their race differences would abort a happy marriage, because before people are eight, they are taught to hate.

We are what we become accustomed to accept. If we wish to have our talented children develop a sense of values and character consistent with our beliefs and with the announced goals of our nation, it is essential to have a quantity of it ourselves. U.S. Senator Jacob Javits, a prime supporter of federal funding on behalf of the gifted and talented, reminded his audience in a talk at the Council for Exceptional Children that educating for high intelligence alone is not enough:

> I hope that all of us will work to provide opportunities for our gifted children to develop their capacities for love, empathy, and communication. . . . Without the development of these neglected traits, the brightest individual is greatly handicapped and much potential is lost.[12]

THE SUBORDINATION OF TALENTED FEMALES

Intellectually gifted and talented females are among the most subordinated, the most underachieving group of people in virtually every society on this planet. In some regions and cultures in southern Europe, in most of Asia, and even in "enlightened" areas in Great Britain and the United States, it is normal for talented women to be respected as "ladies." They are taught, carefully taught, almost from their first breath at birth, not to compete with men in the professions and not to demonstrate their true talents if they wish to retain male companionships. These lessons are learned all too well by women.

In Shakespeare's *King Lear* we learn that Cordelia's

> . . . voice was ever soft,
> Gentle and low, an excellent thing in woman.

Throughout the ages those who control and set the standards of a society have measured a woman's worth in her voice, her beauty, her loyalty, her male offsprings — never in her intelligence. For example, societies have stacked the deck of expectations to discourage girls from approaching the study of mathematics with the same competitive challenge we offer boys. Interestingly, until the beginning of adolescence, boys and girls do equally well in handling mathematics. After the fifth grade, however, and continuing progressively through advanced mathematics in secondary school, gifted and talented boys outdistance gifted and talented girls. We know that there is no genetic basis for this dichotomy. We must conclude that the conscious and unconscious prejudices of parents and teachers motivate boys — but not girls — to work with numbers.

Girls, like boys, need models of success in mathematics. When mothers tell their children to go to father for help with algebra because "I never could understand arithmetic," both daughter and son are learning a pattern of behavior. When teachers turn to boys in the class to answer the tough mathematics problems, when counselors convince girls that majoring in mathematics would be too competitive, other lessons of lowered expectations are learned. With rare exceptions, the typical advanced mathematics and physics classes in U.S. secondary schools will have a ratio of from two to ten boys to every girl.

But there is hope! Harlan P. Hanson, head of the College Board Advanced Placement Program, has reported that for the past several years high school enrollment for both the chemistry and calculus college-level tests has seen "a strengthening of female participation by a percent or two of the total." We are still far from reaching a balance in male-female enrollment. In chemistry for 1979 the AP-test enrollment was 5,306 males to 1,710 females; in calculus it was 16,798 males to 7,929 females; in physics 4,437 males to 602 females. Nonetheless, progress is being made. In this connection I strongly advise concerned parents and educators to write to the College Board in New York City for a copy of an excellent essay by Patricia Lund Casserly entitled "Helping Able Young Women Take Math and Science Seriously in School."

The list of female underrepresentation is endless. One has only to examine the percentage of the society's female doctors, dentists, professors, musicians, business executives, bankers, government legislators, executives, judges, accountants, shop stewards, and brokers to know that the talents of women are not being tapped. Simone de Beauvoir, in her book *The Second Sex,* states,

> To tell the truth, one is not born a genius, one becomes a genius, and the feminine situation has, up to the present, rendered the becoming practically impossible.[13]

The May 26, 1978, issue of the *American Medical Journal* reported that male and female medical students performed in a comparable manner when evaluated. Most assumptions about intellectual and emotional differences between the sexes, states the report, "are not only unfounded but are simply myths unsupported by facts. Whether one looks at general intelligence, creativity, cognitive style, or sociability, love, empathy, emotionality, dependence, and nurturance, the competing sexes show far more similarities than any questionable and overlapping differences." Nonetheless, only 23 percent of U.S. medical school graduates in 1979 were women. Happily this percentage may be a promising augury for the future, because the percentage of women graduating from medical schools in 1960 was less than 6 percent, whereas in 1970 it was just 8.4 percent.

In homes where parents really believe their daughters deserve the same opportunities as their sons, in schools and in communities where models of female excellence are evident, girls are increasingly being encouraged to move ahead despite the constraints of society. But in the main, as detailed in Part V, gifted females either have not been made aware of their talents to compete with men or they have learned to sublimate these talents in order to remain in the mainstream of a male-dominated society. One female summed up her dilemma by observing, "How can we compete with men when we are expected always to be competing for them?" The statistics cited earlier indicate that in at least one of the professions women are more willing to face this competition than was the situation just a few years ago.

THE DELICATE ART OF PARENTING

All children need understanding parents or other adults with whom to communicate. For children who have the touch of talent and giftedness, the level of understanding will determine whether they develop their endowments or settle for anonymity and mediocrity. As part of the painful, wonderful period of growing up, children will alternately cherish and recoil from adult contacts. A poignant poem written for an English assignment by a teenager conveys the ambivalent need youngsters feel to relate, to be loved, and to be themselves:

> Hi, Mama, it's good to see you again.
> It's been some time. I've missed you so. I remember
> the many lonely hours spent at home.
> Can you see how much I've changed?
> I'm not that little girl you used to know!
>
> Oh, Mama, I'm a woman
> and
> I know what love is for.
> Oh, Mama, how I need you
> But I'm not a little girl anymore.[14]

The stereotyped view of family life in which the father leaves for work each day and the mother remains home contentedly with the children is rapidly becoming an anachronism. Someone has observed that home has become a building where people who are biologically related come together, often by accident, as when there is a blizzard. Sociologist David Reisman has pointed out that young people today direct their lives not with a gyroscope of their parents toward a given point ahead, but with radar that flips them back and forth according to the pull of majority taste and opinion.

Here are some interesting statistics:

- More than 50 percent of married women are now full-time wage earners.
- As many as four children out of ten born in the 1970s will spend part of their childhood in a single-parent family.
- Thirty-eight percent of all first marriages fail.
- The average age for menstruation to begin today is eleven or twelve.
- One in ten teenagers will become pregnant this year.
- Fifteen percent of all births are illegitimate.
- Only one out of ten teenage girls in the United States today will not have had sexual intercourse before she turns twenty.[15]

PARENTS AS MODELS

What do these startling statistics mean for the parents and educators living and working with gifted children? Adults cannot prepare these bright children for the kind of world they experienced in their own youth. A remorseful parent observed recently that in her youth children were obligated to please their parents. Today parents feel obligated to please their children. Actually, almost by definition, gifted children can be expected to challenge the values accepted by their parents. After much debate and challenge they may discover that their own value structures are not really so far removed from those of their parents. But debate and challenge there must be, for this intellectual and emotional dueling with parents is one of the testing grounds through which young people sharpen their thinking. And as we have noted, a sharpness of thinking, an inquiring mind and endless rounds of questions are precisely the characteristics that so often distinguish a gifted and talented youngster from an average boy or girl. Because the gifted do question more and do understand more, they are less willing to accept adult explanations that are based on force, age, or lack of logic, such as "Do it because I say so!".

Civilization, in the main, is a system of restraints. Some restraints, like laws, can be forced upon us. Other restraints, such as the concept of honor, are voluntary principles we obey because they appeal to our conscience. These voluntary principles children learn to internalize by emulating the adult models around them. Parents and educators must reinforce the positive ego feelings of gifted children so that they will be encouraged to reach for what adults believe should be grasped. "To know that others believe in them," said Supreme Court Justice Louis Brandeis, "consider them capable of high thinking and doing, and are willing to help them out, . . . may enable them to accomplish more than even they think possible." Kenneth Clark, author of the popular *Civilisation* television series, understood the importance of creating an atmosphere in which his children's growth was a normal concommitant of living. His daughter, Colette, the first woman to be a director of the Covent Garden Theatre in London, recalls that when she and her brother were young, their father never talked down to them.

> "It was always as if we were as intelligent as he was. The effect was to make you clever without realizing it. He always insisted that you have to learn taste — you are not born with it."[16]

Kenneth Clark's children had the benefit of educated parents who encouraged them to learn. Although the struggle is clearly more intense, parents living in poverty areas can also instill a respect for learning in their children. For example, in 1977 William Raspberry, a feature columnist for the *Washington Post,* studied why a number of children who lived in the slum areas of Washington, D.C., managed to make excellent school grades. His conclusion:

> Their families made them understand from the beginning that poverty is a circumstance, like the weather, not a definition of who they are and what they may become. They may be as much victimized by pov-

erty and racism as their neighbors; but they don't dwell on their vic-
timization. They are required from their earliest years to meet high
standards and, as a result, come to set high standards for themselves.
And they are loved.[17]

THE GIFTED IN OUR SCHOOLS

As gifted children move from the home to the school, the shared
intimacies with their parents inevitably fade. Parents learn that they
know and do not know their children. The outside world is sometimes
a formidable rival to the influences and values of the home. When such
situations arise, fortunate is the family that offers gifted children other
adults with whom their momentary truths and their intellectual growth
can be shared and channeled. Our schools should be one such setting
for student-teacher communication. Unfortunately statistical surveys by
the U.S. Office of Education, as well as the results of my own questioning of educators, reveal that not enough progress in meeting the needs
of gifted children has been made in most schools where gifted children
are educated.

It has been said that society determines our status and the educational
system perpetuates it. When Alexis de Tocqueville toured our nation
more that 150 years ago, he remarked that a middle standard was fixed
in America for human knowledge. "All approach as near as they can,
some as they rise, others as they descend."[18] By the middle standard,
de Tocqueville referred to the pattern whereby American people
wished to belong to accepted groups in society and schools directed
their curricula content toward the middle level of intellectual mastery.
This middle standard, still the dominant feature of our schools and our
society, leaves little room for the independent thinking of the gifted and
talented. When we find gifted and talented children, instead of treating
them like flames to be fed, we smother their spirit in order to force
conformity. Not enough schools see the education of gifted children as
representing an attempt to furnish equal opportunity to unequal individuals. Actually nothing is more unequal than the equal treatment of
unequal children.

GROUPING BY ABILITY

Giftedness comes in a variety of packages — all individually wrapped.
In our increasingly complex twentieth-century civilization, few indeed
are the renaissance individuals who possess a natural ability to master
every fact of living. How do teachers feel about the broad spectrum of
ability levels in their classes? A National Education Association teacher

opinion poll revealed that nearly 80 percent of the teaching profession preferred to teach separated average-, high-, or low-ability groups as against teaching mixed groups. The most vociferous objection to ability grouping among teachers came from those who were assigned only classes for students with the poorest retention rates. Unfortunately the dogma in too many schools is to honor those teachers who teach honor students and to show less regard for teachers who deal with slow learners. Teachers of the slower learners often resent their lowly position on the academic totem pole. On the other hand, in schools where all learning and all students are important, all class assignments have equal dignity.

One wonders why the critics of ability grouping of gifted students feel that such a separation is undemocratic. No comparable complaint is aired when schools separate students for remedial reading, speech correction, music, art, drama, vocational programs, and varsity athletics. Can you imagine a football coach offering to place a mediocre quarterback on the team in the name of democracy? How many drama teachers would willingly substitute an untalented actor for a talented one? Nor is there any objection when gifted students, by self-selection, enroll in advanced foreign language, physics, and electronics classes or in the school orchestra. Only when classes for the gifted are based on the accumulated evidence of grades, testing, teacher judgments, and anecdotal records do we hear that the procedure is alien to our democratic traditions. Definitions that interpret democracy as a conformity cult should be recognized as being totally alien to the pursuit of educational excellence.

If it is reasonable to believe that learning is enhanced when students feel they are in comfortable, supportive surroundings, would not placing students in an atmosphere where they feel a kinship with their peers make sound educational sense? Does anyone really maintain that a poor student in mathematics, for example, feels any sense of security or equality when he or she is competing in a heterogeneous class with other students who grasp easily what is being taught? On the elementary level, when a teacher with mixed ability levels divides the class into "bluebirds," "robins," and "eagles," the children need not be ornithologists to understand what such divisions mean. When gifted students and slow students are placed in special separate sections, we have seen that all students benefit. New student leadership emerges in the regular classes as these students begin to look to themselves rather than to the faster students for answers. Slower students are no longer ashamed to participate in class for fear of revealing their inadequacies. Given the freedom to work at their own speed, gifted students are stimulated to go beyond the regular curriculum and to explore individual interests. On each level, minds are stretched.

Certainly at the upper end of ability levels, the students prefer to be learning with others who are their equal in ability. Here are the thoughts of gifted students who were exposed to both mixed-ability and honors classes:

> "I was usually pretty bored, and since there weren't any advanced classes, the teachers tried to give me advanced work, which never worked out because they didn't have time to explain it."

> "We used to go over everything time and time again until everyone knew it."

> "If I didn't study for a test, I'd still get 95 to 100. Now if I don't study, I'd definitely flunk."

> "We always had to wait for the dummies to catch up with what we were doing."

When people talk about being intellectually gifted in academic life, they sometimes refer to the speed in which these students can learn. Piaget's experiments in learning, as well as the common sense of common people generations ago, have led to the conclusion that children grow at different rates both physically and intellectually. One area of considerable variation is in the mastering of new ideas. Some gifted students make instant connections between what they have already understood and new complex concepts introduced by the teacher. By placing gifted students with comparable learning speeds in the same sections, teachers can eliminate the needless repetition and review that cause boredom, disinterest, and disciplinary problems. By no means, however, are all gifted children fast learners. Many gifted students take considerable time to make the necessary connections in order to comprehend an idea. Williams College English professor Fred Stocking has pointed out that in the study of English bright students often go more slowly in examining a subject because they are more thorough than average and slow students. In general, gifted students will see more, think more, say more, qualify more, and dwell more on every major issue. But it would be an error to judge academic ability solely on the basis of a student's speed in learning.

ACADEMIC TALENT AND SOCIAL COHESION

We must also reject the racist thesis that classes for the gifted will result in relegating minority groups to slow- and average-ability classes. We need instead to develop greater sensitivity and sharper measuring procedures so that the potentially gifted in all cultures, in all environments, can be identified and encouraged. Giftedness is not culture bound. Developing social cohesion of youngsters from diverse economic, religious, and racial backgrounds can be a product of homogeneous as well as heterogeneous classes. Listen once more to some observations of gifted students:

> "In my old school they always were sarcastic and called me 'brains,' but here no one does. They accept you as you are here, whether you are black, Chinese, Jewish, Indian, or Spanish."

> "The students at my previous school had never been very friendly with me, because to them I seemed very special. This doesn't mean I didn't have any friends, but the ones I did have were few and far between. They resented me because I always studied and got good marks, yet they didn't. Here the attitude is totally different. I don't stand out, I'm part of the crowd, and I like it!"

Author John Hersey has written that "an aristocracy of talent is dangerous only when it becomes self-perpetuating and dedicated to keeping out newcomers."[19] In schools where there is a conscious commitment to promote intellectual stimulation along with social cohesion, no false dichotomy need exist. When Dr. James B. Conant made his exhaustive study of the American school system back in 1957, he recommended that ability grouping be instituted subject by subject rather than have schools follow the pattern of tracking all children in the same class blocs all day.[20] Under Conant's proposal, a youngster who showed academic potential in English, for example, but was only a mediocre student in mathematics, would be placed in a fast-moving English class and in an average mathematics class with peers of comparable ability in both places. By mixing student enrollment, subject by subject, and by organizing the rest of the school — in home rooms, club activities, social functions, community, lunch, assembly, and recreation programs — so that the interrelationships of students are enhanced, the desired school spirit of cooperation and unity can be achieved without sacrificing intellectual content.

Programs for the gifted and ability grouping are no panaceas. Ability grouping must mean a change, a differentiation in curriculum content and emphasis, otherwise the instructional organization is just another Madison Avenue gimmick to fool the public into believing that significant, new learning programs have been introduced. Some years ago, in one school, previous class grades were used to divide students of social studies into three major groupings — bright, average, and slow. After the classes were organized, the teachers were told that the new arrangement offered unique opportunities to move their classes along as quickly as they could or as slowly as they must. Several weeks later, when a visit was made to one of the social studies teachers who taught all three levels, it was discovered that in each class the teacher asked the same questions, made the same assignments, and covered the same materials in the same way. Programs for the academically gifted without appropriate content and teaching methods will fail to help students grow. Research studies by E. Paul Torrance in Minnesota, Jacob Getzels and Phillip Jackson at the University of Chicago, and Lewis Terman at Stanford University, among others, testify that when appropriate curricula materials are introduced, gifted children grouped together experience a leap in their learning growth. The one thing all gifted children need is to be with each other at least some of the time during the school day. Unfortunately too many school boards, school administrators, and teacher organizations talk about special programs for the gifted only from one side of their mouths. From the other they insist that all teachers be given the same loads, the same number of preparations, the same pay, the same treatment. Teachers, like students, should not be treated like interchangeable mass-produced parts. Some teachers cannot wait to work with gifted students on a poetry unit; others dread both poetry and the challenge presented by keen minds. Some teachers are stimulated when a student with poor mathematics skills finally masters the multiplication of fractions; others have no patience for such minimal progress. Instead of providing flexible arrangements that will permit teachers to teach from their strengths to students with whom they have the greatest empathy, in many schools teachers must try to teach everything to everyone. Teachers have different talents, different approaches to learning, different effects on students. Gifted students need able teachers who enjoy teaching the gifted.

Admittedly there are some teachers who can teach a roomful of tigers, lions, and porcupines, let alone a mixed assortment of young people. They can teach almost anything. They are the virtuosos of the classroom, as rare and precious as a Beverly Sills in the world of opera, a Julie Harris in drama, an Alexander Calder in sculpting. These are the teachers, to borrow Emily Dickinson's phrase, to whom we can lift our hats. While we must treasure these teachers, in no way do they represent the faculties in the overwhelming majority of classrooms. We must carefully match teachers' talents with students' needs.

When we seek teachers for the gifted, we seek people who are themselves bright, who place less emphasis on conformity and more on the unusual in learning. Effective teachers of the gifted welcome the children who challenge them. Such teachers play with hypotheses. They prod their students along with open-minded, broad questioning rather than narrow and limited ones, questions that begin with "Why do you think . . . ?" "What if . . . ?" and "Suppose you could . . . ?" I cannot resist quoting this evaluation by a gifted third-grade Hunter student: "I found that even after the teachers explain things here, you can ask more questions."

Gifted students, indeed all students, desire teachers who know their name, who know the face that goes with the name, who know the human drama and dreams that motivate each name. All teachers must recognize that any grouping of students is still a combination of individuals. In matters of health, in terms of learning the responsibilities of being a citizen of a community and a respect for the opinions, property, and life of others, and in terms of one's honor and pride as a human being, all children have a basic commonality of needs. But gifted children, in addition, have special requirements and potential, which we neglect at the peril of the nation, as well as of the student. We must take full advantage of today's renewed recognition that educating the gifted is important. These are the national leaders of tomorrow, the future innovators, the discoverers, the human resources our country requires.

We must also continue to support programs for the gifted when the educational fashion has changed — and inevitably, change it will. No matter what the mass media proclaims is the latest educational mode, we cannot afford to neglect the gifted. Alfred North Whitehead said it well several generations ago:

> In the conditions of modern life this rule is absolute: the race which does not value trained intelligence is doomed.[21]

When our society and our educators learn to heed Whitehead's warning, being bright will become an asset rather than a handicap for gifted children.

Notes

1. *Webster's New World Dictionary of the American Language,* college ed., 1969.

2. *Education of the Gifted and Talented,* Report to the U.S. Congress by the U.S. Commissioner of Education, (Washington, D.C.: U.S. Government Printing Office March 1972), p. 2.

3. James M. Howard, Jr., ed., *Council for Basic Education Bulletin* 22, no. 2 (October 1977): 12.

4. Jane Case Williams, *Education of the Gifted and Talented: A Role for the Private Sector* (Washington, D.C.: Office of the Gifted and Talented, U.S. Office of Education, March 1974), p. 2.

5. Lewis M. Terman, *Genetic Studies of Genius: The Gifted Group at Mid-Life* (Stanford, Calif.: Stanford University Press, 1959), p. 148.

6. *Education of the Gifted and Talented,* pp. 3–4.

7. Saul K. Padover, *The Complete Jefferson* (New York: Duell, Sloan, & Pearce Company, 1943), pp. 667–70.

8. James B. Conant, *Thomas Jefferson and the Development of American Public Education* (Berkeley: University of California Press, 1962), p. 17.

9. Lorraine Hansberry, *To Be Young, Gifted, and Black* (New York: New American Library, 1970), p. 41.

10. Dr. T. Berry Brazelton, "The Newborn as Individual," *Harper's Magazine,* April 1978, pp. 47–48.

11. Dr. Michael Lewis, *Predicting the Future: Studies on the Growth of Intellect,* (Princeton, N. J.: Educational Testing Service, 1970), p. 11.

12. Harold C. Lyon, Jr., "Talent Down the Drain," *American Education* (Washington, D.C.: U.S. Dept. of Health, Education and Welfare, October 1972), p. 6.

13. Simone de Beauvoir, *The Second Sex* (New York: Modern Library, 1968), p. 173.

14. Leon Botstein, "The Children of the Lonely Crowd," *Change Magazine,* May 1978, p. 4.

15. "Saving the Family," *Newsweek,* May 15, 1978, p. 67.

16. *The New York Times,* May 3, 1978, p. 7.

17. Mary F. Berry, "The Concept of Excellence," *Phi Delta Kappan,* November 1978, p. 197.

18. Alexis de Tocqueville, *Democracy in America,* vol. 1, (New York: Knopf, 1963), p. 52.

19. John Hersey, *Intelligence, Choice & Consent* (New York: The Woodrow Wilson Foundation, 1959), p. 27.

20. James B. Conant, *The American High School Today* (New York: McGraw-Hill, 1959), p. 49.

21. Alfred North Whitehead, *The Aims of Education* (New York: Free Press, 1967).

2

Recognizing the Gifted Child

Willard Abraham

Here is a checklist that can help you to tell whether your child is gifted. It is not necessary to score high on all points, but if your youngster is strong on at least half of them, you can be quite sure he or she has considerable potential.

1. Starts to walk and talk before the so-called average child does. While still very young, demonstrates the ability to put words and phrases together meaningfully.

2. May be somewhat above average for his or her chronological age, in height, weight, physique, and physical endurance, and in specific measurements such as breadth of shoulders, muscular strength, and lung development.

3. Can win rave notices from parents by performing, though not necessarily from a captive audience of visitors! Unusual poise may be one of the first indications of giftedness in some children.

4. Demonstrates an early interest in time. Talks about yesterday-today-tomorrow, days of the week, then and now, calendars and clocks, at an early age. Shows an awareness of time relationships.

5. Has interests that are varied and spontaneous, accompanied by an intellectual curiosity that is broad and expansive.

Willard Abraham, Ph.D., has been a professor at Arizona State University since 1953 and was chairman of the Department of Special Education during most of that time. His writings include the books *Common Sense about Gifted Children, Living with Preschoolers,* and *A Time for Teaching.* He is a syndicated columnist for the Copley News Service and author of a continuing monthly series of articles for parents of young children called *Parent Talk.*

6. Often learns to read before entering school and almost always has an early desire to read.

7. Possesses reading capabilities higher than the so-called average child of the same age.

8. Collects things in an orderly manner (but not always — may actually be among the sloppy, disorderly children too!). Collections, if they are made, may include birds, stamps, chemicals, or pictures of current motion picture favorites. Often these collections are of a complicated or scientific nature.

9. Has hobbies that seem numerous and involved in comparison with other children of the same age. May have as many as three to six different hobbies.

10. Possesses an interest in games somewhat in advance of others his or her age. Shows a preference for those involving rules and system. (How about chess before you'd expect it?) May have a tendency toward occasional solitary play and work. Younger gifted children often develop imaginary playmates.

11. Often shows an understanding of meanings that seem premature for his or her age. Interpretation of current events and of international and political developments demonstrates an ability for abstract, critical, and creative thinking.

12. Shows a mature ability to express himself or herself through creative writing and oral expression and through picturesque ways of getting an idea across; both the vocabulary and content may be unusual.

13. Reacts to comments in a way that indicates a real meeting of minds. Responds quickly.

14. Learns easily, requiring fewer explanations and less repetition by the teacher than most students. May be less patient than others with meaningless drill or "busywork" assignments, often feeling that the time could be better spent.

15. Is able to adapt what has been learned to other situations; transfer of ideas comes rather easily.

16. May be impatient with and rebellious toward the more passive attitudes of others, including adults at home and in school. May prove to be a little "difficult" in this society, which is too often adjusted to the "average."

17. Is shown in some studies to be more trustworthy when under temptation to cheat, higher in honesty, higher in emotional stability, and more adaptable in social situations.

18. Usually shows his or her greater capacity through a higher achievement and mastery of school subjects. But achievement might be much lower than expected just because of boredom with the slow pace and perhaps an uninspired, unaccepting, or even threatening teacher.

19. Usually likes school and shows a desire to learn without prodding. Participates in and seems to have time for numerous extracurricular activities without letting them interfere with academic achievement.

20. Frequently chooses the more difficult school subjects for the simple reason that he or she likes them.

21. Seems to be adept in analyzing his or her own strengths and limitations objectively. An awareness of himself or herself may create unpopularity with students who are not as bright. Not recognizing the cause of this antagonism, may feel a need to withdraw or to associate chiefly with adults.

22. Has a vocabulary beyond other children of the same age or grade and uses and understands the words in reading, writing, and speaking.

23. Asks questions because he or she really ''wants to know,'' and demonstrates that fact by the later use of information acquired through verbal curiosity.

24. Shows a high degree of originality in play, work, planning, and adjustment to situations. (This may even extend to a method for cutting the grass and washing the car.)

25. Has an attention span longer than you might expect.

26. Creates jokes and laughs at the humor of others on a level more mature than his or her age indicates, often on an abstract or imaginary basis.

27. Prefers the companionship of older children, even though they may tend to reject ''a little runt among us big kids.''

28. May show unusual skill or creativity in art or music, carry a tune well at an early age, have a persistent desire to learn music, possess an unusual sense of rhythm, or show a vibrant sense of color.

29. Is less inclined to be poorly adjusted emotionally or to boast, despite his or her superiority.

30. May look much like other children and frequently act as they do — and therein lies a problem. It is so easy to overlook these gifted youngsters.

3
Our Gifted and Talented: What Are Their Needs and What Can We Do?

Ann Weiner

Studies, research projects, statistics! They tend to bore us, turn us off. They appear cold, brittle, even calculating. Yet they are the meat on the bones, the source of change and challenge. Consider what we have here, for example. Here is a seventh-grade boy with social manners that are not acceptable from a four-year-old. Here is a little girl in third grade who has no friends and loathes her teachers. Here is a boy in third grade, terrified each day as he starts for home because of an age peer who is a bully. Then there's a beautiful, mature thirteen-year-old who completed a sentence beginning ''my mother'' with '' . . . never has any time for me''; a sensitive nine-year-old who vomits and has dizzy spells when contemplating a test in school; another nine-year-old, superbly well adjusted in surface behavior, literally gutted inside with hostilities, negativism, and antisocial tendencies.

But there is more. There is Chris, who auditioned on the violin successfully for the local symphony orchestra but was rejected because there was a rule requiring that one must be at least in eighth grade. There is Matt, whose vocabulary was so limited and underdeveloped that he was failing sixth grade; and John, who being only seven and in grade two, failed to understand his teacher's enmity because he had corrected some errors she had made in spelling.

Ann Weiner, Ph.D., teaches a graduate course on the gifted child at the University of Alaska, Anchorage. She works as a consultant to gifted-child programs and sees gifted children privately to help parents make appropriate provision for their education. She is the author of numerous articles on education of the gifted.

There is nothing detached or distant about *these* facts. They relate to a group of gifted children who, with others, present the questions that concern us here: What can we learn from this group about gifted and talented children? What do these findings suggest relative to activity on their behalf both at home and in school?

For the past few years a group at the University of Alaska has been collecting information about bright children. They comprise an unselected group, brought by their parents to be "tested for giftedness." For this article we culled a group of thirty-two children with a grade-level spread of three through seven. This was done because of the uniformity of the tests that were applied.

ASSESSMENT PROCESS

The children were seen alone for sessions lasting no longer than one hour. This usually required three sessions, but in some instances, four were needed. Children, gifted or not, test very differently from one another, and some simply require more time. Without exception the children were absorbed by the testing tasks, and most proffered definite opinions as to preferences among them.

WHAT DO THESE FINDINGS SUGGEST ABOUT MEETING NEEDS AT HOME AND AT SCHOOL?

In common with other children, gifted children reflect their experiences in their academic status to some extent. Parents of young gifted children tend to spend a great deal of time assisting their children in the verbal areas. They seem to spend considerably less time with quantitative situations. Gifted children very early need to have their interest aroused in the matter of counting, numbers, number games, use and value of money, and so on. They then bring dual enthusiasms to school. Once in school, their arithmetic progress needs monitoring to be certain that the child is not becoming confused, having somehow missed a step in the sequential progress of mathematics.

Gifted children are not accustomed to being wrong and dislike intensely asking questions that may expose their ignorance. This attitude has set more than one gifted child on a path to confusion, frustration, and eventual dislike related to anything mathematical. Individual help (tutoring on a one-to-one basis) for a short time can reestablish confidence and sustain interest in mathematics.

REASONING AND PROBLEM SOLVING

Reasoning and problem solving may be successfully introduced to young children in a funtime, relaxed manner when they are very young by interested parents. In a program for the gifted in schools, this is an area probably best pursued in a small-group situation involving gifted children only, where they can operate in an atmosphere of challenge and competitive vying of wits among their intellectual peers.

We see, by a close look at this group of children, that the basic elements necessary in a gifted-child program suggest themselves. One is the need to reduce or obliterate academic-skill deficiencies. Included are mathematics, vocabulary, the latter affecting oral and written communication as well as comprehension. Because of the gifted child's embarrassments at such deficiencies, he or she tends to respond best to individualized study through a tutorial/monitoring scheme. This serves efficiently because when a gifted child is given individual help, he or she tends to improve rapidly.

PERSONAL AND SOCIAL ADJUSTMENT

Another area of need involves improving a child's personal and social adjustment. Most children are interested and concerned with their inner selves and, secondly, with their relations to others. Ego and personality problems concerned nearly 44 percent of the children. These problems involved self-reliance, feelings of belonging, sense of personal freedom, and withdrawal tendencies. Nine children in this group also indicated a low sense of personal worth. All these feelings can be intensely ego-destructive and are demanding of attention.

In the matter of social interrelationships 46 percent of the children designated problems. Within the family these were targeted at one or both parents and/or at siblings. School-related problems encompassed teachers, peers, goals, and lack of success. Social relations were concerned with having few friends, rejection by peers, fear of some peers.

The need expressed in personal and social relationships requires, foremost, understanding and in-depth knowledge of the children by parents and teachers — not an easy assignment in dealing with bright, complex personalities. It is critical that problems not be allowed to become cumulative. At a very early age gifted children can discuss situations, crises, and personal feelings with an understanding adult, and lines of communication can thus be established. In the school setting, both group dynamics and individual counseling could provide techniques to meet these vital needs.

PRESERVING TALENT

Studies of gifted children continually indicate that this group has problems that require assistance. A gifted child, like any other, can founder in a morass of failure, frustration, and maladjustment. He or she can be left rudderless, restless, and unfulfilled, his or her great gifts lost to society. How many millions of persons in the eons of time must have shown great promise? How pitifully few of these found fulfillment! How many of this group survived because of the intervention of an interested concerned person? Marconi's mother found her son space in the attic to work with his wires and contrivances when his rigid, intolerant father, having failed to force him into a military life, wrote him off as a failure. Churchill's English master imbued him with a love of language and the magic of words when he had been excused from Latin and Greek because he was a dullard. Einstein's uncle aroused his interest in mathematics, after he had nearly flunked in elementary school, by teaching him mathematical games and puzzles. The headmaster of Handel's small town school got him musical instruction despite his father's vehement objection to his son's having piano lessons.

Consider the children we have examined here. Who will intervene on behalf of Eric, whose social adjustment is so poor it has ostracized him from peers and teachers? Who will help Matt, who cannot withstand the continued pressure from his father to become his prototype? What about Jim, whose teacher turned him away from mathematics in the second grade when she punished him for taking his book home in the fall of the year and working out all the problems over the weekend? What will become of Karen, brilliant, musically talented, who despises her teachers as being stupid and weeps in agonized frustration because she has no friends?

These findings unmistakably refute the myth that gifted children not only have no problems but can make it on their own. There is also the ample evidence that many eminent persons and their gifts would have been lost to us without the supportive intervention of a concerned mentor. Parents and teachers are in a logical position to provide mentorships when needed by gifted children and thus assure self-fulfillment and societal enrichment.

Selected References

Gallagher, James. *Teaching the Gifted Child.* 2d ed. (Boston: Allyn & Bacon, 1975).

Gold, Milton. *Education of the Intellectually Gifted.* (Columbus, Ohio: Chas. E. Merrill, 1965).

Jansen, Amanda Rohde. *Manual for the Rohde Sentence Completion Method.* (New York: The Ronald Press, 1967).

Moore, Warren D., Hahn, William J., and Brentnall, Lynn C. *Exceptional Children* 44, no. 8 (May 1978): 618–619, "Academic Achievement of Gifted Children: A Comparative Approach."

Terman, Lewis, and Merrill, M. A. *Stanford-Binet Intelligence Scale.* Norms ed. (Boston: Houghton Mifflin, 1972).

Thorndike, Robert L., and Hagan, Elizabeth. *Examiners Manual Cognitive Abilities Test.* Multilevel ed. (Boston: Houghton Mifflin, 1971).

Thorpe, Clark, and Tiegs. *Manual for California Test of Personality.* Rev. ed. (Del Monte Research Park, Cal.: McGraw-Hill, 1953).

Torrance, E. Paul. *Torrance Tests of Creative Thinking.* Norms technical manual, rev. (New York: Ginn, 1963).

4

Concepts of Intelligence

James Borland

Intelligence is an unusual concept in that its understanding appears to be the source of more difficulty for psychologists than for laymen. Two baseball fans discussing Tom Seaver's "intelligence" on the pitching mound or two parents speculating on whether or not their child is "intelligent" enough to get into medical school do not, in all likelihood, feel the need to preface their discussion with a detailed psychological explication of what they mean when they use the term *intelligence.* Each knows implicitly what the other means. Or, as Quinn McNemar put it in his 1964 presidential address to the American Psychological Association, "All intelligent people know what intelligence is — it is the thing the other guy lacks."

Psychologists, however, have a more difficult time of it. What the word *intelligence* connotes to different psychologists varies, not only as a function of theoretical orientation, but sometimes also as a function of such factors as on which side of the political spectrum or even on which side of the Atlantic Ocean they find themselves. To make things more difficult, many believe, along with Anne Anastasi (1958), that one can only define intelligence "with reference to a particular setting or environmental milieu." Thus, one could assert, as Anastasi does, that "there are, not one, but many definitions of intelligence." The result is a cacophony of definitions and theories, some complementary, most contradictory, all attempting to address the same central issue — the concept of human intelligence. So much confusion has been generated that as early as 1927 Charles Spearman was moved to write that "In

James Borland is a Graduate Leadership Education Program Fellow and a doctoral candidate in special education at Teachers College, Columbia University, New York. He also teaches and develops curricula in a gifted program in the Long Beach, N.Y., public schools.

truth, 'intelligence' has become a mere vocal sound, a word with so many meanings that finally it has none."

EARLY HISTORY

The history of the term and of the many concepts that have arisen around it is both fascinating and instructive. From earliest times, human beings have been both intrigued and puzzled by the fact that there are readily apparent inter- and intra-individual differences in mental functioning. It has always been obvious that some individuals adapt far more readily to, and cope more effectively with, the demands of life than do others. In the activities that the culture happens to prize at a given time, whether they be fighting, hunting, propitiating the gods, building bridges, or writing poetry, certain persons are clearly more adept than their peers. What do these individuals possess, it has long been asked, that sets them apart from the rest? Moreover, within the individual there are undeniable inconsistencies. For instance, our senses tell us that a pencil placed in a glass of water is broken at the water line, but our rational faculties tell us that this cannot be so. What faculty within us mediates this conflict? The concept of intelligence probably arose in response to a need to explain or give some order to these phenomena and to answer the questions they provoked.

The first use of the term *mental test* did not occur until 1890 in an article written by the American James McKeen Cattell, a student of the English theoretician Francis Galton. Like Galton, Cattell believed that simple sensory and motor tasks could be measured with a great deal of precision. This latter assertion was undeniably true. Unlike many psychological variables, such things as perception of size, size of head, strength of hand, color vision, and reaction time could, like the phenomena with which the chemist or the physicist deals, allow for exact measurement. And from the beginning psychologists have envied the precision with which physical scientists are able to measure the quantities with which they deal. The only problem with Cattell's approach, as his co-worker Clark Wissler found out when he attempted to validate Cattell's test battery with incoming freshmen at Columbia University, is that it didn't work. These simple tasks, despite the exactitude with which they could be measured, did not appear to relate to anything beyond themselves.

BINET'S TEST

Another approach to the problem of measuring intelligence proved to be far more successful. The French psychologist Alfred Binet began to study human intelligence around 1890, and he soon rejected the idea that so complex a phenomenon could be revealed through simple sensory and motor tasks. Instead, he believed that the most fruitful approach would involve using relatively complex tasks to tap intelligence, which he defined as the "tendency to take and maintain a definite direction; the capacity to make adaptations for the purpose of obtaining a desired end; and the power of auto-criticism."

In 1904 Binet was approached by Paris school officials who were concerned about the large number of children in their schools who were apparently unable to learn. Binet and Théodore Simon, a medical doctor, were commissioned to devise a test that would identify less capable children, who would then be given a less demanding curriculum. Binet and Simon found themselves in what was a virtually unexplored region. Even though they were not certain what intelligence was as a measurable quantity, they had to attempt to measure it.

Starting with the assumption that some children are more intelligent than others and the belief that only relatively complex tasks would reveal these differences in intelligence, Binet discovered that children who were superior on one task — judgment, for example — were also superior in memory, vocabulary, and so on. There was obviously something common to high performance on all these tasks, and he decided that the commonality lay in the fact that intelligence was required for success on all of them.

Binet thus arrived at an empirical concept of intelligence and intelligence-test construction. If a proposed task did not correlate with or relate to other intercorrelated or interrelated measures that seemed to tap this general ability, it was not included in the test. Thus, starting with a rather unclear notion of what intelligence is and including only tasks that related to each other statistically and appeared to be related to general mental ability, Binet and Simon gave birth to the first successful mental test in Paris in 1905. And it was successful; children who scored high on the test tended to do well in school, whereas those who made low scores tended to do badly in school.

Notice that Binet's test appeared to define intelligence as performance on a series of related tasks, while, under different circumstances, Binet arrived at the definition of intelligence earlier quoted involving direction, adaptation, and autocriticism. The former is an *operational* definition; it tells how intelligence is measured. The latter is a *constitutive* definition; it tells of what things intelligence is believed to be comprised. The gap between the two types of definitions is often large, as the gap between the practical and the theoretical sometimes is. In the case of Binet's test, however, the gulf was not really so great, since performance on the test could be shown to be related to school performance, something accepted as requiring intelligence. In measurement terms, Binet's test was *valid;* it apparently measured what it purported to measure.

TESTING IN THE UNITED STATES: THE MENTAL-TESTING MOVEMENT

Although the first mental test was devised in France, it was a characteristically American response to turn the new tool into a "movement." The person who was perhaps most responsible for the success of the mental-testing movement in this country was Lewis M. Terman of Stanford University, who was, incidentally, also the father of the gifted-child movement in the United States. Around 1910 Terman became interested in Binet's test, and in 1916 he published the Stanford Revision of the Binet Scale, better known as the Stanford-Binet. This quickly became, and it remains, the standard test of intelligence, the one instrument against which others are validated. Moreover, the score made on this test, which later came to be expressed in terms of an intelligence quotient, or IQ — the ratio of mental age to chronological age times 100 — was, and is, generally accepted, erroneously, by the public at large as an indication of how much intelligence one possesses.

Terman was not too concerned with defining the nature of the quantity that his test attempted to measure. He referred to intelligence as the ability "to carry on abstract thinking," but he never adequately defined what he meant by abstract thinking. Like Binet, he let his test stand as his best definition. As he stated in 1916, "To demand that one who would measure intelligence should first present a complete definition of it, is quite unreasonable."

The ultimate value of an operational definition depends, of course, upon the validity of the measure upon which it is based. When the measure in question is an IQ test, the question of validity becomes a controversial one. The controversy will largely be avoided here; we will stop only long enough to indicate that it is often as bitter and political, and nearly as old, as the debate over whether heredity or environment, nature or nurture, is the chief determinant of intellectual development, an issue we are also avoiding.

JEAN PIAGET

No conscientious discussion of intelligence can legitimately ignore the strikingly original and immensely influential contribution of the Swiss psychologist Jean Piaget, although no brief summary can do justice to the complexity and profundity of his observations and theories. Piaget was originally a biologist and a student of philosophy, and his use of biological, epistemological, and logical concepts in the study of intelligence resulted in a much-needed cross-fertilization of developmental psychological theory. From the unorthodox procedure of observing in minute detail the activities of children, particularly his own, he developed a detailed, difficult, and compelling theory of human cognitive development.

Piaget viewed intellectual growth as the active adaptation of individuals to their environment. From infancy, individuals are active agents in their intellectual growth. Through interaction with the environment they acquire information and modify their cognitive structures so that the reflexive sensorimotor activities of the infant, such as kicking and sucking, grow into the formal logic of the adult. Indeed, for Piaget, thought was internalized action. Whereas young children must physically manipulate objects in order to deal with their environment, adults can manipulate the mental operations, akin to formal logical operations, which govern their intercourse with the external world. Thus for Piaget intelligence consisted of the active adaptation of individuals to the world around them, this adaptation taking the form of the discovery and construction of knowledge resulting from the development of more and more complex structures and more complexly integrated operations.

Volumes will continue to be written about what intelligence is and is not and how it can be fostered or retarded. As new information is uncovered, we will undoubtedly continue to revise our concepts of intelligence.

Selected References

Anastasi, Anne. *Differential Psychology* (New York: Macmillan, 1958).

Bloch, Arthur. *Murphy's Law* (Los Angeles: Price/Stern/Sloan, 1978).

Hofstadter, Richard. *Anti-intellectualism in American Life* (New York: Vintage, 1963).

McNemar, Quinn. "Lost: Our Intelligence? Why?" *American Psychologist* 19 (1964): 871–82.

Terman, Lewis M. *The Measurement of Intelligence* (Boston: Houghton Mifflin, 1916).

5
Parents, Beware!
The Evaluation of Gifted and
Talented Students

Gladys Pack

When parents of gifted and talented children get together, there is usually a tendency to share "war stories." Through these, parents are often able to help each other.

"My child is three. He's very bright. He's reading. Many people say he's gifted. Where can I go to have him tested?"

"Why do you want him tested?"

"So I'll know if he is gifted. A parent wants to know for sure."

"My child is four. She has been reading for over a year. She can add and subtract. She can do first-grade work. But she's four and the school won't test her. Where can I go?"

"My child is in the second grade. She's been evaluated by the school psychologist. Tests show she's gifted. She does the work my fourth-grader brings home. We suggested they skip her, but the psychologist doesn't believe in it. What can I do? I want to go back, but what can I say?"

"The psychologist told me that my child is gifted. He has an IQ of 149. But he gets failing marks on his report card. His writing is terrible, and I can't get him to do homework. I don't understand."

Gladys Pack is a project director for the Yonkers, N.Y., High and Wide Demonstration Project for the Gifted and Talented. She is a school psychologist and has taught grades two through five in the Yonkers, N.Y., school district. She is president of the Westchester Association for the Gifted and Talented and is currently a doctoral student at Fordham University.

"My daughter has been having a hard time with reading, but I feel
better now. We had her tested and she has an IQ of 130."

"I've just come from the psychologist. She said that my child is gifted,
and I must find a gifted program for her, even if I have to move.
Where can I find a program?"

"My child's in a gifted program. He belongs there, in terms of his IQ,
but he doesn't want to stay. I don't understand."

These are but a few of the reports that are phoned in each day to
parent and advocacy groups, schools, and developmental centers
throughout the country. When a parent calls for help of this sort, he or
she has perceived a need. The child seems to need something different
either at home or at school. Often, the parent initially wants to know
if the need is real. "Is my child really exceptional?" Often this is all that
is asked and all that is answered. When a child is screened and identified
for a specific program, this may be all the information the parent is
given. Once it has been determined that the child is gifted, the need for
special programming still exists. The parent is still left with the question
of the kind of program and activities that meet the child's unique set of
talents and gifts. Identification and screening alone may not answer this
question. Where there are no school provisions for the gifted child
identification procedures may not even exist. Where, then, can you turn
to get the answers you seek?

WHERE TO GO

If your child is of school age or close to it, I suggest you begin with
the school, starting first with the teacher. If you are seeking an evaluation of your child's functioning level and potential in order to develop
a program for your child, the school is the logical place to start. All
schools, including nonpublic schools, have access to some psychological services. The school's psychologist may not see this as a priority; but
if you do and if you can express this as an educational need for your
child, the evaluation your child would receive should result in some
actual program changes designed to meet his or her needs. If you ask
for an IQ test, you will generally not get results. If you describe your
child's behavior and describe how the present program is not meeting
your child's needs, you should get results. Perhaps, like many other parents, you are not sure that an evaluation is necessary. You see what
appears to be precocious behavior, but you are not sure. You need
further information regarding the development of children to determine
whether this behavior is exceptional. You can ask for a conference with
the psychologist to discuss your child. The psychologist is specifically

trained in child development. By sharing what you feel may be exceptional development, the psychologist can advise you as to further evaluation. I suggest the school as a good place for an evaluation, since the psychologist can draw upon your knowledge of the child's development, teacher observations, and standardized-test results. The psychologist is a trained observer of behavior and can sample behavior in a number of different circumstances. The school's psychologist also knows the children in the school. He or she is aware of the talents of various teachers and specialists and is in a position to make recommendations.

I have heard many parents say that school personnel will not look at a child under school age. If your child is close to the entrance age for school, try working with the school administrator and again describe the behavior that has led you to feel that your child is exceptional and in need of special programming. Walking in and asking for acceleration usually does not get you very far, but describing the special achievements of your four-year-old, for example, and your concerns for placement should.

There are times when parents prefer outside evaluations. Perhaps the child is quite young or perhaps there is too long a waiting period for testing in school. Any state-licensed or certified psychologist (depending on state requirements) is qualified to evaluate any child. But many of these professionals rarely work with gifted children. They may not be aware of program possibilities for them. Before choosing a psychologist you should know how much experience the person has had in dealing with gifted children. A number of developmental clinics found in universities or large hospitals have worked with gifted children, both for counseling and research purposes. Before you make a decision, make some phone calls. Try your local parent or advocacy group for the gifted. Many of these groups have investigated evaluation services. Also try the local psychological association and the local university.

TESTING VERSUS EVALUATION

An evaluation of a child is an in-depth investigation of the child's unique style of operating, his or her functioning level, interests, and talents. In an evaluation the psychologist gathers a great deal of data through interview, testing, and observation. This data is analyzed and interpreted to both the parent and the child. This is an involved process, which includes much more than testing. Often, we are most aware of the testing part of evaluation. We mistake a number for an evaluation.

No single test can fully represent a child. Tests are tools designed to point out strengths and weaknesses, to give us direction in program planning, and to allow us to predict success. Tests are but samples of behavior, and we need a number of different kinds of behavior samples in order to know a child and suggest a program. There are numerous means of evaluation to help understand a specific child, in order to further help him or her cope with today and plan for tomorrow. The psychologist is trained to draw upon the parent, the school, the community, and certainly the child, to develop suggestions for a program. Also, the psychologist will use a number of methods to determine which would best sample the behavior needed to make decisions. An evaluation is like a unique puzzle in which the behaviors sampled in different situations fit together to form a singular individual.

IQ: WHAT IT IS, WHAT IT ISN'T

There is no absolute definition of intelligence and no one test that can assure us that we are measuring all aspects of it. The IQ is derived from a score on a specific test. The results of these tests have high correlation with future success in school. Basically, that is what we are measuring when we speak of the IQ test.

There are many things intelligence tests do not measure. They do not measure social adjustment, emotional maturity, creative thinking, leadership ability, artistic or musical talent, or talent in the psychomotor area.

Intelligence tests are designed to make comparisons of children at similar age levels with regard to their ability to learn. There is no nationally defined gifted IQ score. There may be locally determined IQ cutoff scores for entrance into specific gifted programs, but this will differ from place to place. Thus, for example, a child with a score of 130 may be considered gifted in one locality and may not be qualified for a gifted program in another.

Neither David Wechsler, who developed the WISC intelligence tests, nor Lewis Terman, developer of the current form of Stanford-Binet, used a cutoff point to designate giftedness. Both of these tests categorize scores according to the percentage of people obtaining such scores in the standard population sample. Both instruments use descriptive words such as *very superior, superior, bright, average,* and so forth to describe groups of children.

You may now find yourself more confused than before, when you did believe that the "score" would tell you what you wanted to know. But we continue to give intelligence tests, and they continue to yield information upon which we reach decisions. Because of this, you need to know more about them.

THE IQ TEST—PART OF AN EVALUATION

You know that the IQ test is but one tool in a wide range of tools that can be used to assess a child's current functioning level and academic potential. Any standardized IQ test is a sample of behavior under controlled conditions. The group IQ test is probably the one you're most familiar with. It's usually given to a whole class of children by the classroom teacher. It is basically a screening instrument, yielding a numerical score and nothing else.

The level at which a child functions on a group test depends on a number of variables, including the behavior of the whole group. The child's ability to read, visual acuity, and ability to hear and comprehend are all variables that enter into the score.

For a test to be accurate, it must be standardized in administration and scoring. I'm sure that many of you recall taking such tests when you were in school. The teacher would hand out the booklets and the pencils and begin to read directions. Children would interrupt with questions. Some teachers would say that no questions were allowed. Others would answer questions. You may have been very conscious of time limits. Some teachers posted the time on the board every ten minutes. In general the atmosphere may have been less than conducive to optimal results. Rarely do we have controlled conditions.

The most commonly used individual intelligence tests are the Stanford-Binet and the Wechsler scales. The Stanford-Binet is a single developmental scale, spanning ages two through "Superior Adult" levels. Wechsler has developed separate scales at various age levels. Although at one time we compute the IQ using a mathematical formula — by determining an estimate of the child's mental age and then dividing it by the child's chronological age multiplied by 100 (for example, a child whose mental age was eight years and chronological age was six would have an intelligence quotient of 8/6 or 133), we no longer use this formula. Today we compare the child's score with a distribution of scores of all children taking the test in the standardization sample. The average score is given a value of 100, and we determine the IQ score by measuring the variation above and below this number.

In the Stanford-Binet the items are organized by age level. Below the mental age of five the items are arranged in six-month levels, with each subtest worth two months. Above the age of five the items are grouped in one-year age levels, with each item worth two months.

When the psychologist begins working with the child, he or she determines a suitable age level at which to start. Usually this is slightly below the chronological age level of the child. The psychologist first finds the highest level at which the child passes all items. This is called the basal mental age. The psychologist continues with the test, moving from one age level – consecutively – to the next, until the point at which the child fails all items of a single age level. The child's mental age is computed by adding the basal mental age to the total months' credit the child has obtained in items above the basal. The IQ score is determined from a table of mental ages and chronological ages.

The Stanford-Binet is used widely for young children ages three through eight. The test uses a number of manipulative objects at these ages. The child at no time has to read or write responses. There are many psychologists who prefer this test for potentially gifted children, since you can see developmental patterns and the child can continue through the "Superior Adult" level, without being restricted because of chronological age.

This test is heavy in the verbal areas. One difficulty in using this test with gifted children occurs when a child has some strong areas and a number of weaker areas. The child may continue passing one or two items at each age level on through the adult level while at the same time failing a number of items at each age level. The individual test could be long and frustrating for a child with this pattern of development.

THE WISC-R (WECHSLER INTELLIGENCE SCALE FOR CHILDREN—REVISED)

The Wechsler Intelligence Scales are a series of tests, each geared to a specific age. Although the WISC was designed to be used with children from five to fifteen, the test is primarily used with children seven to thirteen years old, while the Wechsler Preschool and Primary Scale (WPPSI) is used with children four through six years of age and the Wechsler Adult Intelligence Scale (WAIS) for adults. Each of the Wechsler scales consists of a set of twelve subtests, each aimed at testing a different aspect of intelligence. Every subtest begins with easy items and progresses to more difficult ones. Each child is exposed to all subtests, beginning with the simple items and staying with a subtest until a specific number of items is failed, whereupon the examiner goes on to the next subtest. The WISC-R has a verbal and a nonverbal scale, providing a separate IQ score for each of these areas. In addition, there is a separate scaled score for each subtest. This allows the psychologist to develop a profile of strengths and weaknesses.

The WISC-R is limited in age span. The test's strength lies in its ability to determine how the child functions in specific areas. This is an excellent test for those gifted children who may be learning disabled, for it gives clues about where to look further and how to plan for an individualized program.

There is much more to test analysis than counting up right or wrong answers. The trained evaluator carefully observes how the child functions during the test, how the child feels about taking a test, and how the child arrives at responses. Even incorrect responses give clues to methods used by children. The evaluator is analyzing the child, not the test.

It is rare for a psychologist to use both the Binet and the Wechsler. Usually the psychologist determines the child's style and then selects the appropriate tool to measure intellectual functioning.

OTHER INSTRUMENTS

As mentioned previously, the IQ is not enough to determine a program. You also want to know more about the academic level on which your child functions. Your child may have scored at a superior level on intelligence tests but bring home poor grades on school tests.

In evaluating the child's functioning, the psychologist must pull together information from teachers' reports, standardized achievement tests, and the child's own views of his or her achievements. Although aiming at individualized programs, the teacher generally sees your child in relation to other children. The standardized achievement tests do the same.

The achievement test is usually adminstered to a group of children. This gives us important information about how the child performs in a group, under the pressure of a testing situation. As a parent you want to know a number of points about your child's achievement. You may ask

- What does my child know?
- How well is he or she progressing from year to year?
- Is the work in the classroom challenging enough?
- What is the best placement for my child for optimal learning?

When the teacher discusses the achievement test, you are usually given two scores: a grade-level score, which may sound amazingly high, and a percentile score, which is usually based on national norms.

Let's look at how these scores are derived. The child obtains a raw score that is equal to the number of correct responses. The raw score is changed to a standard score, which allows you to compare the child's score to others on the same grade level. The grade-equivalent score and percentile are forms of standard scores. The average raw score for all beginning third-grade students in the research sample is the grade equivalent for beginning third-graders. This score is converted into a grade equivalent score of 3.0. Grade equivalents are based on national samples, not local samples. The percentile score is also nationally based.

CONSIDER LOCAL NORMS

In order for you to understand where your child is in regard to what is happening in his or her own class, you must know the local norm. Thus a child in the fifth grade may score at a 9.0 level in math, and be above the ninetieth percentile nationally, but if the local group is bright and moving at a rapid rate, your child may be at a somewhat lower percentile rank on local norms, and the current program may be adequate for your child.

Many parents look at the grade-equivalent score alone and determine that the program is not meeting their child's needs. First ask about your child's functioning on local norms. If you find that your child places well above the local norm and actually has progressed beyond the curriculum provided, alternative programming may be needed.

The standardized achievement test yields a number of separate subject scores, which can give you a profile of the child's strengths and weaknesses. When these are put together with other results, you are able to get a better picture of your child's abilities.

In an evaluation, the psychologist may also use an individual achievement test to determine the level of performance. Here the psychologist may be looking for the process the child uses to determine the response as well as the specific level of achievement.

Another type of test primarily used in junior high or high schools is the aptitude test. This test is designed to determine potential for new learning in specific areas. Aptitude tests are generally used for guidance purposes to predict success in programs.

BEYOND THE STANDARDIZED TEST

In working with a gifted child, it is important to determine areas of interest in order to aid in the development of a personalized program. The gifted child, like all children, needs to be involved in meaningful learning. There are a number of ways to determine areas of special interest. Using the interest scale in conjunction with other measures helps to round out a program and can allow the child to be actively involved in determining the direction of his or her learning by giving the child direction for independent or elective study.

In the course of an evaluation the psychologist may use a measure of creative ability and may also use a number of so-called personality tests. The results of these tests aid the psychologist in understanding the unique coping style of the child. The results of such techniques give clues to the personal and social adjustment of the child. The total evaluation, including projective material, helps us to understand the children's view of themselves in relation to the world, their ways of dealing with their own achievements, and their frustrations.

As parents, you want to have some clues as to how certain programs may affect your child. Your child's unique coping style will give these clues. For example, the question of skipping a grade does not just depend on the academic level of the child. It also depends on how your child copes with a new situation and how your child perceives and works with children of different ages. For some children, acceleration is not the best answer. The results of an evaluation should indicate those differences, which must be considered in an individually designed program. This does not mean that the only answer is a one-to-one program. Through evaluation and teamwork you will be able to see what groupings and what programs fit the child's needs.

EVALUATION LEADS TO JOINT PLANNING

We began this chapter with a number of "war stories," which were all related to two major parent questions:

1. Is my child gifted?
2. What kind of program meets his or her needs?

After the evaluation there will be a conference. Many parents leave the conference satisfied for the moment, only to find themselves frustrated a short time later: They have realized that their questions were not answered. Remember, you have to ask questions in order to get answers.

You initially want to know if your child is considered gifted. You also want to know what the unique areas of ability and talent are. You want to ask about your child's achievement level with regard to a sequence of skills and in relation to his or her peers. You want to know this not so much for comparison, but in order to determine whether there is challenge and a chance to interact with children of a like ability level. If the achievement level of your child is well beyond that of others in the school at his or her grade level, what are the other alternatives? You want to know if acceleration is the best answer for your particular child. If the local school has a program for gifted children, what is the nature of the program and how can it meet your child's needs? If the local program does not meet your child's needs, what other kinds of programs are available? Where? You want to know if there are ancillary programs that you should know about, and you want to know if there are other parents whose children have similar needs.

You want to know how you can explain being different to your child and how you might handle this with siblings. These are but a few of the questions to which you want answers. Ask them.

In an evaluation the psychologist should have a conference with you and also with your child. When a child goes through an evaluation, he or she is entitled to know what comes out of it. Otherwise this may remain a confusing and meaningless experience. Your child does have questions. Ideally, many of these questions will be discussed as part of the evaluation.

Any evaluation should result in a written report that lists results and recommendations. The report should put together all of the information obtained, and the report should be sent to those who will need it for program planning. The school will need it also.

WAR STORIES REVISITED

Although you know all this, I expect "war stories" and phone calls to continue. What I have spoken of here is an ideal situation for evaluation. I suspect that there will continue to be waiting lists and that there will continue to be more screening than evaluation. Today, as we begin to recognize the unique needs of gifted and talented children, it is essential that we have a more aware parent group. The parents of handicapped children have become aware of this and have, through legislation, become a part of the planning process. The parents of gifted children are just becoming aware of the power they must learn to wield on behalf of their children.

Selected References

Fortna, Richard and Boston, Bruce. *Testing the Gifted Child: An Interpretation in Lay Language.* (Reston, Va.: ERIC Clearinghouse, The Council for Exceptional Children, 1976.)

Gallagher, James J. *Teaching the Gifted Child.* (Boston: Allyn & Bacon, 1975.)

Hawes, Gene R. *Educational Testing for the Millions.* (New York: McGraw-Hill, 1964.)

Klein, Stanley D. *Psychological Testing of Children.* (Boston: The Exceptional Child Press, 1977.)

6
The Gifted in Minority Groups

Ursula Thunberg, M.D.

The minorities of the United States generally represent the socioeconomically more disadvantaged groups, be they black, Indian, or Oriental. Coming from various backgrounds, they face many issues that represent a complex interrelationship of historic, cultural, societal, and economic factors. Because I am more concretely acquainted with the problems of the black minorities, which from many angles can be taken as representative of the problems facing a minority child, I will focus predominantly on this group.

More than 11 percent of the total population of the United States is black, with approximately one-third of them under sixteen years of age. Black families with two wage earners have lower incomes on the average than white families with one.[1]

From early youth the typical minority child faces overcrowded, poor sociocultural conditions. Absence, or poor accessibility, of adequate prenatal care affects the minority child at a very early stage.

Data from a book written by M. E. Hetherington and R. D. Parke in 1975 (*Child Psychology: A Contemporary Viewpoint.* New York: McGraw-Hill) indicate that the death rate at the age under one year per 1,000 live births is highest among the black child, followed by the American Indian child.[2] Again, the infant death rate in a survey done in New York City for selected health districts between the years 1966 and 1967 indicates a high death rate especially among the low-income black districts.

Ursula Thunberg, M.D., is chief of Child and Adolescent Services, Bedford Stuyvesant Community Mental Health Center, Brooklyn, N.Y.; clinical assistant professor, Department of Psychiatry, Downstate Medical Center; lecturer, Department of Social Work, New York University; consultant, Department of Pediatrics, Kings County Hospital, Downstate Medical Center, Brooklyn, N.Y.; and member, Advisory Committee, Concerned Citizens for the Education of the Gifted and Talented Children of New York City, Inc.

In spite of the multiple hazards as reflected by the data, comparative early-child-developmental research data indicate that developmentally very young children of African descent are advanced as compared with children of European descent. African children develop psychomotor skills earlier. This advantage seems to get lost past the age of two years, with various environmental influences, such as nutrition and psychological and social factors, being responsible for these findings.

Though these findings may provide avenues of exploration, the fact remains that in reviewing the literature on the gifted and talented, there is a general recognition that the identified gifted are underrepresented among the black, Hispanic, Chinese, and native Indian groups. Various conceptual models have been developed to explain this phenomenon and to develop techniques for reliable and early identification of the gifted among these groups.

PROBLEMS FACED BY GIFTED MINORITY CHILDREN

From the clinical base of more than ten years of on-going child-psychiatric service in minority communities and from encounters with gifted children and their families in those neighborhoods, I would like to delineate some of the problems faced by a gifted and talented child from such a background. I will present some of the gifted and talented children and the special difficulties they, their families, and those people that tried to help them encountered. This, more than any formal argument, will point out those factors in their existence that impede their progress and perhaps their future emergence into public view and available supportive programs.

The children presented were just a few of those encountered accidently in the course of professional work. They, at that time, were not especially looked for, selected, or searched out. Their accidental emergence only raised the following question: How many more like them exist who will never get help or support and will never emerge as gifted people to fulfill their potential development and enjoyment of their unique talents, both for their own enrichment and for society's benefit?

CASE STUDIES

Case 1: A. was a boy three years and two months old, who was referred from a speech and hearing clinic under the impression that he had a receptive and impressive language disorder, possibly with emotional disturbance.

The mother said that the child spoke in a jargon. She brought him to the clinic against the resistance of the child's father and other relatives, because she felt there was something wrong with his speech and she was afraid it might create future problems in school. The father of the child, who was not living in the home, felt that nothing was wrong with him and that he would grow out of it.

In reviewing the child's developmental data we found that he sat up at four months, walked at seven months, fed himself at one year of age, was toilet-trained at one and one-half years, and dressed himself at two and one-half years. He had watched *Sesame Street* since he was eight months old, and was able to read at age two. He liked to use match-sticks and clothespins to spell out words – he had invented this method of spelling himself. He did not use a pencil. He spoke coherently and clearly to a doll but in an unintelligible jargon when relating to others. He was reading clearly any book given to him, from a children's book to any paragraph shown him in the Yellow Pages of the telephone book.

The mother felt upset that the boy was not speaking clearly in social situations. She said that he was a kind of freak because of the contrast between his ability to read and his inability to speak. She also expressed resentment that so much attention was given to his reading capacity by her family.

When A. was eight months old, he started to spend one to three hours in front of the television watching *Sesame Street* while a nine-year-old cousin read the words to him. Shortly after that he began to read the letters aloud to himself.

In the immediate extended family were handicapped family members, family members who received basic technical training, unemployed, and members on welfare. The immediate family consisted of the mother, who had been an adolescent when he was born, two younger siblings, and a father who visited occasionally but did not have a consistent contact with the nuclear family.

At the time A. was seen, the impression was that we were dealing with a gifted, emotionally handicapped child. When this impression was given to colleagues in a professional case conference on this case, it elicited a storm of protest. The suggestions ranged from brain damaged to mentally retarded to idiot savant. At no time was support given to the idea that this minority child from a deprived socioeconomic back-ground was possibly gifted (as reflected by the consistent early devel-opmental data and unusually advanced reading performance). Since he came from a family background that was emotionally highly stressful, and since he was emotionally handicapped as a result of parental and interpersonal conflicts, this child was put in play therapy for four years. He developed completely normal speech in all situations after two months of interaction between the staff and the child and mother and showed consistent advanced conceptual and performance skills throughout the four years of contact.

Case 2: R. was a single, seven-year-old child of an immigrant domestic, who was supporting herself and the child. He spent most of the day by himself. He had been referred for an evaluation by the school because of withdrawn behavior in school, poor participation, and negative attitudes. His school performance was at the top of his class, but his behavior puzzled the teacher. There was an incident of fire setting in the mother's home a few weeks earlier. R. would spend his early mornings by himself, fix his own breakfast, go to school, come home by himself (he had a house key), watch television, and do his homework. His mother generally came home by eight in the evening, tired and irritated. She would fix their dinner and then go to sleep. R. was not allowed to play outside, bring friends home, or visit friends because of the mother's realistic fears of the neighborhood. He often felt sad, sometimes angry. He liked to read books, but his mother was often too tired to take him to the public library, though the teacher had gotten him a library card. Since he appeared to be unusually bright, psychological testing was done, and he was found to be highly gifted.

HANDICAPS OF GIFTED CHILDREN IN MINORITY GROUPS

The cases given are random indicators that highly gifted youngsters exist among low-income minority groups. The clinical cases indicate some of the factors impeding proper emotional and intellectual growth in minority children.

Gifted children are a challenge and sometimes a threat to their parents. A challenge because they demand response from the parent. If the parent is unsure of his or her self-worth and intellectual capacity, the challenge may create anxiety in the parent and be experienced as a threat. This may lead to attempts either to put down the child's performance or to retaliate aggressively because the parent feels the child is challenging his or her authority.

I saw the ultimate of such a reaction in the death by battering of a nine-year-old boy, who at that point was emotionally disturbed. This child had become the pride of his parents in his very early years, because of his intellectual performance. This led to a lack of limit setting and of consistency in limits, which in turn led gradually to the child's uncontrollably teasing and challenging his parents, especially his father, and the teachers, and finally resulted in death when the father lost control during an argument. Neither parents nor teachers had been able to recognize the boy's disturbance in the emotional area, which might have led them to seek appropriate help.

SUPPORT NEEDED IN MANY AREAS

In some cases the gifted child becomes depressed and gives up for lack of emotional support.

Sometimes parents who themselves lack education or intellectual achievement identify with the performance of their child and pressure him or her toward increasingly higher performance, perhaps without providing the proper emotional support, and without understanding the effort involved.

The general home atmosphere will be a large influence on the course of development of a gifted child. Generally, economic and social pressures are higher on minority families. Financial resources are limited and must go for food, housing, and other basic expenses and do not allow for work material, books, journals, travel, and social stimulation.

Many times the general feeling of hopelessness and lack of help from the public school system may create a feeling of defeat at home and have an impact on the performance and growth of the gifted child.

Many minority parents may come from other countries and lack an educated background and are therefore unable to help their children create good study habits or to motivate them consistently.

MYTHS AND RACIAL ATTITUDES

Discussions of the educational problems facing the gifted minority child have repeatedly addressed the difference in perception of special valued talents between the disadvantaged subcultures and the dominant middle class, whose values put more emphasis on intellectual achievement.

There are many suppressed myths and racial attitudes in the unconscious of the dominant middle class culture in America that to this day have not been explored or exposed to systematic study. One result of the power of these unconscious operations is the phenomenon that has been described in the educational literature as the Pygmalion Effect. This is the phenomenon that the positive expectation that a teacher has about a child, based on information given to the teacher, influences the teacher's expectations and results in improved intellectual functioning of the child. Some of the described findings were "that teachers were much less favorable to the lower-class children than they were to the middle-class children, 40 percent of their comments about the poorer children were negative, compared to 20 percent of their comments about the middle class children . . . the teachers were even more likely to talk negatively about black children than white children, 43% to 17%."[3]

Another unusual finding was that "lower-income children who had higher I.Q.'s tended to have teachers who viewed them negatively and this was especially true for lower-income children who were black. Thus, children who are both black and lower-income have a double handicap."[4]

The implications of field studies of this kind help in beginning to isolate some factors in destructive interpersonal interactions and so make them available to intervention. They also highlight the emotional barriers facing a poor, gifted minority child in his or her personal, social, and educational life.

On several occasions, after a clinically referred minority child was identified as talented or gifted, more resistance was met in the school than in encounters with families. Though many times school resources were lacking, alternate suggestions, such as a different class placement or placement in a private school, were often fought by the representative of the system.

There are facilities available that service gifted minority children, but they are unevenly distributed and have their own high set of standards that will guarantee the success of their specific program and approach. They generally do not attempt to shift the focus or improve the awareness of those in the public school system. Frequently the creation of a school center for gifted minority children will depend on the initiative and the capacity of an individual to manipulate the system. Because of the unresolved overlay of prejudice, myth, and racial attitudes, special attention has to be given to the problems of the gifted of the poor minorities. Particular attention should be given to emotional support systems when planning programs, because the poor, gifted minority child may not be able to find these resources at home. Otherwise, untold numbers of gifted individuals will get lost in the morass of our social problems. Time is an essential factor in this effort, since twelve years means one generation of schoolchildren and may mean lost years for many.

Notes

1. Robert B. Hill, *The Strengths of Black Families,* National Urban League, (New York: Emerson Hall Publishers, 1971), p. 12.

2. Amos H. Wilson, *The Developmental Psychology of the Black Child* (New York: Africana Research Publications, 1978), pp. 19, 21, 46–49.
3. Robert E. Shell, *Readings in Developmental Psychology Today,* (New York: Random House, 1975), pp. 248–52.
4. Ibid.

7
Minority Gifted Children

Mary M. Frasier

From past research we can conclude that minority gifted children are found in all areas and are more like the gifted children in the general population than they are like their nongifted peers in their own minority group. The recognition of minority gifted children may be suppressed because many of them come from impoverished backgrounds, but traditional testing procedures will identify disadvantaged minority children who are gifted.

FOR PARENTS AND EDUCATORS

There are many ways that parents and educators can work, singularly or in combination, to provide for the appropriate identification and education of minority gifted children. No deliberate attempt will be made to distinguish between those approaches that might be more appropriate for children who are advantaged or disadvantaged, for many of the problems that must be met transcend social and economic differences. Professor A. Harry Passow summed up this situation when he stated, "When students are black, red, or brown, are different culturally from the majority group, are non-English speaking or have 'non-standard' dialects, those who are gifted or talented among them may be particularly disadvantaged because of discriminatory practices."

Mary M. Frasier is assistant professor of educational psychology at the University of Georgia in Athens. She is co-coordinator of the gifted-child program and teaches graduate courses in the education of the gifted. In addition she is assistant director of the Challenge Program, a demonstration program for the gifted and talented.

ESTABLISHING STANDARDS OF EXCELLENCE

It has been stated that no one is against intellectual excellence for black people, but it is not at the top of anyone's priority list — which is the only position from which excellence has been achieved anywhere. It takes just a brief look at the literature on Mexican Americans, Native Americans, and Puerto Ricans to note that this assertion is equally true about them as well.

The focusing of attention away from the problems and difficulties of disadvantaged and minority groups and toward their potential and how they can be assisted in achieving it becomes the first challenge that parents and teachers must accept. The ghettos that attitudes have created — imaginary ghettos where intellectual and other deficiencies are assumed to exist — must be destroyed.

Many examples are present in the literature to support the value of establishing an attitude of excellence. Educational programs that require the same level of excellence from the culturally different as is required of children from traditional middle-class homes are more likely to provide the environment necessary to challenge achievers. A clear standard of excellence is needed as a model for all areas of study, particularly when working with the culturally different gifted. For example, many of them need to know a well-written paper when they see one.

The home must also play its part. An attitude of excellence is not one that can be turned on at eight o'clock in the morning and turned off at three o'clock.

The challenge to black communities is one of insisting that schools use more effective methods of identifying gifted talent. It is also necessary to combine with other schools in vigorous efforts to develop this talent. Mary F. Berry emphasizes this point when she asserts that above all, the search for excellence means "involving parents and other family members in the learning process. Nothing is a more critical determinant of success than the student's home environment."

Researchers have generalized from the typical socially disadvantaged child to the entire population. The eradication of this attitude as it relates to minority gifted children can happen when parents and teachers adopt and actively promote an attitude of excellence.

EDUCATIONAL PROCEDURES

The problems facing children growing up in disadvantaged families exist not so much because of the things that happen to them as because of the things that do *not* happen to them.

Here are four guidelines that are imperative for educators to consider when planning educational experiences for minority gifted children. They must assume that gifted/talented disadvantaged children

- Are capable of operating at higher levels of thought
- Do need some time in developing lower-level thought processes, such as memory and comprehension
- May exhibit abilities in ways that are not always standard
- Will need more initial support in new opportunities to explore

The challenge to educators becomes one of building on strong areas while also developing weak areas.

Several researchers have asserted that culturally different students need specific types of educational programs. Some have suggested, for example, that these children need strongly structured programs. Others suggest that educational procedures for these children must first both supplement and counteract their social learning if the children are to have an equal opportunity to learn.

Educational procedures that focus on the removal of deficiencies before attention can be paid to the development of potential have frequently been recommended for culturally different children. Such observations are suggested as being more appropriate for stimulating talent among black children. Schools that were successful in producing black intellectuals showed no discernible pattern of teaching methods. Instead, these schools emphasized abstract academic subjects. Successful schools inspired students with *confidence* that they could do anything in spite of anything.

The recommendation gleaned from this observation is that educators must first believe that these students are capable of achieving. That belief must then be backed up with educational procedures that demonstrate this belief.

This same recommendation is applicable to procedures that have been and should continue to be employed by parents. Minorities who have succeeded frequently remarked that their parents constantly impressed upon them that they could achieve.

SPECIFIC EDUCATIONAL AND COUNSELING APPROACHES

Three specific educational and counseling approaches are suggested for use by parents and educators in working with minority gifted children. They are concerned with helping these children develop the skills that are necessary for them to take charge of their own lives.

The first approach is decision-making counseling. This procedure facilitates the development of and reinforces the presence of questioning attitudes. A recent assessment of successful black and Mexican-American achievers from disadvantaged backgrounds revealed that one of their characteristics was their questioning orientation. At critical junctures during formative years the individuals tended to ask questions such as ''Who am I?'' ''Where am I going?'' and ''What do I really want in life?'' This type of introspection invariably led them to do the seeking necessary to become aware of alternative paths. Futuring, the science or art of trying to learn about the future in order to best cope with and live in it, is a critical skill for minority gifted children to develop. Future problem solving is a technique recommended for use with disadvantaged minority gifted students especially. In future problem solving they would be given a chance to explore a problem of the future systematically, using creative problem-solving techniques. By learning how to follow through from the identification of a problem to the development of a plan to implement a solution, these children can have a chance to create their own future.

Finally mental imagery and guided fantasy are two counseling approaches that can be used to assist minority gifted children in developing an awareness of alternative careers. The value of these approaches is further enhanced by the fact that explorations can be done in the psychologically safe environment that can be provided in the home or at school.

MENTORS

An important person in the life of many gifted chidren is that person who can — formally or informally — assist them in their development. This person often serves as the confidante with whom gifted children can discuss their ideas as well as share their fears.

Educators and parents can either serve as mentors or assist minority gifted children in finding a suitable one. By using techniques such as interviews, analyzing responses to open-ended sentences, analyzing stories regarding heroes, and examining responses to interest inventories, educators can direct the search for an appropriate mentor. Parents can observe hobbies and activities freely pursued by their children to get cues regarding who might be a good mentor for their child. Even communities can provide financial support, opportunities for talent development, and moral support.

Programs that can be developed for gifted black children and youth are limited only by the creativity of teachers and administrators working with parents. This is true for all gifted minority students. The challenge is for educators and parents to mobilize their efforts in the promotion of achievement. The task of identifying and nurturing talent wherever it is found is a challenge we cannot refuse to accept.

Selected References

Berry, Mary F. "The Concept of Excellence." *Phi Delta Kappan.* 60, no. 3 (November 1978): 196s–197s.

Davidson, H. H., and Greenberg, J. W. *Traits of School Achievers from a Deprived Background.* Project No. 2805. Contract No. OE-5-10-132. (New York: The City College of the City University of New York, May 1967).

Gallagher, James J. *Teaching the Gifted Child.* (Boston: Allyn & Bacon, 1964).

Glaser, E. M., and Ross, H. L. *A Study of Successful Persons from Seriously Disadvantaged Backgrounds.* Contract No. 82-05-68-03. Final Report. (Washington, D.C.: Office of Special Manpower Programs, Department of Labor, March 1970).

Jenkins, M. D. "The Upper Limit of Ability among American Negroes." *Scientific Monthly 66* (1948): 339–401.

Marland, Sidney P. *Education of the Gifted and Talented.* Report to the Congress of the United States. (Washington, D.C.: U.S. Office of Education, 1972).

Mercer, J. R. "Pluralistic Diagnosis in the Evaluation of Black and Chicano Children: A Procedure for Taking Sociocultural Variables into Account in Clinical Assessment." Paper presented at the meetings of the American Psychological Association. Washington, D.C., September 1971.

Passow, A. Harry. "The Gifted and the Disadvantaged." *The National Elementary Principal* 51 (1972): 22–31.

Riessman, F. *The Culturally Deprived Child.* (New York: Harper & Row, 1962).

Taba, Hilda and Elkins, D. *Teaching Strategies for the Culturally Disadvantaged.* (Chicago: Rand McNally, 1966).

Terman, Lewis M. "Mental and Physical Traits of a Thousand Gifted Children." In *Genetic Studies of Genius.* Vol. 1. (Stanford, Calif.: Stanford University Press, 1925).

Torrance, E. Paul. "Broadening Concepts of Giftedness in the 70's." *Gifted Child Quarterly* 15, (1971): 75–80.

Torrance, E. Paul. "Torrance Tests of Creative Thinking." Norms Technical Manual. Rev. (Lexington, Mass.: Personal Press, 1974).

Torrance, E. Paul. *Handbook for training future problem solving bowls.* (Athens, Ga: Georgia Studies of Creative Behavior, February, 1976).

Watley, D. J. "Multipotentiality among Bright Black Youth." In R. H. Fredrickson
and J. W. M. Rothney. *Recognizing and Assisting Multipotential Youth.*
(Columbus, Ohio: Chas. E. Merrill, 1972).

Witty, Paul A. "Some Considerations in the Education of Gifted Children."
Educational Administration and Supervision 26 (1940) 512–21.

8
The Underachieving Gifted Child

Willard Abraham

Parents of gifted children sometimes face the dilemma of the under-achiever. Before the problem gets to the counselor, a discussion like this might have taken place:

"I tell you he's lazy! Not stupid — just plain lazy, that's all."

"Don't be ridiculous! You saw his report card last month and the month before that. All A's and B's. What's so bad about that?"

"Plenty. He didn't deserve one of those grades. They were gifts from teachers he's fooled."

"Oh, that's not true! How about his examination papers?" Nothing below 85 or 90. Tommy's doing fine, just fine."

"But we're expecting too little from him, and he's perfectly satisfied to do as little as possible."

"He's a happy boy, though, and if we put on too much pressure, we'll do more harm than good."

"Tommy will be happier if he realizes how much more he can accomplish. Remember when he was in Little League? You thought he really wasn't a good catcher or hitter. But I practiced with him, he really worked at it — he became one of the best on the team.

"And what about those piano lessons that seemed such a waste of money at first? When we demanded more, encouraged more, and expected more, he came through. Now he not only plays well, but enjoys it as he never did before."

"Let's just leave well enough alone. He's doing all right. There's no sense in asking for trouble."

The truth — and therefore the solution to the problems of a youngster like Tommy — lies somewhere between these two extreme and uncompromising points of view. There is some validity to the arguments of both parents in this illustration. For example, the husband is correct in his contention that grades sometimes do not give a clear picture of whether a child is working up to his or her capacity. Neither an A nor a C may accurately reflect what a child is really learning. At the same time, the wife is correct when she contends that undue pressure to "make" a child work to capacity may be dangerous. Pressures that create tensions can, of course, result in less rather than more learning.

On the other hand, what the mother in this instance may not realize is that the careless, sometimes even slovenly, habits of childhood might lead to adult unhappiness and unfulfillment.

Parents are often limited in their objectivity, not seeing their own child in clear perspective. That is why the experienced teacher who views a child as one of thirty-five to forty — and in the context of years of experience — is a valuable and objective professional source of help. Even more important may be the skills of the competent school counselor.

Tommy and other bright ones like him are underachievers. They perform below what can and should be expected of them, a danger that can lead to later frustration if not noted and corrected in early years. Repetition and lack of challenge dog their daily tracks.

A child with a fine, logical mind who could have brought luster to the legal profession may settle into a routine clerical job because his parents were satisfied with his average work in school.

Another youngster was pleased at accomplishing his goal of never taking a school book home at night, never preparing for an examination, and still "making it" through school.

A gifted child may be a member of this "pseudo slow-learner" group for many reasons. While there is time, one might follow the advice given by a teacher a few years ago: "If you want Gulliver to rise, look at the ropes that bind him."

PHYSICAL

Sight. Does he squint, strain, rub his eyes, or complain that they hurt, water, or itch? Does he hold his book very close to his face when he reads?

Hearing. Does she often ask you to repeat a question or statement? (That may have nothing to do with hearing, of course. Many children know we will say something a second, third, or fourth time! We often encourage the habit of not listening!) Does she sometimes miss, or seem to miss, a point made in a movie or on television?

Other. Has he had an infection, disease, or accident the effects of which may linger on? Is there a possibility (as farfetched as it may seem to you at first) that malnutrition may be holding him back, limiting his enthusiasms, interests, and capabilities?

Is it time for a thorough physical examination to help discern why she is not performing beyond the "adequate" plateau she now occupies?

EMOTIONAL

Could it be that squabbles, nagging, or bickering between parents are upsetting her more than one may be aware?

Is divorce or separation a possible limiting factor on his working to capacity? In other words, is the parent's failure now leading to his?

Is it possible that the relationships with her brothers or sisters are more disruptive than they appear?

Has the family moved around so much that deep inside he harbors the feeling that nowhere is home?

Does satisfaction with her limited output provide all the justification she needs for not exerting herself and for developing that habit of doing "just enough to get by?"

SCHOOL

Is the teacher who is satisfied with "adequacy" rather than "capacity" destroying his incentive to work up to the latter?

When it comes to new educational materials and techniques, is the school's lethargy a sufficient excuse for her lethargy in school performance, permitting a creative spirit to wither before it has a chance to mature?

Many other reasons may hold back a child's performance. Shyness can make children fearful. Physical or emotional immaturity can make them incapable. Educational pressures at school or unrealistic expectations at home can make them rebellious, even though in a quiet, submerged way.

Or it may be a hidden distaste for school imposed by insensitive teachers or demanding parents, laborious and discouraging study habits, failure to read assignments in what to them is a reasonable period of time, irregular attendance due to illness that results in a burdensome academic load, or a curriculum that fails to challenge their fertile, searching, pushing desire to learn.

To motivate a child who is performing more slowly than he or she is capable requires a cooperative effort between home and school. Neither one can do the job alone.

Additionally the youngsters themselves can help. From them may come the most insightful view of their own limited performance. They may quickly put their finger on the cause, the damper that has held them back. It will be to a parent's credit if a child confides that it is their pressure, lack of interest, or partiality to a sibling. What is identified might not be the real reason, but it may be enough to warrant careful thought.

Together they can seek answers to questions that may help move gifted children toward the achievements their abilities deserve.

Can "Inspiration" Turn the Tide? Don't discount it too quickly as a naïve idea, for the one-to-one, adult-child relationship and expression of interest and concern may help loosen the lid on performance. A parent — even a teacher or counselor — may not be the proper adult for the job, however. Sometimes a neighbor, aunt or uncle, cousin, or friend may provide the one bit of stimulation that is missing, the one link toward helping the child realize that he or she is more capable than has been demonstrated so far.

Can One Be Realistic in Starting with the Child Where He or She Is? This question is far from an educational cliché, for "where the child is" must be determined by discovering interests, fears, ambitions, and dreams. A knowledge of the subject of the child's current absorption (whether it is Ian Fleming or one of the many successors to the Bee Gees, or both), concern about proving masculinity or femininity (whether through sports, sex, smoking, liquor, or drugs), worry about the future (and whether acceptance by the university he or she wants is possible with a school record that is merely adequate) — these are the kinds of feelings and attitudes sensitive parents must be aware of if the breakthrough is to be made. It is a matter of knowing where children are before one can help them get to where they should be going.

Are There "Earthy" Kinds of Motivation That Can Be Used Effectively? You may not like to resort to them, but the end may be worth the means. For example, how about the fact that the average university graduate has lifetime earnings far in excess of that of the average high school graduate? (This is a factor that may be in the process of change.) To get the necessary university preparation, one must have top grades plus a list of creditable scholastic and extracurricular activities.

Can Motivation to Perform Be Stimulated by Deprivation? Parents sometimes almost suffocate their children with an overburdened, cocoonlike environment where almost every whim is satisfied, perhaps even saturated. Slowing down the stream of supposed necessity and frequent luxury may be the healthiest step one can provide toward a child's taking a look at a world that is not fully cushioned. And that one look may lead to activities that previously he had not been stimulated to perform.

Can We Shake Ourselves Loose from Some Psychological Verbiage That May Have No Relevance at All for This Child? *Overprotective, dominant, aggressive, Oedipus complex* — the terms may be interesting, but they and their kind might be totally unrelated to youngsters and the chains that bind them. Too often words get in the way of action.

Gifted underachievers may *seem* to be satisfied, but how can they really be if they have any inkling that they can work at a higher level and that their professional goals could be raised and reached? They may show no resentment toward school or family, but dissatisfactions may be deeply ingrained in them. Perhaps their disappointment and discouragement lie far below the surface, ready to burst loose when they suddenly realize that they have wasted themselves.

As all youngsters do, the gifted want the three A's — Affection, Achievement, and Aspiration. Your controlled help toward acquiring them will give them a step up in respect to whatever goals you encourage them to set for themselves.

2 GIFTED CHILDREN IN THEIR HOMES AND FAMILIES

The Prayer of the Mother

Peg Rix

Lord,
I am the mother.
I have much to teach these children
without their knowing
they are being taught,
and time is short.
They must learn to perceive clearly,
and to dream goldenly.
Help me to teach them courage, Lord,
without forfeiting the gift of tears.
Show me the way
to nurture in my children the spirit
and the curiosity to search
beyond the horizon
for Truth.
Help me to share with them, Lord,
the joy of discovering Beauty —
of sound, color, scent, and touch.
But most of all, Lord, I need your help

in letting them grow away from me,
creating their own images
and not mirroring
mine.
Thank you, Lord,
for allowing me to make a contribution
to Eternity.

Amen

Dayton, Ohio

Reprinted with permission from *Prayers from the Classroom,* edited by Evelyn Copeland.

9

Modeling Behavior

Eleanore Fisher

Reversing the adage "Do as I say, not as I do," a group of fifteen parents embarked upon a child-rearing endeavor geared toward developing a home environment in which gifted children would be encouraged to "do as I do."

This effort was an outgrowth of a parent-education study group conducted in a Westchester County, New York, public school as an integral part of a "special projects" program designed for intellectually gifted elementary school students.

Fortunately the concept of parents as partners in the education of precocious youngsters is gaining acceptance in the early 1980s.

In the past much of the research and educational effort was almost exclusively directed toward the gifted child in school. The implication was that education takes place in school, and therefore if we wanted to know why and how these children achieved, it was necessary to look to the schools for answers.

Recently, however, educators have been investigating the proposition that schools are not the exclusive agency of education in our society. There are many influences other than schools that affect children's education, and that learning takes place in a host of varied ways and places. Family counselors have long been aware that the family is among the most influential of all the educative institutions. There is

Eleanore Fisher, Ph.D., is a school administrator in Westchester County, N.Y. Her involvement in the education of the gifted includes working with parents, faculty, and students in workshops, demonstrations, and group sessions at Columbia University, SUNY, Pace University, Virginia State University, and many school districts. Her articles on education have appeared in educational journals and magazines.

mounting evidence that children not only receive an education from their families, but that the family also serves as the agency that prepares them for their future educative experiences. A child's experience in his or her family can set the stage for the manner in which further education will be received in the many other educational institutions encountered throughout life.

The family can be seen as the "home-base" institution, where children have the freedom to sort out all the other influences. Depending upon the climate, the message they receive can be hostile, supportive, or ineffective. Clearly the atmosphere of the family has more to do with the kind of a person the child will become than any other single factor.

Accepting this point of view can be challenging, exhilarating, and a little scary for parents. Young people are often leery about their ability to be parents even with "normal" children. Parents of gifted children may feel particularly inadequate because of their precocious offspring. They are proud of having gifted children, it's a boost to their ego, they feel blessed; yet they are beset with problems. Gifted children are often hard to handle, cause family friction, don't conform, have special needs. They characteristically have incredible energy and unrelenting persistence. In pursuing something, gifted children can "wear out" even a doting parent. Frequently they walk, talk, read, and conceptualize at a younger age than other children, before the family is "ready" for them to develop these skills. Parents often cannot call upon their own experience as children in a family to help them deal with the many anxiety-provoking situations that can occur when there is a gifted child in the family.

Because of these concerns, it is becoming increasingly popular for parents to join together in self-help affinity groups. Within the framework of a trusting, supportive atmosphere, parents have the opportunity to share common concerns, exchange successful coping skills, and gain some insight and perspective.

This is a report of a plan of action that resulted from one such parent group in Westchester County, New York. After four two-hour sessions, this group of fourteen parents zeroed in on one aspect of child rearing. We developed the idea that parents modeling certain behaviors might serve as a wonderful learning tool for their gifted child.

Following is a discussion of some of the areas that parents identified as behaviors that needed attention. Parents agreed to try to model their own activities in the hope that their children would emulate the desired behavior.

FEAR OF TAKING RISKS

We know that a number of gifted children are reluctant to take risks. They are self-critical and resist trying new things for fear of not being best or first. We need to help them to feel enough psychological freedom and safety to take chances, make mistakes, be wrong. Children need to see their parents risk new things, fall flat, and engage in activities where success is not guaranteed. A little girl watching her mother learn a new skill, take up a new sport, go back to school, apply for a high-level job — all activities fraught with the chance factor, all possible failures or rejections — is learning more about risk taking than any lecture could provide. Even a small example makes the point: One mother reported that she was never good at map reading and frequently got lost when driving alone. In the group she indicated this as a real problem area, since it curtailed her movement and prevented her from visiting many interesting places. The family was aware of her reluctance to venture too far from home and had come to accept her unwillingness to risk getting lost. What they hadn't realized was the lesson she was teaching her daughter: "If you don't know the exact road, the correct direction, don't take a chance. It's better to hold back than to risk a mistake." In addition, she reported that on family outings to unfamiliar places, when her husband drove and she had to provide directions from a map, she became so tense for fear she would give misleading directions that she frequently couldn't read the map or became so anxious that she refused to do it for fear of embarrassing herself in front of the children or incurring her husband's wrath and disdain. By helping this very intelligent, competent mother realize that the problem was not inadequacy in terms of map-reading ability but rather an old, ingrained fear of making a mistake, of not being her usual smart, efficient self, the group opened up an area of self-awareness for her. She decided to concentrate on this one small area of risk taking for herself in order to model that behavior that she said was indeed a problem area for her child as well. Hence, in order to encourage children to experiment, to become freer about searching for creative, original solutions, parents began attempting to become risk takers themselves. They let their children see them taking chances, trying new things, experimenting with new methods, developing a tolerance for their own possible failure.

MISUSE OF LEISURE TIME

One of the most common concerns aired was the amount of time children wasted watching TV. When parents began to examine their own behavior in regard to TV watching, they began to see that in effect they were setting the very standards of which they were so critical. Hence, the father who spent his evening watching TV because it "was more relaxing, more enjoyable, less taxing than reading" was sending a message to his children about his attitude toward reading. That's okay as long as he hadn't just finished lecturing about the virtues and values of reading. In other words, having one set of values that you espouse for the children and a different one for yourself creates problems for children. Recent research has shown that in families where children watch TV excessively the parents usually do too. The group members helped each other accept the idea that they were indeed wasting as much time as they accused their children of wasting. Parents became more conscious of the amount of time they spent engaged in activities they would not be pleased to see their children doing. Developing an awareness of how each parent relaxed, played, and used his or her leisure time helped them to adopt new codes of behavior. Hopefully, by demonstrating healthful, constructive, enjoyable ways of using their spare time, parents were teaching children that sports, hobbies, friends, family, and reading were all wonderful alternatives to TV.

POOR SOCIAL RELATIONS

It is not uncommon for gifted children to be hypercritical of anyone they perceive as slow to grasp ideas or inadequate in any way. Such children frequently ridicule teachers, friends, and siblings. They are not especially patient or understanding. Parents revealed a lack of knowing how to help their children be more humble, more accepting, more appreciative and sensitive to differences in abilities and potential.

During the discussions on this topic, parents became aware of how frequently they voiced prejudicial, unkind remarks about checkout clerks at the supermarket, gas station attendants, and post office employees, for example. Even co-workers and the professional people who crossed their paths during the course of the day were subject to ridicule, sarcasm, and innuendos over the dinner table. They began to realize that they had created a hierarchy of valued persons, with low-level workers receiving the brunt of the criticism. In effect the parents were setting up a social "we" and "they," with the individual family members being at the top – select, intelligent, open, correct. While no parent truly meant to paint such a picture, they were embarrassed to admit how many times teachers, principals, and peers had been put down by them in front of their gifted children. One father, a lawyer, reported asking permission to take the class to court to observe a judicial procedure. When the teacher refused to grant permission because of insurance and safety concerns, the father told his son to pick six classmates, whom he took despite the teacher's position. He told his gifted child that the legal experience was valuable, he was a responsible adult, and that the teacher was wrong. However, the lesson he taught his child by his behavior may have had a greater effect on his son than anything the children learned that day in court. By his actions, he taught his son a great deal about authority, about obeying regulations, and about interacting with significant people in one's life.

As a result of examining this incident, parents became acutely aware of how much incidental learning takes place by children, who concentrate not on what their parents say but on what their parents do.

OVERDEPENDENCY ON ADULTS

Parents yearn for their children to be more independent, to be more competent, to tackle hard jobs themselves. Parents urge their gifted youngsters to try things out, to seek creative solutions. They refuse to answer questions routinely; they don't provide solutions; they encourage discovery. Yet in their own lives they model behavior that is quite the opposite. One mother sheepishly reported that immediately after she had done all of the above with her young son, she complained aloud that she couldn't take a bath because of some problem with the water heater, and she wouldn't even attempt to go down to the basement to look at it because she was so sure she didn't have the skills to solve the problem. "Let's wait for Daddy to fix it" or "I won't even try to figure that out" are ways of approaching problem solving that are in direct contrast to the goals we have for our children. The group helped this mother to see that her modeling independence, her reaching out to find solutions by herself, would probably be a more valuable lesson for her son than merely preaching. The best way to have a competent, independent child is to be a competent, independent person yourself. Children will then have a living example of the kind of behavior for which you are striving.

The group sessions dealt mainly with feelings and attitudes. The goals were to

- Help parents become aware of the special nurturing needs of their family because of the presence in it of a gifted child
- Help parents appreciate the unique characteristics of their family dynamics
- Understand the importance of their own behavior because gifted children are exquisitely sensitive to pretense and are tuned in to every nuance

- Learn from their peers, from the literature, and from the group leader some of the successful ways in which others have dealt with similar problems
- Internalize the learning so that it becomes relevant and useful in rearing their own children in their own family
- Take action in the direction of effecting change in their own behavior and begin to model those behaviors that they deem desirable and/or absent in the behavior of the gifted child

As a result of the group experience parents came to realize that one powerful way of nurturing their child's potential was to demonstrate by their own actions the kind of behavior they wanted to encourage in their children.

10

Parents—Do Your Children Like Themselves?

Kim Elizabeth Davidson

Ronnie enters my classroom, head hung down between his shoulders, face drawn and tight, shyly hiding behind his mother. She walks him to the door, pats him on the head and says, "See ya later."

"Good morning, Ronnie," I say. Ronnie looks wistfully after his mother as she leaves and then sinks into a chair, watching. "Ya," he replies. "Why is he so disagreeable?" his mother will ask me later. "He seems bright, but he doesn't try or anything. I don't get it. He should do more things."

And in fact Ronnie's mom is right. Ronnie is bright, very bright, but life is tough for him. Why? Because he isn't very happy about himself and he senses that his parents feel he isn't very successful.

When Lynn comes to my room in the morning, she too hangs her head shyly. Yet there is an apparent twinkle in her eye as she looks around, still holding tightly to her mother's hand. Together they walk over to the reading table, and Lynn's mother says, "Let's see what you might like to read today. I'll say good-bye, and when you get home, you can tell me about the book you chose and about the rest of your day." Together they pick out a book, and Lynn waves good-bye — not an easy thing for her to do. Though her eyes follow her mother to the door, her face says she's ready. Lynn seems prepared for school and confident about the things she is doing.

Kim E. Davidson, formerly a teacher in the Newton, Mass., Community Services Program, is head teacher at the Ridgewood, N.J., Child Care Center. She has a particular interest in special education.

SELF-IMAGE

The personalities of children are affected by the ideas they hold of who they are and where they stand in relation to their world. This is a very powerful force, and it motivates their behavior. Children who are fortunate enough to be encouraged and supported from birth in an atmosphere of love, caring, and security develop feelings of confidence and self-esteem. If, on the contrary, children live in an atmosphere of reproach and disapproval, they may become crippled — socially, emotionally, or intellectually. When such children look at themselves, their reflections are unclear, and in their hearts they feel confused and inept.

Parents are the primary and most significant influence on the development of a child and are the child's major support system, spokesperson, and caretaker. Parents supply the constant, consistent guidelines, limits, and directions needed to ease the child into independent life. They have the keenest sensitivity to a child's needs as well as the responsibility to act on the requirements. This is not at all an easy job. But it is of fundamental importance, since positive feelings, nurtured from birth, permit children to venture forth with courage to try things on their own, to fail, and to try again — in short, to grow. Children welcome challenging tasks, work things out for themselves, and confront their world realistically if they have love and guidance supporting them.

PARENTS' ATTITUDES

Parents ask, "But how do I help my gifted child to feel confident?" Often the first thing that comes to mind is praise and recognition — a very basic tool in helping to bolster a child's self-esteem. Children need to be encouraged, appreciated, and complimented. But praise must be sincere and deserved. For example, Patrick's mother praises the compositions he brings home from school by saying, "Okay, Patrick, that's fine. Another good paper!" Patrick's mom doesn't realize that her comment means little to him. He knows his work isn't improving, and he pays little attention to her.

There are times when parents put children down unconsciously, ignoring their efforts to gain attention by repeatedly asking for help or commendation. "Mommy, Mommy, Mommy", says Sharon, pulling at her mother's sleeve. But her mother ignores her and goes on talking to her friend. This kind of thing we see over and over again.

Belittling a child is deflating and humiliating, especially if it comes from the person the child cares most about. Some children who have special abilities and interests perform at a very high level, but parents are not always satisfied. One father commented to his son, Eric, who had just completed a piano performance of high quality, "It would have been better if you had worked harder on your left hand as I told you."

WORKING TOGETHER

Making choices and decisions about actions and observations encourages competence and adds to a feeling of respect for oneself and for others. Self-confidence is created through honest communication, cooperative planning, and decision making in which parent and child together examine various alternatives.

For example, Peter loved to write stories about his friends and asked his mother to read them. She was enthusiastic about his writing, but one day said, "Your story is very exciting, but it is hard for me to read your handwriting. Let's think about what we can do to improve it and work together on it this afternoon."

Parents provide experiences that result in the mastery of skills and tasks that help to build the feelings of competence and achievement that are the stepping-stones to the next learning task. It is a challenge to parents to find a variety of ways to help a child experience success and to allow for individual creativity.

Darren and his son, Gordon, collect stamps. It is a way for them to spend special private time together. It also provides an opportunity for Darren to teach his son about history and geography and to expand his knowledge and understanding of the countries involved. In a loving and caring way he opens his son's eyes to new developments and challenges.

Parents who are aware of the significance of self-esteem will provide sincere praise, assist in the mastery of skills, and create situations that challenge thinking. Then future Ronnies will find it easier to walk through the door confidently, wearing a smile that says, "I'm ready."

11

Private Time

Barbara Hirst

Every gifted and talented child has an enormous need for private time. There must be some time during each day for a child to do as he or she pleases, with no stimulating ideas and plans from parents, grandparents, teachers, or other concerned individuals. So many of these children are programmed, planned, and scheduled so rigidly that many grow up without ever knowing what it means to relax, to be by themselves happily, to daydream. They have become totally dependent upon others and upon external stimulation to be busy and productive. Their own internal resources cannot be marshaled for individual thought and reflection.

Music lessons, dance lessons, religious instruction, trips to cultural events and institutions are all valuable and can be integrated into a child's life, but certainly not all of them each day or week. They become much more valuable and important to the child if they are chosen carefully, with an eye toward the child's interests and talents.

Just as valuable is time to be by oneself, to be able to reflect on the day just past or the new day just beginning. The child who seems to be daydreaming can be doing some very important personal thinking. Learning is acquired in hundreds of ways. It is not limited to schools, classrooms, or planned activities. Free time, personal time, enables a gifted child to devote energy to exploring new — or old — areas of interest. It can also provide for a transition from prior involvements.

Parents must help provide this personal time for their children and prevent the tyranny of overscheduling.

Barbara Hirst has been a teacher in the New York Public Schools, a staff associate with the American Association for Gifted Children, and coordinator of the Astor Program for the Gifted in New York City.

12

Parents of Gifted Children: Coping with Anxieties

William M. Greenstadt

GROWING TOWARD INDEPENDENCE

All parents look to their children to fulfill their own often frustrated and unattainable childhood dreams for achievement, gratification, and happiness. In some cases the parents' unconsciously imposed life goal for the child is to confirm a memory of their own mythically perfect childhood. But those parents who can find pleasure in diversity, and who also prize their own individuality, are relatively immune from such anxieties. It is not necessary to feel totally identified with a thing of beauty to take pleasure in its perfection. By the same token, from the state of closeness and nurturing identity with the newborn, the healthy parents obtain their greatest satisfaction in those aspects of the child's growth toward independence and individuality that seem to both parents and child like new discoveries, unique and unpredictable.

Each step forward in the child's growth presents parents with a bittersweet dilemma. The earlier pleasures of the preceding stage of development must now be relegated to the parents' memory, while newfound pride and pleasure are experienced in the child's new personality attributes and achievements.

The gifted child, perhaps more so than one who is not, represents a greater temptation to the parent for vicarious gratifications of dreams of glory and favor in the eyes of the world. The child's quick respon-

William M. Greenstadt, Ph.D., is an associate professor of school psychology at City College, City University of New York, and is vice-president and on the faculty of the New York Freudian Society. He is also a consulting school psychologist at the Hunter College Campus Schools.

siveness, delight in learning, and the seeming ease with which a wish is transformed into an achievement are potential hazards to the parent. Such parents, possibly more so than those of less-than-gifted children, must be prepared for the puzzled rage that such children may encounter when tackling something that is, after all, beyond even their capacities. Fortunately many intellectually gifted and talented children also possess a greater-than-usual tolerance for frustration and an enviable persistence. But the parent should be ready to temper the child's stubborn insistence on immediate success with his or her own patience.

In some instances a parent may possess an unconscious memory of an early sense of omnipotence. This attribute may now be transferred onto the gifted child. The result is that the parent fears to exercise his or her role as an inhibitor and controller in the service of the child's better adaptation to the exigencies of reality. The parent is afraid to "stunt the child's growth." But the child ends by feeling unprotected and exposed prematurely to a recalcitrant world. The child's only defense against such distress and helplessness is to accept the dubious gift of the parent's fantasy of omnipotence as a magic talisman against even legitimate and tolerable disappointments and failures.

TALENT IN CHILDREN MAY CAUSE ANXIETY IN PARENTS

A number of parents, when confronted with a child with a truly unusual ability, such as musical or artistic talent, may be placed by its early indications of superiority into states of anxiety and guilt. For example, a boy was admitted to the kindergarten of a suburban school who had already developed a remarkable skill in reading, such that he could read *The New York Times* with adult fluency. To the psychological consultant who was called in to evaluate the boy's general abilities, the child seemed embarrassed by his own awareness of his unusual talent and also aware that his mechanical skill in reading was not fully matched by a comparable level of comprehension. He wished to hide his ability from the other children for fear that it would alienate him from them, since he sensed that they were socially and emotionally not too unlike himself. The parents of this boy worried about his schooling and asked the psychologist for advice both on how to prevent his superior intellectual talents from languishing and on how to handle the problems arising when the other children were learning the elements of reading that he had long since mastered. The most pressing problem seemed to be that of the parents' guilty sense of responsibility in being the custodian of an extraordinary talent and their fear of somehow stifling it without meaning to. They had apparently reacted to this feeling of guilt by alternating between worrying about developing their boy's talent and treating that same talent as if it did not "belong" to them. Counseling with the parents focused on this issue in addition to making specific suggestions to them and to the school personnel about special enrichment activities for the boy. It was hoped that both the parents and the school would develop a feeling of shared, cooperative responsibility for the boy's productive and happy school life. Ultimately, the parents came to understand something of the sources of their anxiety and felt better able to take satisfaction from the boy's superior achievements. In addition, the school staff was alerted to the youngster's fear of being thought "too smart," and alternative classroom groupings were initiated to defuse the problem.

GIFTED CHILDREN MAY THREATEN PARENTS

Some parents whose own competitive zeal is intense may feel unconsciously threatened by a gifted child and may transmit to this child anger and hurt pride at the child's early display of talents that exceed their own. Early failures in competition with a sibling may accentuate the danger to the parent's pride. When parents play competitive games with a very young child, they may (under the guise of preparing the child for realistic competition) strive, even against their better judgment, to beat the child in the game. This may occur regularly at a time when the child interprets being defeated as a rejection issuing from the parent. It is entirely possible for such children to withdraw from the competitive field and to express their abilities only in the safe, private world of fantasy, where no competitor can subject them to humiliation. Or they may, at a later point, abandon the competition of work for the solitary reassurances of play. Even competitive play may retain for the child the significance of a field of endeavor where it "really doesn't count."

The ability to lose and to handle the blow to one's pride of having been defeated is developed in children only relatively late. It becomes a securely integrated trait perhaps only during the latter part of the elementary school years. At this time, the child's love of truth and reality has achieved a preeminent value, where *knowing* that one has lost has become more worth retaining than the avoidance of any sense of shame attached to losing. In a child's early years of growth, parents need to stress activities and accomplishments that focus more on cooperation than on competition and to minimize incidence where the only options are winning or losing.

PARENTS SOMETIMES IDEALIZE THE TALENTS OF CHILDREN

It is sometimes the case that the talents of a child are idealized in such a way that the parent expects that all possible undertakings by the child will meet with the same success in each instance. The notion thus developed is that "giftedness" is a general endowment. Actually one of the theoretical positions about the nature of intelligence holds that it represents both a general, inborn factor, distributed with comparative evenness throughout the variety of abilities by which we measure "intelligence," and an assortment of special abilities.

It is, however, more frequently the case that an otherwise "gifted" child may indeed show quite remarkable talents in many areas but less-than-outstanding ability in one or more other areas of functioning. In order to promote a healthy and realistic sense of self, the gifted child must come to learn where these strengths and relative weaknesses lie and to tolerate the rather greater effort necessary for attaining mastery in those areas of intellectual functioning where one is less well endowed. If the child's parents have not developed an analogous tolerance for differences (including the sense of the child's basic difference from the parent), they will find the task of helping to develop a greater sense of patience in the child beyond their emotional and intellectual scope. Once again, we have a sphere in which the joys of raising a gifted child and taking pleasure in the development of the child's uniqueness may be spoiled by overidealization.

PLATEAUS IN LEARNING

A similar problem is presented by the universal tendency of all people to learn in what appears to the uninitiated observer as "spurts." The normal plateaus in learning, often accompanied in the child by an apparent loss of interest in the learning process or a shift in the sense of excitement in learning a new skill, may be misunderstood as a loss of motivation, or worse yet, a display of "laziness."

A general concept in the theory of human development is the sequential manner in which mastery takes place. The child's first approach to the task of adapting to an environmental situation is almost always *global*. From global reactions the child begins to *differentiate* both the characteristics of the environment and his or her own reactions to them. The final stage is one in which differentiated but relatively uncoordinated units of behavior are now *integrated* into more complex performances. In addition to this general sequence should be added the evolution in thinking from the *concrete* to the *abstract*. The interplay of these trends often results in periods during which the integrative process goes on "silently," without any apparent or overt signs of learning.

The parents of any child, including those of a gifted child, must sensitize themselves to this intermittent process of learning and develop an awareness of when a child is in a "resting" state as contrasted to when he or she may have utterly given up.

TOLERANCE OF SLOW DEVELOPMENT OF SOCIAL SKILLS

Most parents tend toward greater tolerance of slower development of social skills when their child has clearly demonstrated the capacity for advancing rapidly in intellectual pursuits. Such complacency sometimes is a product of the child's having given the parent ample gratification of the latter's idealized hopes for achievement and competition while also providing the parent with equally gratifying experiences in remaining the "tending" adult. Such children are unconsciously permitted to continue to be spoiled, clinging babies as "payment" for their having satisfied their parents' needs. Although gifted children are often as precocious in social development as they are in the intellectual sphere and will demonstrate a willful need to strike out on their own in splitting themselves off from their all-too-brief babyhood, it is not always sound for the parent to rely wholly on this self-assertion. Such social skills as self-control over the normally egotistic outlook toward the world, the child's feeling of brotherhood and identification with all other children, the capacity to share and to give — these must be consciously fostered by word and action in the gifted child.

IMPLICATIONS

During a youngster's periods of growth and change, should an emotional conflict develop leading to some form of adjustment problem, intellectual functions and achievements are almost always pulled into the orbit of the conflict. Once embroiled in it, mental growth may be inhibited or distorted in its expression. Thus an emotional or personality problem may encroach upon the field of intellectual development and prohibit it from achieving its full and characteristic potential. It has been discovered, for example, that very early emotional as well as intellectual environmental deprivations can *irreversibly* interfere with and distort intellectual growth. Such children are destined to find the tasks of school learning an unremitting agony. The child who has already shown a high level of intelligence at an early age, but who seems to have fallen back as he or she grows older, may have this potential "restored" if the slowing down can be shown to be primarily of emotional origin and if he or she then receives appropriate psychotherapeutic treatment. It may be added that some children with emotional problems experience considerable anxiety both in tutorial and in testing situations, which predictably results in evidences of lowered measurable ability and academic achievement. Parental anxiety and guilt about a child's apparent slowing down in intellectual development should be applied to a careful assessment of the reasons for the lowered functioning. Such an apparent slowdown may be completely predictable and understandable.

A gifted child may offer the receptive parent an incomparable stream of pleasure and satisfaction as the child's growth and individuality unfolds. Perhaps a recipe for joy in the parenting of a gifted child may be offered: One of life's sweetest pleasures is to be given a gift one did not really think one could hope for or deserve. Parents should allow themselves to savor the gift and even to express the gratitude they feel toward the one who gave it — their own child.

13
Recognizing Creative Behavior

Felice Kaufmann

Creativity is a word that is used widely by persons both in and out of educational circles. We speak of a creative child, creative writing, creative drama, and the like. Too often, however, this term is applied only to an end product — an artistic work or musical composition, for example — without much thought being given to what the creative process is really all about.

The rapidly changing demands and challenges existing in the world today have almost necessarily been accompanied by an upswing of interest in and a broadening of the concept of creativity. Consequently we are now able to look to a variety of activities and behaviors to locate our creative children, rather than the usual means of looking at academic performance alone. Some of these behaviors can be especially well observed in a home environment where the child is relaxed and relating to people and things with which she or he is familiar and safe. It is here, then, that parents can be most instrumental in developing the kind of situation in which creativity can truly flourish.

WHAT IS CREATIVITY?

Dr. E. Paul Torrance's definition of creativity has wide currency in educational circles. He defines creativity as

> becoming sensitive to or aware of problems, deficiencies, gaps in
> knowledge, missing elements, disharmonies and so on; bringing

Felice Kaufmann, Ph.D., is an assistant professor in special education at Auburn University, Auburn, Ala. She has served as research assistant to Dr. E. Paul Torrance, directed a gifted-child program, taught gifted children at the elementary and secondary levels, and completed an internship at the USOE Office for Gifted and Talented.

together available information; defining the difficulty or identifying the missing element; searching for solutions, making guesses or formulating hypotheses about the deficiencies, testing and restesting these hypotheses and modifying and restating them; perfecting them and finally communicating the results.

Here we see limitless situations in which parents might recognize and encourage their children's creativity. Anything from solving problems with brothers and sisters to finding unique methods of cleaning out comic book collections might be considered good indicators.

The realization that creativity is a natural, healthy process and a strong human need is one good reason for parents to want to provide for creative experiences in the home, much as they would provide for their children's physical or psychological needs. Creativity should be viewed as a tool that has real life relevance on application. Any opportunity that a child has to sense problems and create solutions can be helpful to his or her growth as a creative person.

HOW PARENTS CAN RECOGNIZE CREATIVE BEHAVIOR

It is, of course, no easy task for parents to devote close attention to their child's creativity when so many other areas of development need either obvious or immediate attention. At times parents may even feel that working on the creative aspect of their child's personality may interfere with other types of learning. But there are things a parent can do without extensive or exhausting effort. It is important that parents become familiar with certain signals of creativity so that they will be able to recognize and encourage creative behavior when it appears. Torrance suggests the following indications:

- Intense absorption in listening, observing, or doing (''But I didn't hear you call me for dinner!'')
- Intense animation and physical involvement (''But I can't sit still — I'm thinking.'')
- Use of analogies in speech (''I feel like a caterpillar waiting to become a butterfly.'')
- Tendency to challenge ideas of authorities (''Why do I have to go to school until I'm fifteen?)
- Habit of checking many sources (''Mom, I looked at all the books and watched a TV special and asked my teacher, and I still can't figure out where God lives.'')

- Taking a close look at things ("Hey, this centipede only has ninety-nine legs!")
- Eagerness to tell others about discoveries ("Guess what, guess what, guess what!")
- Continuing in creative activities after the scheduled time for quitting ("I did my artwork right through recess today!")
- Showing relationships among apparently unrelated ideas ("Hey, Mom, your new hat looks just like a flying saucer.")
- Following through on ideas set in motion ("Tomorrow I'm going to dig for gold in our backyard.")
- Various manifestations of curiosity and wanting to know ("I just wanted to see what the yard looked like from on top of the roof.")
- Spontaneous use of discovery or experimental approach ("I thought flour and water would make bread, but all I got was white goo.")
- Excitement in voice about discoveries ("Flour and water make paste!")
- Habit of guessing and testing outcomes ("I put detergent in the birdbath, but no birds came to clean up. Can I try some bubble bath today?")
- Honesty and intense search for truth ("Mom, I hope this doesn't upset you, but I've come to the conclusion that there is no Tooth Fairy.")
- Independent action ("There are no good books on racing cars, Mom, I'm going to write my own.")
- Boldness of ideas ("But I think that children should be allowed to vote.")
- Low distractability ("I can't come out to play — I'm waiting for my chemicals to dissolve.")
- Manipulation of ideas and objects to obtain new combinations ("I'm going to take this string and this pencil and make a compass.")
- Penetrating observations and questions ("When the snow melts, where does the white go?")
- Tendency to seek alternatives and explore new possibilities ("This old shoe would make a great flowerpot.")
- Self-initiated learning ("Yesterday I went to the library and checked out all the books on dinosaurs.")

- Willingness to consider or toy with strange ideas ("What if dogs were masters and people were pets?")

Knowing these behaviors, it is important that parents watch their children for their natural tendencies in this direction. Behaviors such as those mentioned may show up in unexpected places or at unexpected times — at the dinner table, at bedtime, in the playground. But wherever or whenever they surface, it becomes crucial for parents to appreciate that creative thinking has taken place. Using creative potential that children have and demonstrate is always easier and more productive than teaching these behaviors from scratch later on.

HOW A PARENT CAN HELP

There are some positive steps a parent can take toward setting the stage for creativity to grow. The following list is adapted from some suggestions provided by Torrance:

- Provide materials that develop imagination, such as open-ended stories or drawings.
- Provide materials that enrich imagery, such as fairy tales, folk tales, myths, fables, nature books.
- Permit time for thinking and daydreaming. Just because children don't look like they're busy doesn't mean that their minds are not.
- Encourage children to record their ideas in binders, notebooks, and the like. Even playing secretary for them by having them dictate their stories to you can be a special way of showing that their ideas are valuable and that you care about what they are thinking.
- Accept and use the tendency to take a different look. There are really many things one can learn about the world by standing on one's head.
- Prize rather than punish true individuality. It is always possible to find little details about children's work or behavior that might make them feel as though you noticed them as special people.
- Be cautious in editing children's products. Sometimes a word corrected in the wrong place or too many times can stifle a child's creative energy and feeling of worth as a creator.
- Encourage children to play with words. Even in such a common setting as a car ride or a shopping trip, word games such as rhyming, opposites, and puns can be used to their full advantage.

TEACHING CREATIVE THINKING IN THE HOME

In addition to the general setting of tone and opportunity for creativity to develop, it is also a challenge for parents to learn and reinforce some of the specific thinking processes that go into a creative act. This knowledge is helpful not only in its direct effect on children but also in the parent's understanding of creativity as it applies to toys, materials, experiences, and problems in the home.

The four main thought processes of creative thinking are fluency, flexibility, originality, and elaboration. Each of these plays a specific role in the development of creativity; all are vital to its production.

Fluent Thinking is the ability to produce a quantity of possibilities, ideas, consequences, or objects. The importance of this process is that it builds a large store of information or materials for a person to select from or use at a later time. It is fun and exciting to be challenged to think of new ideas, and little or no materials are required to create games for this purpose.

Asking a child, "I wonder how many different ways we can figure out to use these old plastic bags? that shoe box? those extra milk cartons?" is a good way to stimulate fluent thinking and also produces some interesting and helpful solutions for everyday problems. Questions like "How many words can you remember that begin with *bl?*" or "What would happen if animals could talk?" have kept many a child occupied on long car trips. And the benefits of "How many different ways can you think of to remind yourself to take out the garbage?" should go without saying.

The point is quantity of ideas, not whether a child comes up with realistic or practical solutions. Once thoughts flow, the child may want to go back and work on these ideas, evaluate them, and develop one or two. But even if she or he does not get to this stage immediately, the process will have begun. Practicing fluency in a variety of situations leads to greater ease with creativity.

Flexible Thinking is the ability to use many different approaches or strategies in solving a problem. It allows for changes in thinking to include alternatives, contrasting ideas, various points of view, and so forth. Some examples of questions that foster flexible thinking would be "How many sentences can you think of that begin with the word *yellow* and end with the word *forest?*" or "In how many different patterns can you arrange this triangle and circle?" As with fluent thinking, the development of this process helps children produce many approaches to a problem so that their final solution comes only after the consideration of many possible ideas. This process can, of course, be useful in solving all kinds of problems, from academic to social, and thus is an especially important tool for learning and growth.

Original Thinking is the ability to produce unusual, unique, or unanticipated responses. This, too, is a process that requires few materials. Asking a child to think up new names for common objects, comic strip characters, or animals, or having them make up titles for books or movies are good ways of encouraging orginality. Some parents have been able to use lists of children's excuses for not doing chores as a take-off point for some original thinking by manipulating the humor of the situation to reduce conflict. If children feel that their excuses are being appreciated for their originality, the chore itself may seem less awesome. Good-natured comments like "Well, last week it was that you were coming down with the plague. . . . What is it this time?" can be just as effective as "Don't tell me that you're too sick to clean this room!" If the household schedule can stand it, it might even be possible to use a vacation from a particular chore as a reward for the most original excuse, provided that the children know that this procedure is just a game.

Elaborative Thinking is the ability to expand, develop, and embellish one's ideas, plans, stories, or products. It is important in the development of creativity because it promotes communication, which is vital to the process. Asking children to discuss details in their stories or having them create inventions from various objects are two good ways of provoking elaborative thinking. Children might help in making elaborate and detailed plans for their birthday parties or in cataloguing things in their rooms. It is also possible to encourage elaboration by playing memory games at bedtime. Opportunities to discuss the events of the day become a challenge to active young minds, especially when they are pressed for details concerning their senses and feelings.

Besides specific training in each of these four areas, there are other creativity tools that can be easily used in the home. One of these is creative problem solving. This technique, originated by Alex Osborn and developed by Sidney Parnes and other members of the Creative Education Foundation, in Buffalo, New York, follows the aspect of Torrance's definition of creativity that relates to the sensing of problems and gaps. The five main steps of problem solving can be applied to almost any kind of problem and are fun and productive at the same time. As outlined by Torrance and R. E. Myers, these steps include

1. **Sensing the Problem or Challenge.** This first step is usually brought out by a specific incident or situation, such as "How shall I spend my allowance?" or "How can I make sure I get up on time for school?"

2. **Analyzing to Find the Real Problem.** This step involves finding

facts about the problem, restating it in broader terms, changing the wording, and finally breaking the problem down into smaller subproblems. For the second question just mentioned this might mean asking questions such as "Why am I not getting up on time?" "What don't I like about getting up?" or "By what means do I get myself up?"

3. **Producing Alternative Solutions.** The next step requires brainstorming all the possible solutions to the problem, no matter how off the track the suggestions might appear. Criticism at this stage is absolutely forbidden. Alternatives for this problem might be anything from "Use three alarm clocks" to "Buy a rooster" to "Drink lots of water so I'll have to get up to go to the bathroom" to "Don't sleep at all."

4. **Evaluating Ideas.** At this stage comes the selection of criteria for the most promising ideas generated in the previous steps. The criteria for the sample problem might be expense, annoyance to the family, physical space, or health.

5. **Preparing to Put the Ideas into Use.** This stage requires the refinement of the selected solution. Questions such as "How can I make the solution attractive or appealing to other people?" or "What will be the consequences of the solution?" now become appropriate. In this case it might be "How can I convince my father that a rooster is better than an alarm clock?"

Different aspects of this model may be adapted to fit the age of the participants, making it usable for people of all ages and abilities. It is exciting to see the process in action in any variation. It is also an excellent way to train creative thinking.

Another interesting type of creative training is the SCAMPER Technique developed by Robert Eberle. The letters SCAMPER represent seven types of clues for fluent, flexible, original, and elaborative thought. They are:

S	Substitute	To have a person or thing act or serve in the place of another: Who else instead? What else? Other place? Other time?
C	Combine	To bring together, unite: How about a blend, an assortment? Combine purposes? Combine ideas?
A	Adapt	To adjust for the purpose of suiting a condition or purpose: What else is like this? What other ideas does this suggest?

M Modify	To alter, to change the form or quality: change meaning, color, motion, sound, odor, taste, form.
Magnify	To enlarge, make greater in form or quality: What to add? Greater frequency? Stronger? Larger?
Minify	To make smaller, lighter, slower, less frequent: What to subtract? Smaller? Lighter? Slower? Split up? Less frequent?
P Put to other uses	New ways to use it? Other uses if modified?
E Eliminate	To remove, omit, or get rid of a part, quality, or whole: What parts can be taken out? To keep the same function? To change the function?
R Reverse	To place opposite or contrary, to turn it around: Opposites? Turn it backward? Turn it upside down? Turn it inside out?
Rearrange	To change order or adjust, different plan, layout, or scheme: Other sequence? Change pace?

The advantage of the SCAMPER method is that it can be applied to many situations with a minimum of materials. For example, as simple an item as a toothbrush may become the object of a SCAMPER adventure:

- If you needed a toothbrush and did not have one, what else could you use? (Substitute)
- What could you make with six toothbrushes and six feet of string? (Combine)
- How would you change a toothbrush for someone who had no hands? (Adapt)
- What would the Jolly Green Giant use for a toothbrush? (Magnify)
- What else could you use a toothbrush for? (Put to other uses)
- What would happen if you removed the bristles on a toothbrush? (Eliminate)
- How would a toothbrush function if the bristles were at the bottom? (Reverse)

SCAMPER has been known to fascinate children for many hours and is highly recommended for the rainy Saturday afternoon blues. It is also a helpful technique because of the many exciting and functional innovations that can be produced in the name of fun.

WHAT ABOUT FAR-OUT IDEAS?

In order to develop creative skills, children must feel that they are psychologically safe. This means that they must know they can indulge in fantasy and take risks with their thinking and not be judged harshly or punished. Statements like "Don't be silly" or "You should know better" should be avoided at all costs, because they squelch imagination and playfulness. Comments like "You have so many ideas" or "What else can you think of?" or "That's really different!" take about as much energy to say and are much more conducive to a climate that breeds creativity. If children's ideas seem potentially dangerous, a gentle "How would that work?" or "Can you explain that again?" or "Maybe you'd better get some more facts" would encourage them to come to their own conclusions. Statements like "That's terrible" or "What a ridiculous idea" only kill the effort.

WHAT ABOUT CREATIVE TOYS?

With so many "creative" toys and games on the market today, it is no wonder parents get confused. Half of this problem is not so much knowing which of the items to select as understanding how to make the selection. The best way a parent can judge products on their creative value is to look for open-endedness. For example, a set of blocks with parts that interlock with only a few specific parts would be less open-ended than a set with limitless possibilities for arrangement. It is also possible to turn a standard product into a more creative one by applying the techniques that have been discussed here. For example, questions such as "How would you change that game so that younger children could use it? or "What would happen if that doll were five feet tall?" or "How many uses can you think of for dice?" or "Can you invent new rules for that game?" provide many opportunities for creative thinking and prove that a parent does not have to buy new toys to get the job done well.

Most important, parents must know children, their interests, how they think and learn, the kinds of creative thinking they enjoy, and the kinds they need to develop. This may be accomplished by observing children, but it is even more effective if parents themselves begin to practice creative thinking. As parents become familiar with many points of view and themselves experience more enjoyment of words, images, colors, and senses, children will naturally follow. Creativity training can be hard work, but it can also bring happiness and productivity. It literally depends on how you look at things.

14

The Creative Child at Home

Gertrude Howell Hildreth

Normal children are curious by nature, and their behavior is quite spontaneous in activities such as block building, drawing, carving soap, experimenting with inclined planes, trying out kites and rockets, working with the number system. Fantasy is a prominent feature of the play life. A young child's expression reflects inexperience and ignorance of the everyday world. The inventiveness of childhood results from sensorimotor impulses, that of older persons from mental reflection and intellectual reasoning. For example, at first, knowledge of fractional parts is gained through experience with blocks, pies, and other objects. In later years a child no longer needs experimentation with these objects because the rules of mathematical computation with whole numbers and fractions have been learned.

Creativity is talent for original thinking that generates novel ideas, inventions, and products that significantly affect people's lives. Creative minds, the world's greatest source of social change and human welfare, are considered to be the rarest and most valuable of human characteristics.

Among inventions that have changed the course of history and influenced human progress are the telescope and microscope, steam and electric transportation, the cotton gin, the linotype printing press, harvesting machines, the bicycle, the sewing machine, and the "gas buggy," to mention but a few examples. Creative thinking is demonstrated in every field of human endeavor — in all the arts and sciences,

Gertrude Howell Hildreth, Ph.D., was formerly a psychologist and associate in research at Lincoln School, Teachers College; a Fulbright Lecturer at the University of Istanbul, Turkey; and a visiting professor at American University in Beirut, Lebanon. She is professor emeritus of Brooklyn College, N.Y. She is also the author of books and articles concerning gifted children.

in every professional career: government, economics, social welfare, health care, architecture, research, biology, anthropology. Pressing problems of our world today — the use of available energy, population control, the food supply, health improvement, international relations, universal education — can be solved through the application of creative intelligence. As old ideas, customs, and modes of life become obsolete, new devices and ways of thinking take their place.

ORIGINS OF CREATIVITY

Creativity, psychologists agree, is learned ability that emerges with social facilitation rather than a unitary skill that can be taught to children and young people by a formula or a particular course of study.

The ability to do creative thinking, along with other human attributes, is a product of both nature and nurture. Some individuals are born with superior intellectual equipment; everyone is subject to environmental circumstances, the effects of which are not readily predictable. Home and school experiences, with instruction by parents and teachers up to the age of maturity, prepare children for each new step in development.

A notion prevails that all forms of giftedness are merely the result of luck or chance; gifted kids are the ones who "got a break." Fate, like a throw of the dice, leads to fame and fortune or to the reverse. The British physicist Lord Rutherford, on hearing someone say, "Lucky Rutherford, always on the crest of the wave," responded, "Well, I made the wave, didn't I?"

CREATIVITY AND UNUSUAL APTITUDES AS DEVELOPMENTAL TRAITS

Dr. Sidney L. Pressey, noted American psychologist, was the originator of a unique theory to explain the emergence of exceptional abilities and performance in any category, mental or physical. According to Pressey, superior aptitudes and talents develop by a process of cumulative success. Dr. Pressey believed that genius is produced by giving a capable young person encouragement, intensive instruction in special areas, and continuing opportunity for creative work. The cumulative effect of the total experience leading to successful experience is what matters most.

Early in life bright, clever youngsters get on the "gifted track," where they continue to develop through continued persistence, effort, practice, and rewards until they become experts or champions. By age eight or ten the children have become accelerated for their age, and through continued success, by the late teens, the particular trait has become well established.

Dr. Pressey was convinced that the same principles of learning and habit formation account for star status in athletics, stage acting, and other types of performance that combine physical and mental prowess.

Does the Pressey theory hold for so ephemeral a characteristic as creativity — that is, a promising display of originality that gets nurtured by praise and reinforcement, congenial educational stimulation, and constructive parental guidance? A survey of biographies of eminent inventors and original persons gives an affirmative answer to the question. Continuity appears to be the rule. Once on the creative track, the individual is inclined to stay there.

WHAT ARE THE MOST CREATIVE YEARS?

Studies of the most productive and creative years indicate that the greatest productivity in the arts and sciences comes in the late twenties and early thirties; for literature and philosophy, a little later.

Creative achievement of lasting value seldom appears before the adolescent years, but on reaching early adulthood young people have achieved maturity for signal accomplishment. As in the case of physical strength and agility, after age thirty-five the pace begins to slacken.

IDENTIFICATION OF THE CREATIVE CHILD AT HOME AND IN SCHOOL

Some children at an early age are busy with unusual productions that represent more than chance performance. Kindergarteners may show signs of original thinking and talent for making little discoveries or inventions or may devise unique games and occupations. Parents may recognize a child as unusual because of skill in drawing or handwork, exceptional memory, mature flow of language in narration, talent for the violin, but they can overlook potentiality for creative accomplishments. However, reliable predictions can scarcely be made without the test of growth itself and how the child responds to guidance and environmental circumstances.

TRAITS OF CREATIVITY IN YOUTH

Creative young people have unusual traits that distinguish them from others — intensity of purpose, strong drives, high mental energy, vivid imagination, and the ability to bring new ideas to fruition in practical form.

Although traits of the creative thinker are similar throughout all age levels, some are more characteristic of one age level than another; for example, collecting things, reading adventure stories, building objects to play with. In early childhood, creativity is associated more largely with gross motor activity and control, later on with mental processes growing out of school experiences.

Here are some predominant traits of creative youth: unusual powers of perception, reasoning ability, special insights, flexibility of thinking. The trait of studiousness is characteristic. Bright young people like to engage in theoretical speculation.

High intelligence is unquestionably an ingredient in early creativity, but to have a high IQ does not guarantee originality of thinking. Originality is the outcome of superior intellect combined with certain habits of mind, scholarly methods of problem solving, and requisite background of experience.

PARENT ATTITUDES TOWARD A CHILD WITH CREATIVE IDEAS

Some parents may need advice about maintaining a positive attitude toward the child with precocious ideas who delights in novel experiments. Instead of harboring suspicions about the child's sanity or protesting, "I don't want my child to be a little genius, a freak of nature, an infant prodigy who attracts attention. Better to be entirely normal like his friends and classmates," parents should realize that even to harbor such thoughts may engender attitudes toward the child that could thwart the ambition to become a great leader or original thinker in adult life.

Instead, parents should show tolerance, confidence, and understanding of the child's little discoveries. Praise any signs of originality. Comment favorably on an original map, a block tower, a costume, a painting showing originality in design or color.

FOSTERING CREATIVITY AT HOME AND IN SCHOOL

Early identification of gifted children at home and in school makes it possible for parents and teachers to do long-range planning for the child's educational needs and to provide suitable guidance for all phases of development from year to year — physical, mental, and personal. With predictive data to go by, there is less cause for concern when the child's actions seem unusual or abnormal. The children themselves will be less likely to "give out" or "give up" for lack of direction of their energies. Suggestions for training and guiding these children necessarily vary with the age level under consideration.

ADVICE TO PARENTS OF THE CREATIVE CHILD

Thoughtful parents of children with unusual ideas and creative tendencies seek first to create a congenial home setting for the development of promising traits. The children are full-fledged participating family members rather than subordinates of inferior status. The story is told that the famous American philosopher Dr. John Dewey called his family together for weekly meetings to discuss problems that arose from time to time. How did the water in the bathtub happen to run over and leak through the floor? How can we arrange to pay for the damage? What suggestions has anyone for preventing such an accident in the future?

Discovering how to deal with problems for oneself is half the answer to developing independence of thought and action. Avoid dictation when a problem is within the child's grasp. Rules for home conduct should be made by parents and children together, a process that requires some independent thinking and exercise in self-control.

Giving children an increasing measure of independence and self-responsibility is essential for maturation. In every way cultivate the child's individuality, his or her unique tendencies and preferences. No matter how farfetched a child's idea or creation may seem, it may be a good one. Better to risk praise than to discourage originality. The family household may be even more influential than schooling in the early years when freedom of expression and cooperation among family members are considered essential traits to be developed. Some measure of freedom gives the youngster a chance to experience making choices and his or her own decisions.

Dr. Albert Szent-Györgyi, the Hungarian-born scientist, attributed his drive toward science research to growing up in a family of scientists and an intellectual atmosphere that fostered interest in discovery. In such a household, children's questions are welcomed and freely answered on the level of the child's understanding. Children's suggestions are welcomed when planning for activities is under discussion. The children are given freedom to do as they wish on consultation with their elders, depending upon their age and stage of reasoning.

The children are given space of their own where their possessions are kept and free play is permitted. Assist the child in setting up his or her own den or studio with a desk, table, workbench and equipment, blackboard, and good lighting. Even a corner of a room may suffice for the kindergarten years.

Play life is indispensable for wholesome growth, mentally and physically, for socializing and character development, for muscle building and coordination. Play stimulates the mind and gives the creative child an outlet for experimenting with ideas and materials. Through their play, children gain in exploratory behavior with objects, events, and relationships. Constructive and dramatic play may, in fact, underlie preparation for an inventive career.

Younger children enjoy devising their own play materials from exploration with household "throwaways": spools, plastic bottles, pots and pans, wheels, boxes, crates that cost nothing and are disposable.

When the entire family plays together at a cookout, a picnic, or on a camping trip, there are advantages both for the older and for the younger members. The young ones test out their agility and thinking powers with the grown-ups; in turn, the adults gain better understanding of immature members of the group.

For example, in a city household with three children and limited floor space, parents gave up the idea of having a parlor always ready for guests. Instead they turned the sun-lit room into a playroom for the children until they were in the teens. A backyard with some equipment or neighboring playground space for play under supervision extends recreation resources for active children. Space reserved for hobby interests gives incentive for learning in many categories.

A creative child who enjoys handwork may find in weaving, sewing, knitting, or papercutting an outlet for imaginative thinking as well as an offset to chain reading and TV viewing.

For the child with literary interests there are many outlets for expression, from scribbling enthusiastically to class-newspaper editing. Such a child may enjoy making a scrapbook, starting a diary, keeping records with illustrations, serving as scribe for class and club meetings, or "just writing" to record fanciful ideas. Such were the juvenile endeavors of eminent literary figures.

THE DEVELOPMENT OF READING SKILLS AND INTERESTS AT HOME

Most highly creative persons — certainly all the great writers — became literate in early life not so much by "teaching themselves to read" as by having been attracted to print by their elders and by repeating sentences read aloud.

Children who show interest in reading for themselves at home in the early years are encouraged by parents and older children who read stories and poems aloud. Progress is rapid when reading and handwriting are taught together, using the vocabulary of daily events for recording words and sentences on a large blackboard in the playroom or on the porch. Avoid showing concern if the child, in trying to record ideas in a familiar vocabulary, comes up with somewhat fanciful spelling. As vocabulary recognition increases, supply the beginner with well-illustrated "I Can Read" books, which have simple vocabulary and plenty of repetition. Also, read aloud from stories of magic and from biographies of inventors and explorers.

General conversation among all members of the household, storytelling, reading aloud, and asking and answering questions are all means of building fluency in oral language.

The elementary and junior high school years are the right time to reinforce language usage skills in the mother tongue, and perhaps in a second language as well. A person with a head full of innovative ideas that he or she is unable to express adequately will be at a distinct disadvantage in competition with other gifted people who can also speak and write with ease. Children's ability to speak grammatically improves in association with those who pronounce words correctly and habitually use good grammar.

THE MENTOR

Home and school educational guidance of the young brings into focus the teacher, whether a qualified and certified expert or a parent who has natural talent for instructing children. The Greeks had a word for it, the *mentor,* an adult experienced in imparting learning, manners, and morals to young persons and who sometimes serves as a friendly companion, tutor, and personal counselor. A wise, patient grandparent may be eminently fitted for the role. In the mentor a gifted child has continued contact with a mature mind. One-to-one instruction at the hands of a learned person tends to develop the traits of a scholar, enthusiasm for learning, and interest in original problem solving.

INCIDENTAL AND SELF-INITIATED LEARNING AT HOME

Much of a bright child's learning outside of school is incidental, the result of observation and questioning rather than instruction from adults. Counting, telling time by the clock, using scales, a calendar, the telephone, a thermometer or a calculator, and observing the stars are examples of such learning. Even, to some extent, learning reading and writing through alphabet play, recognition of labels at the store, and observing traffic signs are the result of the child's own initiative.

A recommendation to parents and older siblings is that they utilize all these resources for the child's incidental learning by keeping the equipment in sight, using correct terminology, and answering children's questions. Children learn new words, common terms, and proverbs incidentally when they are used repeatedly in their presence.

Primary facts about economics can be learned in the process of putting money in a bank account, buying and selling, and using and accounting for money. The cultivation of good study and work habits begins at home when a child becomes used to the idea of planning a job to be undertaken, considering the best use of time, avoiding interruptions, exercising care in using materials, and keeping things in order in the study and work space.

TEACHING FOR CREATIVITY

Can creativity be taught? The answer in general is no if the term implies the assumption of mental discipline or instruction in a separate subject apart from the rest of the curriculum.

The experience of eminent creative persons as young scholars indicates that none of them had a ''course in creativity,'' but all absorbed, from varied studies, certain skills, attitudes, and proficiencies that made them competent scholars in the first place, then led them on into fields of work and study that engaged their ability to identify problems and to apply reflection and imagination in dealing with them.

Prompting children to raise pertinent questions is a means of stimulating novel thinking on some topic. When Dr. Isidor Rabi, physicist and Nobel Prize winner, was a schoolboy, his mother would inquire on his return from school, ''Did you ask any good questions today?'' Children must be stimulated in their intellectual pursuits at each age level. Research still has much to discover in determining how to enhance creativity. In the meantime parents can work with the resources at hand to encourage their children along paths suggested in this essay.

15
Gifted Children and Their Siblings

Sylvia Sunderlin

"We are all alike, in different ways," said a mother while being interviewed by an educator about her family, which consisted of a gifted son with a splendid academic record; a daughter who, while still in high school, was already making a name for herself as an artist; and twins, a boy and a girl, born nearly ten years after the daughter, both with average IQs. Her seemingly cryptic remark was not a defense but a wise expression of the philosophy of that family. What she meant, the educator had already discerned, was that parents and children had faced up to their differences and had built upon them to strengthen a family founded on love, mutual trust, and a determination to let nothing stand in the way of family solidarity.

VARYING ABILITIES IN ONE FAMILY

While the identification of the gifted and talented has been explored, expressed, and reexpressed in dozens of different ways, the identification of the not-so-gifted child remains more elusive. The child of somewhat less than median intelligence may not be markedly noticeable or different in a family of children who all have about the same degree of intellectual capability, but in a family where there is one brilliant child or perhaps two who are differently but equally gifted, the child of lesser capability may be egregiously noticeable.

This child's learning difficulties may stem from one or more reasons —

Sylvia Sunderlin was formerly a staff associate at the American Association for Gifted Children and is presently a consulting editor for Association for Childhood Education International, Washington, D.C. She is the author of *Antrim's Orange,* a book for children.

speech, hearing or sight disorders, disability lingering from the effects of a severe childhood illness, or because the child has a limited capacity to learn. The child may also be shy, clumsy, frail, anemic, or overweight. An inferior physique, unpleasant personal habits, or a poor self-image can be additional handicaps to the child who has to struggle, or perhaps has not the will or heart to struggle, to keep up with gifted brothers and sisters.

Even in families where all the children are gifted and there appears to be minimal variation in their intelligence and skills, there are likely to be problems of rivalry among them, each one vying for parental attention. But in families where wide gaps exist between a gifted child and his or her siblings, problems may be more numerous and of a different order. Many parents experience unusual stress and anxieties in trying to establish harmony in the family and equitable relationships among widely different children.

Parental attitudes are as varying as the family patterns themselves. Some parents go to extremes in ignoring or pretending to ignore their gifted children. Through a kind of perverse detachment they hide their pride in their child's giftedness as if they were afraid of being accused of taking credit for the child's intellectual attainments, or perhaps through fear of being found wanting by comparison.

Parents who focus attention upon the gifted child while neglecting the less-well-endowed child foster bad feelings for everyone.

Still other parents face the conditions of each child individually, spreading their love over all their family while striving to do for each child what is right, just, and needed.

What are some problems parents of differing children have to face? How do some parents cope with great differences among their children?

The Cooper family is an example of widely divergent natural endowment among siblings. The father is a lawyer and the mother is a successful businesswoman with a prosperous real estate firm. Their daughter was eight and their son four when the third child, a girl, was born. The older two were difficult and perhaps "disappointing" children to bright, successful parents, for they showed no special aptitudes, no inclination to succeed academically or in any other way. The third child showed early signs of giftedness. She walked, talked, and learned to read at an early age. She was beautiful and charming; she could sing in a clear, true voice, and by the time she was eight showed extraordinary skill and grasp of music. She progressed rapidly in both piano and violin.

From the time she showed unusual promise, the Cooper parents were aware of their problem. The two older children exhibited constant resentment and jealousy, voicing their bitterness openly and frequently:

"Grace gets everything her own way because she knows how to sing."
"Why is school so easy for her and so hard for Tom and me?" By the
time Grace was nine and sailing blithely through school and music lessons, accomplishing everything with ease in contrast to her older sister
and brother, the Coopers realized they must act quickly. Could they
suppress Grace's enthusiasm and skill? No, they must get help. With the
counsel of a school psychologist and a private professional advisor,
they launched a skillful campaign within their own family to set matters
right.

Without ignoring Grace, they began to concentrate on the older
ones, taking more notice of their strengths. Barbara, now seventeen,
would be finishing high school this year. Then what? At first she showed
no interest in anything beyond high school. What would happen to her
if she could not go to college, if she did not want to go? With the help
of the school guidance counselor they talked and worked with Barbara,
supporting her in every positive move, encouraging her social life, praising her for each accomplishment: completing a piece of needlepoint,
serving as a leader for a class first-aid program. And then Barbara began
to reach out. She wanted to be a nurse. Once that desire was indicated,
the Coopers bolstered their elder daughter with support, praising her
for her worthy ambition, letting her know that she was a valued and
achieving daughter. She was on her way.

At the same time they were working with Tom's guidance counselor,
probing and watching to discover their son's as-yet-unrevealed gifts.
They showed their enthusiasm and interest for everything he tried. Up
to this time they had been rather indifferent to the many interests he
had tried and discarded, with many failures. He began to show signs of
developing in his "tinkering," which he had been engaged in since early
childhood but which they had failed to notice. He liked to fix things, his
own toys, broken lamps, small motors. He surprised them the day he
admitted that he wanted to be a mechanic of some kind, but he was
afraid that his college-trained parents would disapprove of such a
"lowly" calling. Once they convinced him of their absolute approval
and, furthermore, delight in his admirable choice of occupation, he
began to improve both in his schoolwork and in his relations with his
parents and siblings.

Grace would happily have gone along, basking in everyone's
approval. The counselor suggested to the parents, and they quickly
agreed, that Grace be made aware of her responsibility within the family. She was drawn into the family project by being made to understand
that her older siblings had a great deal to offer her: examples of
patience and precepts of unselfishness.

The Bensons were the parents of Jonathan, a frail, partly crippled boy whose handicap resulted from a rare case of poliomyelitis. The trauma of his handicap was tragically compounded by their guilt, for they were a doctor and a former nurse, who blamed themselves bitterly for having neglected at a critical stage in Jonathan's life to have given him a repeat immunization shot. Their guilt was intensified by the fact thay they had a daughter four years older, academically brilliant, a vivacious and attractive girl who was becoming a well-known competitive swimmer. By sixteen she had won many championships in local and state competitions and was talked about as a likely competitor for the next Olympic games.

The staggering contrast they could never eradicate. By the time Patty had won her seventeenth swimming medal, the Bensons had sunk to a state of such despondency that they did not know where to turn. Jonathan sat in patient silence, his very silence an accusation for the aching gap between their two children in both giftedness and accomplishment. Professional advice had failed to provide a solution in narrowing the gap between their two children. They felt they could not bear to go through life watching one child flash ever upward in shining glory while the other stayed immobile, an everlasting accusation to their neglect.

Finally, for these two medical professionals who thought there was no answer save in their own profession there came an answer from the least expected source, an old college friend who had become a clergyman. When he came for a first visit, he saw the situation, saw their distress, and he spoke frankly: "You cannot work a miracle in the way you would want to. Jonathan will never have the full use of his legs. But he is a person with talents of his own. Why don't you help him to find himself?"

That was the moment of enlightenment. They threw off their self-pity and began to concentrate on Jonathan. They drew Patty into the situation, enlisting her support, convincing her of her share of responsibility in making Jonathan's life worthwhile. What had once been a mild water therapy prescribed for Jonathan now became a major project. Daily, giving up much of her time from extracurricular activities, Patty worked with her brother. It was an act of true and unrelenting devotion. She taught him, strengthened him, until he could achieve a strong mobility in the water with the upper part of his body. From there he went to working with oars in a fixed rowing shell and learned the rudiments of coxmanship, so successfully that he was able, later in college, to cox his varsity crew to a successful championship.

As for the parents, their efforts were constant in finding every means possible to help Jonathan discover for himself a way of growth, a satisfying mode of living. With his success in learning to swim he began to take pride in himself, worked harder at his studies, improved his academic record to such a degree that when he was ready for college, he proposed to prepare himself for a career in law. He is now in law school, where he expects to specialize in advocacy for the handicapped. Patty's spectacular swimming career stopped short of the Olympics when she decided, halfway through college, that she would marry and raise a family.

The three Schmitt boys were all gifted, the eldest in mathematics, the second in chemistry, and the youngest outstanding in all his studies and exhibiting from his early years exceptional leadership ability. The fourth child in the family, a girl, had suffered brain damage at birth. From babyhood it was evident that she could never attain success in mastering ordinary skills. She was listless and inattentive, she read poorly and seemed insensitive to the success and triumphs of all her brothers in school and athletics. The father was a Korean War veteran who had gone into the army after two years of college. Upon returning from the war, he was so disillusioned with college and life in general that he went into business and eventually became prosperous. The mother, who had never gone to college, had had a brief career as a stenographer. In his achieving sons the father's own unrealized hopes were fulfilled three times over. As for his daughter, he babied her, humored her, but did not treat her as a person to be respected. His attitude was reflected in the actions of the sons, who were inclined to be rude, impatient, and scornful of their doltish little sister. It was a male-dominated household, in which the mother suffered for years in silence as she watched the sons flourish and the little daughter growing physically, but only a little intellectually. Since she was not an educated woman, she found it hard to voice her complaints or to express her deep conviction that it was all wrong to treat the child as if she were half pet animal, half doll. She had the sense to seek help.

At a parents' meeting at school she heard a lecture on a topic she had known nothing about, the potential danger of mental illness in neurologically handicapped children. Overcoming a natural timidity, she armed herself with the opinions of experts. Assured that psychological counseling was on her side, she tackled her husband and sons. In one stunning outburst of eloquence she let them know what she thought of them for their treatment of Karen all these years. She meant to change things. "She's a human being!" she cried. "You start treating her as if she were as smart as you are. You'll see!"

There was a change in the Schmitt family. Mother took over, led the way, inspired by her own passionate commitment to Karen's welfare. It must not be too late. They began to talk to Karen, to include her in their games. The boys took turns helping her learn to ride a bicycle, swim, skip rope. They read to her and played simple board games.

Above all, they were patient. The most noticeable change was that they talked to Karen as one of themselves, not down to her. It took time, many months, but gradually Karen responded. Her reflexes seemed sharper, her expression was brighter, her speech improved. She was evidently a much happier and better adjusted child. When the school psychologist examined Karen about six months after the mother's "revolution," she commented to Mrs. Schmitt, "You have done wonders with this child. She has come a long way." "I know she will never be as smart as her brothers," said the mother, "but I will never treat her as if she were any different. Nor will anyone else if I can help it."

The three hypothetical cases might be labeled "success stories." For every Cooper or Benson family that makes life better for their less-than-gifted children there are a hundred who do not. Ignorance, indifference, and chronic temperamental conflicts are only some of the reasons that the less-than-gifted are not reached, worked with, or influenced positively so that they can help themselves to make their own distinctions within the family.

CHILDREN CAN HELP EACH OTHER

It is important that parents realize that the responsibility for striving for equality among their children is not theirs alone. Their gifted children should assume a large part of this responsibility for helping the less-gifted sibling. How can there be whole-family involvement if the able ones are not drawn in, as Patty was with her crippled brother, to assume a large share of the task?

It is probably harder for parents who are themselves gifted to have children not as smart as they themselves are than it is for parents of ordinary intelligence who do not expect to engender genius. It is those gifted parents who are likely to suffer most when they have a child who is seriously handicapped by brain damage, neurological dysfunction, or any of the congenital disorders that are likely to lead to chronic failure. These are the disorders that, if not treated as soon as they are diagnosed, may lead to serious mental breakdown. Psychotic symptoms of schizophrenia are likely to appear in early to mid teens in children with such basic handicaps, who, as they enter adolescence, become increasingly aware of their failures and shortcomings. Depression and paranoia can appear almost without warning, the forerunners of serious mental illness. Young Karen was a likely victim for such a fate. Her mother's timely action probably forestalled a severe personality disorder. These are the less-than-gifted who most need care.

Perhaps the gifted child with a not-so-gifted sibling is the lucky one. Lessons learned within the home, within the concerned family, where constant patience, tolerance, and selflessness must be exercised, are lessons that tend to help build sound character, which even the most brilliantly gifted child in the world needs more than anything else, no matter how shining the gift.

16

Personal, Physical, and Family Traits of Gifted Children

Roy L. Cox

Perhaps the most important trait of gifted children is the fact that they are so much like other children their own age and sex. It is simply not true, as has sometimes been implied, that gifted children possess traits that cause them to be easily recognizable in groups of average children. On the contrary, giftedness is perhaps the most difficult of all exceptionalities to identify and evaluate.

The only trait common to all gifted children, and one that is missing in all others, is an intellectual potential significantly higher than that of most of the population. And yet myths about strange, unattractive young "geniuses" have abounded for years. Among the most common of these have been beliefs that only a thin line separates genius from insanity, that gifted children tend to be small, sickly, and unattractive, and that unusual ability in the very young tends to deteriorate rapidly, resulting in low ability and failure in adulthood. While it seems likely that the colorful but unflattering characterizations of child and adult "geniuses" by writers of fiction may have encouraged the persistence of some of these myths, they cannot explain the apparent willingness of so many individuals to believe or partially believe that handicaps and unattractive physical traits are related in some way to giftedness. Researchers and writers have been providing information that refutes such claims for a great many years. And yet, in spite of considerable evidence to the contrary, misconceptions about the gifted continue. I

Roy L. Cox, Ph.D., is professor and director of Research and Special Services, School of Education and Psychology, Western Carolina University, Cullowhee, N.C. He is co-author of two books, contributor to several others, and author of more than forty articles, critical essays, and reviews in such journals as *The Gifted Child Quarterly, Peabody Journal of Education, Educational Leadership, Phi Delta Kappan, The Kappa Delta Pi Record,* and others.

would suggest that jealous individuals may find that scoffing at real or imagined weakness in the gifted acts as a balm, soothing the irritation of their feelings of inadequacy by giving them a basis for feeling equal, if not actually superior, to these "strange creatures."

FAMILY TRAITS

It should be clear at this point that gifted children, and even highly gifted children, can be found in virtually every type of home and community environment. As Stanford Professor Lewis Terman once stated, "No race or nationality has any monopoly on brains."[1] We would agree and quickly add that children of the wealthy, the educated, or of any other group of parents do not, either. However, we are by no means implying that some family characteristics, especially in certain combinations, do not influence the statistical possibilities that gifted children will be found or will not be found in those family units. Terman, who found two families with five gifted children each, ten families with four gifted children each, and twenty families with three gifted children each, suggested that such unusual numbers of gifted children in single family units, together with those large numbers of families who contributed two gifted children each to his study, represented strong evidence that "something besides chance was operating such as common ancestry, common environment, or, more probably, both of these influences".[2]

A number of writers have discussed the influence of "good" home environments. It is interesting that in describing favorable home environments, the emphasis has often been placed on the absence of certain negative influences, such as divorce, low family income, unfavorable community life, and illiterate or poorly educated parents. Satisfactory incomes are usually listed as positive influences in any description of good family environments. Satisfactory family incomes are important not only for the good nutrition, good health care, and enrichment opportunities they are capable of providing, but also for the freedom from feelings of insecurity and even fear that the struggle for survival can produce in children from poor families. However, the manner in which the family income is acquired may be a more significant single clue to the nature of the home environment than income, since occupations usually suggest things such as educational level, social status, and attitudes concerning the appropriate use of income.

References by writers to family type have been noted from time to time, but most of these have been very general statements about the "freedom" enjoyed by gifted children in their families or the influences of "democratic" families on the desire of their children to achieve in school. In an effort to acquire more specific data, we asked the parents of some forty gifted children to discuss these topics with us in several small group sessions. While the number of participants was small and the method of collecting and evaluating the information highly subjective, a summary of the results seems worthy of consideration.

Wtih few exceptions, children in these families seem to have enjoyed a considerable degree of personal freedom. However, in most instances, these freedoms were clearly not unlimited. A majority of the parents indicated that rather firm lines were drawn at some point beyond which their children understood they must seek permission from their parents. Little or no agreement appeared to exist concerning where this limiting point should be established, and it was not possible to determine the extent to which these children, as a group, actually participated in decision-making activities. No evidence of the strong patriarchal control typical of yesterday's family could be detected, but the patterns that emerged were neither democratic nor equalitarian in the classical sense. Instead, decision making seemed to be partially shared and partially divided between the parents in a variety of complex patterns, with wide ranges of participation by the children permitted, depending upon the family and the age of the child.

Many family activities were centered around the mother, especially in those families with younger children. However, in spite of the fact that a large number of the fathers were at the point in their lives when male parents are often most deeply involved in establishing themselves in their businesses or professions, the interest of these men in their families was most unusual, as is suggested by the fact that they took time off from their work to attend these two-day conferences. In fact, the unusual interest of both parents in their children, their almost aggressive quest for information, the candor with which they provided the information requested, and their obvious pride in and affection for their children were perhaps the most impressive patterns that were found.

It was interesting that these parents did not seem to believe that their gifted children had encountered unusual problems in developing satisfactory relationships with their age peers and that only a small number were aware of expressions of resentment toward the gifted child by any of their other children. Serious problems of interpersonal relationships would seem much less likely to develop when parents are as well informed and interested in their children as were these parents.

The importance of family traits that combine to form good family environments cannot be emphasized too strongly. The influence of these types of family units not only seems to decrease the probability of problems involving the gifted child, but appears to stimulate desire on the part of all children to achieve success in school. Of course, gifted children as a group seem to have unusually favorable attitudes toward school, although there have been some notable exceptions to this rule. The influence of family status is not limited to immediate members of the family and their associates, but often extends into the classroom, influencing many aspects of the school and its educational programs. Thus, through the direct and indirect involvement in school programs of families whose home environments are favorable to the gifted, the classroom environment can be made to favor the special needs of gifted children.

PERSONAL TRAITS

Just as many differences exist in the characteristics of families of the gifted, the personal traits of these children differ enormously. However, some traits tend to appear more often than do others, and a number of them will be discussed in the sections that follow. It must be kept in mind that these traits appear in various combinations and to various degrees in average as well as in gifted children and that none are present in all gifted children.

HEALTH AND PERSONAL APPEARANCE

Gifted children are no smaller, weaker, less well developed, or in any way inferior to other children. Those who have worked with and studied gifted children generally agree that, as a group, they are average or above average in height, weight, physical development, coordination, and general appearance. In fact, with the possible exception of the need for corrective lenses, researchers have found no evidence of any of the stereotypes that have often been associated with gifted children.

Some gifted children, like some average children, develop physical handicaps, health problems, and mental and emotional difficulties. However, there is no evidence that any of these are more likely to occur in children who are intellectually superior. Terman found no evidence of relationships between giftedness and either poor health or physical abnormalities. Not only did he find that his subjects did not tend to be physically handicapped, undersize, or sickly, he reported that, as a group, they had better postures, fewer abnormalities of the heart and lungs, and fewer headaches and dental problems than did the unselected group. In fact, the physicians who examined Terman's gifted subjects reported that they were found to be generally "physically superior" to the unselected group.[3]

When physical handicaps do occur in able children and youth, their superior intelligence frequently makes it possible for them to compete successfully with their classmates in spite of even serious limitations such as blindness and to participate in extracurricular activities not ordinarily believed possible. In fact, borderline handicaps, such as hearing and visual losses, are often more difficult to recognize early in gifted children because their superior abilities make it possible for them to minimize the influences of their handicap and to compete successfully with their mentally average classmates.

The belief that only a thin line separates "genius" from "insanity" is among the most interesting of the myths about the gifted and may have even served as a reinforcement for other misunderstandings. The "mad genius" has been a popular subject of writers for generations and has not contributed very favorably to the image of gifted children. While the gifted can and do develop mental and emotional problems, when this occurs, the same influences that result in poor mental and emotional health among the mentally average are usually responsible. Researchers such as Terman and Oden and many others have stressed the fact that gifted children are no more likely to develop poor mental and emotional health than are other children in the population. We are aware of no research that would in any way support the myth that gifted children are more likely to become insane or to become emotionally unstable than would be the case if they were not gifted.

DEVELOPMENTAL TRAITS

As a group, gifted children appear to have motor abilities that are at least as good as those of other children the same age; they begin to walk and to talk at least as early as their less-able age peers. In my studies I found a wide range of ages at which gifted subjects were believed to have begun to speak.[4] Some of these children were extremely young. This can be explained in part by the fact that proud parents often believe they are hearing speech when they are only hearing pre-speech, wordlike sounds (da da, etc.). However, most of these parents had kept unusually good records of their children's early years, and in most instances we are convinced that they were trying to be as accurate as possible. For example, twenty-five parents reported that their gifted children did not begin speaking until the age of two or later, a point at which average children have often developed vocabularies of as many as fifty words.

A considerable range of ages was also reported at which these gifted children began to walk. It should be noted that even though the point at which children take their first unassisted steps is also subject to some interpretation, the influence of this interpretation would appear to be less significant than in the case of beginning speech. Three parents indicated that their gifted children had begun to walk at the age of six months, the earliest age that was reported. The legs of most children will support their weight at this point, but beginning to walk at this stage of development is unusual. At the other extreme, more than 4 percent of the gifted subjects were reported as not beginning to walk until the fifteenth month or later, and one child was reported as not beginning to walk until the eighteenth month.

Reports of delayed speech and delayed walking, even though relatively small numbers were involved, are interesting. We have heard many reports over the years of gifted children who walked or talked quite late but who mastered these tasks quickly once the process was initiated. It is possible that similar patterns appear at about the same level among all children, and that parents and others may be attaching undue significance to the matter after they find that the child is gifted. In view of the problems of early identification, the small percentage of the population that is gifted, and the even smaller numbers who have exhibited the developmental patterns described, finding an answer to this interesting question will be difficult.

SPECIAL INTERESTS AND ACTIVITIES OF GIFTED CHILDREN

In contrast to the seclusive, inactive child frequently envisioned by the public, gifted children are active, curious, and frequently outgoing. They tend to involve themselves in many activities, some of which require a considerable amount of group activity. I found that many gifted subjects were active in their religious groups and that they participated in a variety of social and special-interest clubs and youth groups. Many of these children enjoyed sports of many types and a wide variety of outdoor activities. Male subjects tended to be more interested in sports than did female subjects. In all these areas, gifted children showed the same general participation and interest that was found among their age peers who were academically less advanced.

Perhaps the leisure-time activity most characteristic of gifted children, except for the very young, is reading. Terman found that gifted children began to read earlier, that they read more, and that they read more widely than did the unselected control group. I found reading to be the favorite free-time activity identified most often by gifted subjects. In fact, it has been theorized that the tendency for gifted children to wear corrective lenses more often than do mentally average children could be the result of earlier and considerably more reading.

In addition to reading for fun, gifted subjects read selective topics to gather information for special projects in school, to support their interest in a great many hobbies, to explore new interests, and to further their understanding of a sport or some other recreational activity. While the idea would be difficult to support empirically, we suggest that one of the most important reasons for the extensive and broad reading of so many gifted children is that books represent a readily available means of satisfying the great curiosity that they have about almost everything around them.

As was emphasized initially, gifted children are much like other children except for their unusual intelligence and matters related to high intelligence. Terman found that his gifted subjects were more interested in intellectually oriented activities than those in the unselected group, but he found no significant differences between the two groups in the extent of their interest in play activities. Thus I am convinced that gifted children select leisure-time activities for the same reasons other children do, because they find them interesting and enjoyable. The major difference between them and mentally average children is that their interests are not only much broader, they are larger in number, and they tend to pursue these interests with more vigor and determination than do many of their less-able age peers.

Notes

1. Lewis M. Terman and Melita H. Oden, *Genetic Studies of Genius,* vol. 4, *The Gifted Child Grows Up* (Stanford, Calif., Stanford University Press, 1947).
2. Lewis M. Terman and Melita H. Oden, *Genetic Studies of Genius,* vol. 5, *The Gifted Group at Mid-Life* (Stanford, Calif., Stanford University Press, 1959).
3. Lewis M. Terman, *Genetic Studies of Genius,* vol. 1, *Mental and Physical Traits of a Thousand Gifted Children* (Stanford, Calif., Stanford University Press, 1925).
4. Roy L. Cox, "Background Characteristics of 456 Gifted Children with I.Q. Scores of 130 and Above," *The Gifted Child Journal* 21 (1977): 261–66.

3

GIFTED CHILDREN IN
THE COMMUNITY

Halls of Learning—Anonymous tenth-grade student

When from these halls of learning
My sheepskin I receive,
Math, physics, frogs, and chemistry
A lot I've learned of these.

What have I learned of people
whom every day I see?
I'm sure they're more important
than some cat's anatomy.

What have I learned of people?
I'd really like to know
In years of progress we have missed
what most we need to know.

17
Gifted Children and the Public Library

Kathryn Farnsworth

Sing me a song
of a golden child
    with a golden key
to a li-brair-ee . . .

    Norma Farber

    "Sing Me a Circular Song"

A golden key to the library indeed — a gift for any child, but an inestimable treasure for the child who is gifted and talented!

The library is a special place. It has to be used to be appreciated. No more the rows and rows of carefully spaced and tended volumes, the "shushing" caretaker librarian. Libraries reach out to people; they are easily available as a community resource for all. A library can furnish a child with a whole world of information and imagination that will last through a lifetime of growing and learning. Parents, especially, can help a gifted child to develop the habit of wise use of all the resources that the library makes available.

> Steven at age twelve has never heard the term *gifted* applied to himself. He knows he's smart, that school is a breeze. But, asked to describe himself, he says he's a boy who likes books and libraries. He reads several books at a time, likes to keep a few ahead "so he won't run out." And he keeps contact with libraries, favoring those in which he feels acceptance and a warm welcome.

Kathryn Farnsworth is a library consultant in preschool and family services, reading support programs, and storytelling. She is also a teacher, children's librarian, and nationally known storyteller.

THE LIBRARY BEGINS AT HOME

Most libraries today do make children, as well as their parents, feel at home. Parents are treated as partners in this important task of keeping bright young minds alive and curious. Of all institutions the library is the one in which parents of gifted children can best involve themselves in their children's education. Librarians increasingly recognize the parents' role as the child's first and most important teacher, the adult who spends the most time with the child throughout his or her growing years. Most parents welcome this opportunity for partnership.

However, the experience of books starts long before the first visit to the library. Parents begin by crooning and sharing nonsense syllables with their infant. Mother Goose rhymes provide a good foundation for later reading and other language experiences. Youngsters respond to books that picture simple objects they can point to and name. Sharing "lap" books – simple stories and wordless picture books – best communicates the joy of reading to a small child.

Reports from parents vary concerning the best time to begin reading aloud to a child. Some families gauge this by the child's interest. But in other homes the parents cuddle the child from a very early age and just share whatever they happen to enjoy reading. The key idea is *sharing* – sharing what is enjoyed, because the quality of the experience is what counts. A certain father contentedly read Conan Doyle's Sherlock Holmes stories to his small son. Years later that experience is still warmly remembered by the boy.

As the child grows, regular, unhurried visits to the library suit the early years. Toddlers are enthusiastic – coming to the library is an event in their lives. They have just begun to push out boundaries of home and neighborhood.

In response to pressure from parents many libraries are planning group experiences for the very young. Whether that is in the best interests of children, gifted children as well as others, has yet to be evaluated. Meanwhile, parents have a wonderful opportunity to guide their children's growth as they explore the library, suiting materials to their interest and temperament, making choices together and taking time for conversation about books and other media. This one-to-one sharing allows children to be the active, busy, talkative creatures they are at two or three years – exploring on their own with the reassurance and support of their parents.

> A two-and-a-half-year-old was greatly upset by a move across country. One day he and his mother visited the library in his new community. On the shelf he discovered Marie Et's *In the Forest*. It was his favorite in the library "back home." Quite magically this slender pic-

ture book became the bridge to adjustment in his new surroundings, thanks to this family's wise and appropriate use of libraries.

Picture-book or story hours for preschoolers are a staple in most library diets. Socialization, moving out from family and home, learning to trust adults other than one's parents — story hours provide all these experiences. But their primary goal is to build on the introduction to literature children already have had at home.

Some libraries recognize the value of sharing this experience with parents by inviting them to join the story hours, not as observers but as participants. Parents can tactfully encourage this practice. It is good for the children; it is a learning experience for the adults.

Parents can also serve children by requesting separate story hours for older and younger preschoolers. Fours and fives have the attention span for stories with more content than younger children will listen to. If groups include three-to-five-year-olds, the older children are most likely being shortchanged.

Borrowing books or other media for home use is an important part of the library experience, beginning with the preschool years. Parents should allow time for children to make choices. To judge their choices in terms of "too long," "too easy," or "you've had that before" does not help them grow. Of course, parents want to provide children with quality books. But children at all ages are individuals; their choices may not be the same as their parents'. Most children, gifted though they may be, will want sometimes to read what is popular, what is easy. An eleven-year-old boy thoroughly enjoys Susan Cooper's Newbery Award–winning *The Grey King,* but he saves his allowance to buy books from the Hardy Boys series. Another child varies his diet of adult history and biography with comic books. Both learn to distinguish quality from mediocrity.

As a child grows, the library becomes increasingly important in representing options. Gene Maeroff, writing in *The New York Times Magazine* of August 21, 1977, tells of a four-year-old whose application for early entrance to school was turned down. "While he was waiting to be old enough to begin kindergarten, Jeffrey spent a good part of each week in the public library pursuing personal research projects in astronomy and geography."

Choices of other kinds are possible for children in the library. At the very least the child "chooses" to be there; attendance is not required. Nor does the library assign a grade to what is done there. This nonrestrictive openness and freedom are very important to gifted children, who often live with pressures of many kinds. They need this opportunity to experience an atmosphere quite different from that to which they are exposed in school. The library need not be a haven, though sometimes it is, for a gifted child to escape boredom, frustration, or anger. Mostly it is a place where emphasis is placed on the life of the intellect and where gifted children can feel at home and find others like themselves.

Library service is by nature individualized, matching materials to particular needs. Recreational reading is only part of a child's experience. Independent study represents enrichment for the gifted child. Librarians are challenged by the diversity of gifted children's interests. Their interests are both deeper and more extensive than those of their peers. That is not to say that gifted children are equally talented in every area. They have an intensity of feeling about choosing for themselves at the same time that they may need the help and guidance of adults. Librarians do well to cultivate understanding, patience, and tolerance.

CRACKING THE LIBRARY CODE

What a gifted child needs most from an adult, whether parent or librarian, is knowledge of the library's resources and the opportunity to learn to use them. The catalog, whether in card or book form, indicates what is in a library and where to find it. Access may be had through author, title, or subject. Arrangement is orderly, with books divided into main divisions and subdivisions in nonfiction titles. When children understand the "plan" of library materials and how to use the catalog, they can quickly locate the books they want by themselves.

Children benefit from learning how to use reference books on their own. Parents and children together can browse through these "fact" books to determine their scope and arrangement. Is it alphabetical? Is there an index? A table of contents? There are interesting appendices in dictionaries that are often overlooked — abbreviations, rhyming words, biographical data, grammar, punctuation.

Encyclopedias represent small libraries in themselves. Many list related articles that may entice the gifted child to study a subject in depth.

Newspapers and periodicals have indexes of their own. Children and parents together can practice until they feel at home with the form and abbreviations of these indexes. In research using newspapers and periodicals, the child gains experience in distinguishing fact from opinion. He or she learns to read with an open mind, critically. The child is continually finding material and learning to select and organize it. When children begin to think about what they read and reflect on it, they will discover the means to forming judgments and making decisions. These are the skills they need for a lifetime of learning.

This kind of library service to children precludes a cutoff of materials at a particular grade level. Gifted children must have access to ideas well beyond the limits of a children's department or the school library. Users of small libraries whose children's and adult services operate out of one area have an advantage in access to the library's total resources that often outweighs the size of the collection. When this is not the case, parents need to see that, at the very least, their children are treated courteously, and that their right to information is recognized by adult reference librarians. Sometimes a parent's presence is enough to ensure equal treatment for a child. But if a librarian cannot respond to the legitimate needs of the gifted child, parents would do well to use (and improve) their own research skills, unafraid of any limitations they may feel. A dedicated, understanding parent can find his or her way from source to source more satisfactorily than a reluctant professional. In libraries large or small, it is ease of access that counts, and parents can help their children enormously.

> Janie was a dejected underachiever in sixth grade. Her father began accompanying her to the library whenever a report was assigned. While he sat beside her at a table in the reference area, he read the daily newspaper. But when she needed his help, he was available, whether to listen to Janie or to call a librarian's attention to her needs. Janie gradually gained confidence in her own ability to manage research assignments. It is not surprising that she made an outstanding scholastic record in high school.

This should not suggest that parents and children usually must "go it alone." There are librarians, in both children's and adult services, who gladly respond to the opportunity to help all children acquire research skills. The gifted child has a greater need for library skills than other children. Learning how to learn is of great importance, since work done independently is vital to such a child.

Gifted children are not always easy to deal with. Adults must look beyond the label to see the child who has the same needs as other children and some additional ones as well. Librarians note that many gifted children who focus on an intensive search leave bookshelves in disarray. They may ask for assistance and then seem to spurn it when offered. They may act out their anger and frustrations in the library. Sometimes the greatest need a child may have is for solitude, a place to be alone or to reflect — without pressures. As Peppermint Patty of Charles Schulz's *Peanuts* strip says to her teacher, "Daydreaming? No, ma'am, I wasn't daydreaming. I was just conceptualizing!"

County library systems, library federations, and reciprocal borrowing privileges now permit library users the facilities of many libraries. There is yet another option. While membership in most libraries is free, membership in some libraries, for example, college libraries, may be obtained for a nominal fee. This is a good investment for the entire community if the local library cannot meet the needs of the entire family.

Experiences with different libraries present an unusual opportunity to the gifted child. Some families take "field trips" to libraries of special interest. Others visit and use the library near where they vacation. If parents take the time, gifted children are challenged by solving the mystery of how and why the unfamiliar library is arranged as it is. They can "crack the code." They can also observe the structure that all libraries have in common. With experiences like this it is unlikely that later on they will be overawed or fearful in the college, the city, or the university library.

A LIBRARY OF ONE'S OWN

The personal ownership of books is important in the child's experience. To have a library of one's own means that favorite titles are there at hand, that a new book is always there to beckon. If a family can afford a set of encyclopedias, their availability encourages the whole family to "look it up." Gifted children use them for browsing. A library representing his or her own unique interests is necessary to the gifted child. Birthdays and special holidays may be occasions for adding books to this collection.

Perhaps a group of parents and community leaders serving as advisors to the library staff may talk about specific needs. They may determine that the community lacks afterschool and summer recreational activities. Or that competitive sports represent the only out-of-school choices for children in their town. In one community the public library developed "curiosity clubs" from just such a need. Included were small groups for stamp collecting, journalism, mime and drama, filmmaking, creative writing, and puppetry. Gifted children, who are usually "interest oriented," stand to gain most from such offerings.

Playing games like backgammon and chess with opportunity for instruction is a popular activity at many libraries. Again, this means a chance for gifted children to find partners at their own level of accomplishment. Field trips, demonstrations, hobby shows, and special exhibits provide occasions to share interests regardless of age levels. Recognition is given for the child's special skills, perhaps an opportunity to teach others. This is often the greatest reward of all.

Parents have often been responsible for the development of unique programs in the library. One mother concerned with helping her six-year-old grow from a beginning reader to a child who enjoyed reading now sees her plan implemented in several public libraries. During one summer she and her son used federated libraries for access to over a hundred "Easy Readers." Encouragement, taking turns reading aloud, and pursuing the many exciting activities suggested by the books' subject matter were the key to success for the boy. Now other beginning readers can have the enrichment of "I Can Read Clubs" during the summer months in their public libraries.

PARENTS AS LIBRARIAN VOLUNTEERS

Aliki's *June 7* (New York: Macmillan, 1972) has inspired young children to write their own books of birthday experiences, leaving pages for additions in later years. How proud a child is if a librarian shows him or her how to produce a clothbound book for his or her personal library. The same book-binding activity (with blank pages this time) can be the start of journal keeping for other children. When librarians lack the time or talent for these activities, parents might consider volunteering their services.

Stories told in the folklore tradition represent a form of literature with an unusual potential for response by the gifted child. Ask about and search out, if you can, such unique experiences for your child. The library often has such a program (not to be confused with reading aloud, however). Folklore societies and park or recreation commissions sponsor storytelling. For centuries folktales have been told to all ages; it is another experience that parents and children can share. Not only are children's imaginations stimulated by the choice and combination of words and phrases, but it has been observed that children who frequently hear stories told aloud unconsciously grasp the story form and are able to apply this knowledge to their own creative writing.

Pilot programs have shown that readers of any age can learn to tell stories and share them with others. Children are challenged to read widely as they search through folktale collections. They develop criteria for choosing a story and then learn how to tell it effectively to others. Storytelling is a rare opportunity for the gifted child, whose interests are often difficult to share with others and may in other activities suffer feelings of isolation.

"I told it four times," says a sixth-grade girl. "It was simply amazing to see how the children could listen to me. The teacher told me that not even she could keep the children this quiet." A boy in the same class expressed his feelings this way: "The experience was new — just standing in front of a whole class with all eyes on me, sometimes getting a laugh or two, sometimes so interested that they don't know when to laugh. I would encourage every child to take a course like this. The librarian knew what she was doing, and she never told you to hurry up with your stories. She helped us with problems.''

Parents who already have this skill or are willing to practice it could share with gifted children either individually or in small groups this stimulating and creative art form. It takes hard work and time. Often librarians don't have this time when they must meet other demands. But skilled volunteers have traditionally extended the boundaries of library service to children. And often the most willing volunteers have been parents.

What a natural and creative partnership it is — libraries, gifted children, and their parents! A partnership that blesses every child with a ''golden key'' to enjoyment, to knowledge, to life.

18
Satisfying Insatiable Curiosity: The Use of Community Resources with Gifted and Talented Children

Barbara Rollock and Naomi Noyes

Like Kipling's Elephant's Child, gifted and creative children often keep their parents in a perpetual state of siege as they badger them to answer questions and to produce new ideas for activities, expeditions, and projects. Rather than the frequent spankings the Elephant Child's relatives resorted to, most parents and other involved adults struggle to provide a steady stream of stimulation. Whether families are urban, suburban, or rural, the identification of community resources for gifted and talented children can be difficult. In addition, taking advantage of these resources is close to a full-time job. When parents work, another dimension of difficulty is added.

To help busy parents add depth to their children's experience, the resource identification process must be telescoped. A simple (though often gargantuan) identification tool is the local telephone company's Yellow Pages. Headings will not only lead to information about the obvious kinds of places to visit (museums, art galleries, animal farms),

Barbara Rollock is coordinator of children's services at the New York Public Library, a position she has held since 1974. She has served as president of the Children's and Young Adult sections of the New York Library Association and as president of the Children's Services Division of the American Library Association.

Naomi Noyes is children's specialist, Manhattan Borough Office of the New York Public Library.

but even the unsuspected (pottery studios, dairy farms, stores, and craft and trade shops). All kinds of serendipitous journeys can start here.

Without doubt, however, it is the public library that can help the most. It is actually the root of enrichment; indeed, its materials enrich any experience before, during, and after. It is, moreover, often nearby, open when school is not, and it is free.

Quite possibly the library, while to some the most obvious community resource, will come as a revelation to others. As an institution it is often taken for granted, even by those who ought to know better. Its all-too-often grim and elderly exterior can hide a treasure trove of significant information, enrichment, and delight.

Obviously libraries provide books. Here are mentioned three that will certainly be useful to the busy parent, who may be helped thereby to pinpoint children's special interests and talents beyond those already known.

One is *Alkema's Complete Guide to Creative Art for Young People* by Chester Jay Alkema (Sterling Pub. Co., 1971, $14.95). It is a potpourri of ideas that use performing arts as a springboard for painting and drawing. Another is *Children's Media Market Place* edited by Deidre Boyle and Stephen Calvert (Gaylord Professional Publications, 1978, $15.95). This describes such areas as periodicals for children, juvenile bookstores, juvenile book clubs, talent agents, and children's television-program sources. Still another prolific source of ideas is *The Whole Kids Catalog* by Peter Cardozo, (Bantam, 1975, $7.50). Its cover description says it all: "The great new catalog of super things to find, to do and make. The book for kids that all grownups have been waiting for. Thousands of amazing adventures and amusements. Moviemaking, arts and crafts, puzzles and games, kite flying, Indian lore, hobbies, magic, sports, photography, moneymaking secrets and more."

In addition to books, in some libraries parents may borrow framed art reproductions, toys, sculpture, and 8-mm and 16-mm silent films. One parent discovered the film *Nanook of the North* and used her 16-mm projector to show it to her children and some of the neighborhood youngsters. The library's film collection provided an excellent respite from poor TV fare, and showing well-selected films became a weekend activity for the neighbors and their children.

In addition to the public library's wealth of ideas presented in a variety of forms, there is a new force at work. A current trend in public library service is the presentation of community information in forms more easily used by the public than are card files or even printed directories. The library as a source of information on community resources for gifted and talented children can, therefore, prove more fruitful than it did as recently as five years ago. Suggested community resources can appear to be obvious at first, but for children who have not yet had the experience of visiting the firehouse, the museum, or even the public library itself, the whole world is new. The fact that resources are obvious is not the issue; it is the quality of the use of those resources that makes them significant in a child's development. A bright child may be moved along to above average, and a sleeping genius may even be awakened by conscientious parents' dedication to providing a broad spectrum of experience to their children. It is the depth and richness of that experience that makes the difference.

As a beginning, parents and their children can explore the immediate neighborhood to identify those agencies that deliver services vital to the economic, social, and cultural life of the community. A local business such as the neighborhood supermarket may provide the preschooler with a first lesson in consumerism. His or her first financial transaction and knowledge about loss and gain may occur at the corner candy store. (Newspapers, radio, and television are mass communication media that contribute to the formation of attitudes or information in the life of the gifted and talented.) Cultural and educational institutions such as schools and libraries are obvious, but others, such as the local police station, should be considered, for they often provide a link between young people and community projects. Energy and environmental agencies aim to instill a sense of community service or impart lessons about conservation.

Literature about a particular community agency can be obtained directly from the agency, since most of them print and distribute free brochures about their services. Inquire about the possibility of scheduling visits, attending free lectures, exhibitions or other visual presentations offered to the public.

Find those agencies that encourage children to participate voluntarily in specially designed programs, for example, museum art classes, library programs, student art exhibitions or competitions, creative writing or poetry workshops, filmmaking projects, and so on.

ARTS AND HUMANITIES

Because of the intellectual differences of the gifted from those of similar age and their capacity for independent and often self-directed learning, some educators feel there is an obligation to develop in these children an appreciation of those areas of the arts and humanities that symbolize the best of human culture. Such studies in an age of technology provide the necessary balance between arts and sciences, which are more commonly stressed in the education of the gifted. The child interested in music and art should certainly participate as a performer or spectator in concerts, theater performances, puppet shows, or cultural festivals in the community.

MUSEUMS

Outreach is the key to success in most of today's museum programming, since museums, like other nonprofit organizations, have to compete for public support and funding. Attention to the needs and interests of children is evidenced by the emergence of children's museums or "junior" museums, "see-and-touch" exhibits, and exhibits that invite the young museumgoer to participate actively in the display.

In their function as exhibitors and preservers of the monuments of the past, museums provide an avenue for study of the cultural endeavors and accomplishments of people through the ages. Many museums provide guided tours for groups of children. Some museums involve parents in classes with their children. Most of their programs use slides, films, or audio-phones to accompany individual viewing of an exhibition. If parents belong to an organization in the community, it is possible to get speakers from the museum for special programs that can enrich all the community's children. Museums' sale shops are a source of interesting material: catalogs, reproductions of art and artifacts, announcements of future programs and classes.

BUSINESS AND INDUSTRY

In Japan interest generated by a traveling puppet theater for preschoolers so captivated local businesspeople that they undertook to subsidize the production costs of the performers. In New York a local bank provided the printing costs for publication of a brochure directed to parents, "Reading Begins at Home," published by the Brooklyn Public Library. Business and industry have a stake in the future intellectual and economic life of the community. Some business corporations provide scholarship aid to gifted students or grants for innovative programs in community agencies. When public funds have been insufficient, community agencies have often looked to the business community for support.

Gifted children may be curious about the relationships of business with other community services. They should learn that certain skills are necessary to sustain business operations in the production of consumer goods and in furnishing occupational or vocational opportunities for large segments of the population. Without the technicians, mechanics, and marketing specialists life in our highly industrialized society would not be possible. Some facilities, such as candy factories, clothing mills, and automobile manufacturers' showcases, welcome visits and honor requests for brochures.

HEALTH CARE RESOURCES

Since many health care agencies are eager to foster community education among residents in their area, arrangements for some kinds of visits may be made. Groups may visit laboratories and hospitals where children can observe the work of therapists (physical, occupational, or recreational), medical social workers, laboratory technicians, dieticians and nutritionists, health aides, science or medical writers, and paramedics, to mention a few. Charitable organizations such as the United Fund and United Way offer films that describe the work of health agencies, and many organizations distribute literature about health services.

EDUCATIONAL INSTITUTIONS

Families fortunate enough to live near colleges and universities have the potential for a really significant resource for their children. With an increasing interest in the gifted and talented as a group entitled to educational attention, colleges and universities, in recognition of this need, are beginning to open up their courses, either in the regular undergraduate program or in adult education programs, such as Hunter College's Center for Life Long Learning, to promising children.

RELIGIOUS ORGANIZATIONS

Long before the complex structure of present-day society, churches formed the focal point of community activity and assumed the responsibility for the spiritual and social life of the members of the congregation. Today, although many agencies offer community services, many churches have opened their doors to the young for other than religious pursuits. Churches and synagogues are still the hub of social life for some, and the traditional picnics, outings, and suppers continue. The call to social action, however, on the part of religious organizations has prompted many churches and synagogues to take part in social welfare programs of benefit to the community, culminating in sponsorship of day care centers, head start groups, or the administration of their own church or parochial schools. It is not unusual for a church or synagogue to encourage its members to promote cultural activities such as young people's choirs, organ recitals, concerts, or dramatic presentations. Some religious centers even offer meeting space to the community and promote family discussion groups or adult education lectures on problems affecting the family. Such activities may be a positive element in the life of gifted children, not only because of the religious factor but because it encourages belief in a code of ethics, influences their emotional growth, and further defines their relationships to others in their universe.

RECREATION AND SPORTS

Play is an important factor in the development of all children, and to the gifted and talented it may be the necessary socializing element in communication among their peers.

Parks are most frequently associated with outdoor activities. Whether they are local, state, or national, parks are usually equipped for sports and outdoor activities such as boating, swimming, or ball playing. Some parks have zoos where children can see animals and learn valuable lessons about conservation. Botanical gardens are often found in park settings and may help interest the future botanist. The Little League ball clubs, Boy Scouts, Girl Scouts, Campfire Girls' organizations, and YMCAs or YMHAs help develop principles of physical health and sportsmanship in athletics or similar competitive sports activities. In rural areas the 4-H clubs involve girls and boys in the care of animals and other worthwhile projects.

National parks are a good source for family recreation and education and for families who enjoy camping and communing with nature. There are numerous publications available from the National Park Service about activities such as following nature trails, nature walks, and other valuable outdoor activities to suit the recreational needs of the family. (Recreation may span activities from leisure-time reading to participation in neighborhood softball games.)

Local newspapers and magazines such as *Cue* (now part of *New York* magazine), *Parents'* magazine, and others list opportunities for recreational pursuits. The gifted child may respond to theater performances or football games, chess competition or street art shows, model building or coin collecting, skateboarding or soccer.

No matter what the leisure-time activity, play for the gifted child is a valuable part of his or her total development. Information about resources that may help extend or develop the potential of a gifted and talented child are within reach in a variety of forms and from numerous sources. It is necessary only to be alert to their presence.

In conclusion, let us return to the public library and its relationship to gifted and talented children. Above and beyond providing materials in many forms for the enrichment of a child's experiences, it is within the library's power to provide contact with gifted and talented adults. It can provide a forum for authors, illustrators, and others who create books and wish to share their experiences with children. Often these visitors give insight into the creative process. From such programs and others in which creative people demonstrate their talents, fruitful and significant mentor relationships between adults and children can develop.

And as a very last word, when all such places and activities have been located, visited, and found — whether they turn out to be successful or not — this hard-won information should not be lost but rather should be shared with others who have gifted children.

Out of the information gathered and evaluated by parents and their children, a new information file can be added to the public library's collection. It will add considerably to the public library's place as a prime community resource for the growth and development of gifted and talented children — and, indeed, for all the community's children.

19
Parents, Children, and Museums

Daniel S. Sapon

Museums are unique among cultural resources in that they afford visitors an experience of "the thing itself." The tangible objects collected and exhibited by museums may be the products of human behavior or they may be the products of the natural world. While the works of human beings are called *artifacts* and *art objects* and the works of nature are called *specimens,* all share the common property of their authenticity and their presentation in association with other objects or specimens in a manner intended to instruct or to illuminate. While the stated purpose of most museums is the fulfillment of educational and aesthetic goals, it is clear that additional elements are necessary before these goals may be fulfilled.

The parents of all children, at every possible level of skill, are in a special position to help make a visit to a museum a valuable educational experience for their children, and, more important, to prepare their children for the effective use of museums as a source of independent learning. There are a number of principles of approach common to *all* museum settings that are useful to parents in seeking to guide their children toward more rewarding learning experiences in museum settings.

FRACTIONALITY

The vast majority of the artifacts and specimens that we see in museum settings should be approached with the question "What's missing?" The earthenware jar is broken, and a small piece of it is miss-

Daniel S. Sapon is director of the Cultural Voucher Program, Museums Collaborative, Inc., New York City. Formerly he was director's assistant for grants at the Jewish Museum in New York and, prior to that, director of education at that institution.

ing. The curator looks at the jagged edge of the break, at the smooth contours of the pot, and makes a hypothetical reconstruction of the missing piece. It is vital to understand that the pot was once intact and that the missing piece may be imagined while viewing it. Parents may ask their children to look at museum objects, determine what is absent, and then describe what they think the missing components looked like.

SOURCES

When examining artifacts or works of art, it is important to talk about where they came from and how they were made. If we return to our example of the pottery jar, we would want to imagine the moist clay from which it was made, the potter's wheel upon which it was placed, and the hands of the potter that shaped the clay. Indeed, we might wish to discuss the potter, his training, his experience, and his life. All of these things preceded the existence of the object exhibited before us.

USES

Returning once again to our jar, let us now consider its function as a container. What did it contain? Corn? Oil? If it was used to cook in, what was cooked inside it and by whom? Here we can discuss who the cook might have been and who might have eaten the meal prepared in this pot.

CONTEXT

A true understanding of our jar will now require a look at the total context in which it existed. Who used it, who handled it, who looked at it? How was it made and how was it used? Beside what did it sit on the hearth? Where did this small object fit into the greater human and physical contexts? I would like to suggest that all of these questions are vital to an understanding of this modest museum object.

These same underlying questions may be applied to specimens from nature. When we look at a stuffed animal in a diorama and ask our children to describe what's missing, the most obvious feature is the lack of movement. A living, breathing, eating, moving animal is now still. While the shape of its body is accurately presented, any opportunity to study its behavior is absent. In a good diorama, however, the museum staff have gone to some lengths to provide answers to certain of the questions of context. The landscape, vegetation, and other animal species may all be included in the diorama. A zoo, of course, is a kind of museum, and the contrasts here are interesting. In a zoo there is an opportunity to observe living, moving animals, although they are seen in settings that are generally not characteristic of the animal's natural environment. Thus the same animal viewed in both a zoo and a diorama is presented with important features missing, but the fractionality is of a different kind in each type of museum.

Discussing these issues with children is important, not because we must emphasize the limitations or imperfections of the learning situation, but rather because their explicit delineation allows us an opportunity to develop imagination and to supplement the absent elements.

BRINGING QUESTIONS TO THE MUSEUM

There is an old joke in which two men meet and one asks the other, "Does your watch tell time?" The second fellow replies, "No, I have to ask it." It is my belief that this situation is characteristic of the experience of the museum visitor and that the exhibits do not "speak for themselves." Rather, differences in the quality of museum experience have much to do with the kind of questions visitors bring with them.

Parents can facilitate this process by posing such questions as those just outlined and by encouraging their children to pose their own questions. One way to do this is by demonstrating the vital role of *labels* in museum settings. Every good label should lead the visitor's eyes back to the object and should respond to some of the questions posed. Labels do not give answers to all questions, but they are a point of departure for further enquiry.

It is also important to discuss the relevance of the museum object to the child's experience in the outside world. Relating the discussion to home, school, travel, friends, excursions, visits, or any other topic strengthens the impact of museum learning.

The essence of a good museum experience is that it is multidisciplinary. There are things to see, to touch, and to talk about: objects of art, all kinds of human creations, and specimens from nature. These objects have often been transported across large gaps of space and time. Parents, by discussing these underlying notions with their children, not only enrich the current experience but also build vital skills for their children's effective use of museums in the future. Drawing upon an awareness of the great scope of human activity and the many dimensions of the natural world, the application of a few basic notions can greatly enhance the quality of everyone's museum visit.

20

Rural Advantaged Youth

Lenore Higgins Worcester and
Patricia O'Connell

Webster defines *rural* as "pertaining to, or characteristic of, the country or agriculture; rustic." Some city dwellers would equate rural with such terms as *disadvantaged, cultural poverty,* and *isolation.* Still others view it nostalgically in the context of family reunions during the holiday seasons or warm summer nights by the lake. Each view may be accurate depending upon the perception and experience of the individual. This article is written from the positive experiences of two consultants who have worked and continue to work in a rural state developing programs and providing services for the gifted and talented.

Rural, as we use it, does not mean a suburb of New Haven, Boston, or Philadelphia. In this case it means the state of Maine, whose total population is still below one million inhabitants and whose largest city, Portland, has approximately eighty thousand people. Maine is a large state geographically with many unorganized towns and plantations and vast tracts of timberland. Winters in Maine are as rough as the stories have described them, if perhaps told with just a bit of enlargement to tantalize and entertain city folk. However, it is true that from November

Lenore Higgins Worcester, Ph.D., is on the University of Maine at Orono graduate faculty, teaching and publishing in the fields of the gifted and learning disabilities. She is chairperson of the State of Maine Gifted and Talented Advisory Board, which developed Maine's first legislation for the gifted and talented. She has done extensive in-service training throughout Maine, specializing in the topics of rural and underachieving gifted children.

Patricia O'Connell is a state consultant for gifted and talented in the Division of Special Education of the Maine Department of Educational and Cultural Services in Augusta, Maine.

to April conversations concerning programs, workshops, and in-service meetings do end with such comments as ``if the weather is good or weather permitting.''

A word of caution might now be appropriate. Rural people do not consider themselves disadvantaged, nor would they describe their culture as impoverished. They would probably be the first to agree that theirs is a different culture. But this would be said with pride, not with deference or feelings of inferiority. There is a rich culture that varies subtly and at times markedly from one region of the state to another just as it does from one section of this nation to another.

In urban centers parents of gifted and talented children tend to view the city as Utopia and all its richness as the only worthwhile environment that could possibly aid them in fostering their child's potential. In this context urban or suburban living is viewed positively, whereas rural living is viewed negatively. There certainly are differences between city and country living. Two key features or strengths of urban life can also be considered as strengths of rural life. These are people and resources. Basically we're saying that when the school confirms your suspicions that your child is indeed gifted, you don't have to despair, pack your suitcases, sell the house and depart to the city. There are distinct advantages in raising a gifted and talented child in a rural setting.

THE NATURAL ENVIRONMENT

The most pervasive resource for people in rural communities is the environment that surrounds them. The professions of most of the adults in the community are in some way connected to the natural environment, and the children often have an in-depth knowledge of specific aspects of this world. For example, a child of a fisherman will know a great deal about the tides and the weather and the habits of the fish. This base of information can be enlarged to cover so much more. The environment can become a laboratory for the child in which his or her knowledge is expanded. One of the qualities of gifted children is their ability to think on a higher conceptual level. Therefore, using the natural environment as a vehicle, you may increase this knowledge. You may pose questions that have to do with the food chain in the sea, or you may have the child study the effects of the moon on the quantity of fish that are caught over time. These kinds of activities expand on what the child already knows and use the environment that surrounds him or her as a complex learning laboratory. Too often the familiar is taken for granted; yet this is clearly one of the great advantages of rural communities.

THE INDIVIDUAL CHILD

Gifted children tend to have friends who are both younger and very much older than themselves. All too often parents appear uneasy when their young child forms a friendship with a young adult. One positive feature of rural living is that communities appear to have less age segregation, a distinct advantage for the gifted child living in a sparsely populated environment. It naturally allows for a wide discrepancy of ages in a child's friends and acquaintance. This means that a gifted second-grade student is able to play with a fifth-grader who is his or her intellectual peer.

Another positive aspect is that all children are well known by everyone in the community. This knowledge can be, and is, used very constructively by teachers of gifted children living in rural communities. It allows teachers, parents, other adults, and children to be aware, to recognize, and to accept individual differences rather matter-of-factly. It also encourages children by word and action to grow, to stretch, to reach, and to be themselves. An in-depth knowledge of children and their families is the only way teachers can plan and project for the children's total growth and development. More often than not in metropolitan schools large sections of a child's history is unknown.

A few examples will illustrate the subtleties of this point:

Mary is an extremely bright second-grader who is a happy, outgoing, achievement-oriented student. Her parents are newly separated. During the school session she lives with her mother, and during vacation periods with her father. Approximately two weeks before her vacations she becomes argumentive, fussy, and unproductive in school. The teacher's telephone contact with the parents confirmed her suspicions. Mary has a good relationship with both parents but initially needed assistance in making the transition from one parent to another. Now the teacher gives extra support and makes allowances for Mary's behavior. Knowledge of Mary and her home situation allowed the teacher to relieve pressures at school rather than add to them by exerting too many demands during these periods.

Carl is a highly gifted boy living in a small rural Maine community. He is very academically oriented. As a fourth-grader his achievement ranged from the ninth- to the twelfth-grade level. He is in love with the sciences and has his own scientific technical library at home. He has friends and is accepted by his community. He has always been viewed by everyone as extremely bright. Carl's adult and perceptive comments, his vast achievements and accomplishments, are taken in stride by his peers and neighbors with an understated comment such as, "That's just Carl."

Tom is another gifted elementary student living in a small town. His parents own and manage a tourist fishing camp whose season begins before the end of school and ends after the beginning of school in September. Tom helps his parents run this isolated camp, which is accessible only by seaplane. While Tom's absences from school are real and could constitute a problem, they do not because the school has an intimate knowledge of the child and the circumstances. Tom is fortunate to be forming friendships with his family's clients, a variety of individuals from many professions who have established and maintained lasting ties with Tom and his family.

An intimate personal interest in and knowledge of a child and his or her family over a period of time is a significant feature of what a rural community can offer a gifted and talented child.

THE ACCESSIBLE RESOURCES

While a large number of people and resources is clearly an advantage of which urban areas may boast, rural areas have the edge in another way. Although the people and resources may be fewer in number, they are physically more accessible to children in rural towns. The library may be small, but generally you can walk there from home safely. This intimacy is very important.

A man who grew up in a rural town and is presently very much involved in museum work and natural history tells this story of his childhood: There was a small museum in his town filled with stuffed birds and rocks and arrowheads, which were displayed erratically at best. Yet to him it was a magical place, and he went there at least twice a week all through his childhood. He developed a love for and an intimate knowledge of the collection, which has been valuable throughout his adult life. Further, as a teenager he was able to work after school with the curator in many different capacities, and he came to know the collection as well as the curator. This probably would not happen in city museums. They are too large to allow students this overall exposure to their workings.

This leads to another very important advantage of rural life. Children with ability have an opportunity to perform adult tasks in rural communities. The man with the interest in museums was able to take over the responsibilities of the assistant curator. In other instances an able actress would be able to develop her talents in community as well as school productions. An able writer could publish in the local paper in addition to the one at school. There are opportunities for gifted youths to serve as apprentices with whatever organization or business is in the community. Such children also have easy access to people who live in the community. There are often people with specific expertise. In a small town everyone knows people performing a wide range of skills and involved in a diversity of occupations. If a child is interested in a given topic, there is often someone in the community who can work with him or her. For example a boy was interested in the history of railroads, and his father knew a retired railroad engineer who was also a history buff. The student spent a great deal of time with this man and as a result developed an oral history of the railroads.

An outgrowth of these firsthand experiences is a sense of confidence that the child develops. Gifted children from rural settings can have many opportunities to perform as professionals rather than as students. They have access to whatever resources are available and can become a working member of whatever pursuit they are interested in. There is not the rigid segregation of roles one often finds in urban areas. Rather, in small towns one can often find a local high school student with an interest in writing covering local sports events for the town paper. The need, then, is for parents to help children take advantage of these opportunities or to help them channel their interest.

TOPICS FOR ACTIVITIES

There are an infinite number of possible enrichment activities available in a rural setting. These may be short singular experiences or some of a longer duration. In Maine any of the following could be considered a suitable topic for exploration: forestry, the fishing industry, potato farming, town meetings, general stores, toothpick factories, blueberries, game wardens, farms, barns, fences, architecture, lobstering, maple syruping, mountains, inland waterways, fly tying, genealogy, and gravestone rubbing. Remember to allow for your child's interest, personality, and need for structure when developing activities.

Here are two possible topics you may wish to develop with your child.

Town Meetings In some small towns local affairs are run through town meetings. This is a form of government that is accessible to young and old alike. Thus it can serve as a natural vehicle for the consideration of many issues related to government. Elsewhere there are meetings of school boards and zoning hearings, which offer similar opportunities. The basis of a project could begin with any of the following questions:

- Does this form of government work?
- Are issues clearly and rationally discussed?
- Is this the 'real democratic process'?

- What are the similarities and differences between this form of government and the town council form of government?

Some of the activities centered around this topic could include

- Interview the moderator of the town meetings. Find out how he or she was selected; find out what is the philosophy about selecting people to speak and controlling the meeting and how the moderator feels about the effectiveness of this method of government.

- Look at the town records and look at the issues brought up in each warrant over the past twenty years. Make a chart of those issues that are consistently brought up and those issues that are less frequently brought up. What assumptions can one make about what is important to the town? What is not important?

- Survey random members of the community and ask them how they feel about the town meetings. Survey questions could ask whether they feel that all the issues are allowed to be fully discussed; whether they feel they had a fair say in town policy; what they consider to be the most important issue that the town deals with, and so on.

- Have your child follow an issue from the beginning to the end to see how it is dealt with and what steps it must go through in order to be accepted by the community.

The possibilities are endless. Your child could gain many valuable skills, including interviewing, surveying, writing, and charting as well as gaining a real insight into town government. Likewise your child could develop a very interesting product from this, including such things as a newspaper article, a play centered around a town meeting, or a short story with the town meeting as a focus.

Wild Flowers There are many aspects of nature that could be developed into short- or long-term projects. One such example, wild flowers, is illustrated here as a model:

1. During what months do the various wild flowers blossom? Make a chart of this to see how they overlap and how long they blossom.

2. Identify all of the flowers by color and put them in place in a color spectrum.

3. Many flowers are associated with certain ceremonies, festivals, or occasions, both happy and sad. Try to discover or to hypothesize why these particular flowers are associated with these

events. For example, lilies given at Easter and at funerals and roses given to lovers.

4. There are Indian legends related to flowers. Find these out and correlate them with what Anglo-Saxons associated with the same flowers.

5. Create a collection of drawings and information about the flowers in your area. This would include drawing them and providing information about them. Make this into a book.

As a parent there are several things that you can do to help your child foster his or her many talents. The first is to know how gifted children in general learn and then more specifically how your own child prefers to learn.

Next, look at what is available in your immediate surroundings. Finally, and perhaps most important, you must take responsibility for your child's learning both in school and out of school. Build on the resources that are available. There are many.

21
Never Underestimate the Power of Parents

Gail B. Robinson

Many people have responsibility for the education of gifted children, but parents have the greatest responsibility of all. Sometimes appropriate education in the schools and adequate resources in the community develop only when parents demand them.

Parents can suggest that such community resources as libraries, museums, and theaters be made available to gifted children. Mini-courses, after school or on weekends, can be offered at community centers. Courses and classes such as chess, guitar, foreign languages, creative writing, and great books could be sponsored. Museums don't have to limit their offerings to exhibits, but should also contribute by offering courses in art media, art history, and anthropology. Many of the courses offered in both museums and libraries can be taught by members of the community who have expertise in a given area. By meeting with these people, gifted students are sometimes able to find a mentor — someone with whom they can establish a close working relationship. To provide these experiences, parents must frequently be the initiators of such courses.

Being an advocate for education of the gifted and talented can be frustrating, time-consuming, patience-exhausting — but certainly rewarding. Trying to convince teachers, principals, school superintendents, boards of education, and legislators that there is an urgent need for gifted children to have a special education is no easy task. Yet one cannot tackle this project with anger or defensiveness. Tact, diplomacy, and patience are essential.

Gail B. Robinson is administrative consultant to the American Association for Gifted Children. She was formerly teacher/coordinator of the gifted program in the Mamaroneck, N.Y., school system. She is an adjunct instructor at Manhattanville College, Purchase, N.Y.

You may hear arguments from many people stating that gifted children can learn anywhere, at any time, and that they do not need a special education. When nearly every community is faced with budgetary problems, you may be told that there is not money for special programs for gifted and talented students. A successful advocate must be sympathetic to the existing limitations, yet be able to offer specific suggestions as to why a school program for the gifted must be implemented.

Dr. Madeleine F. Coutant, executive director of the Susquehanna Manpower Corporation, suggests that parents can become part of a group designed to advocate programs for gifted children or to organize an association if none exists in their area. Since all this is best accomplished and more effective if you are not trying to do it alone, you can "advertise" your intentions to form such an organization in many ways.

- Place an announcement in your PTA newspaper describing your intentions to form a local association.
- Place similar announcements in newsletters of local churches and synagogues.
- Make an announcement at a PTA meeting, telling the time and place of your meeting.
- Place an advertisement in your local newspaper. In this way you will reach the broader community.

When your meeting does take place, have someone act as secretary by taking minutes. Be sure that you establish a mailing list, including everyone who is at your meeting. Discuss the objectives of your organization and how you can reach other parents. Perhaps an interested parent is an attorney and will help you draw up by-laws and a constitution for your organization. Such an organization provides opportunities to work for public awareness and to build an even larger and stronger base of support. This group should include both parents, professionals, and interested members of the community.

Assess the needs of your gifted children in your community and report the findings to the local board of education. Specific needs will vary from community to community. Having an advocacy group attend school board meetings demonstrates determination to implement the needed programs. Additionally it is imperative that parent groups, and the community at large, write to local, state, and federal legislators indicating why legislation is needed to provide special programs for our gifted and talented children.

The procedure takes time, but with persistence parent advocates will eventually be successful in their efforts. Let no one underestimate the determination and power of parents acting as advocates for the appropriate education of their gifted children.

22

National Programs for the Gifted

Jane Case Williams

Meeting the educational needs of exceptional children, whether gifted, handicapped, or both, has come to be recognized as the appropriate role of those agencies at the state and local level that hold responsibility for public education. This has come about in recent years through the passage of legislation, both state and federal, that identifies the needs of exceptional children as an important, and often neglected, educational priority requiring the provision of services to children within specified age ranges, commonly five through twenty-one.

Enactment by the Congress in 1975 of Public Law 94-142, called the Education for All Handicapped Children Act, was a landmark in national recognition of the specialized educational needs of exceptional children. This law requires that each state requesting federal funding seek all handicapped children and provide individualized education plans (IEP's) to address their specific learning problems. While this federal legislation did not include gifted and talented children in its provisions, it is interesting to note that a significant number of states, in recognition of the need for individualized services to children of high ability, have voluntarily included the category "gifted" in implementing their searches for exceptional children and development of IEP's. Further, some states, such as Connecticut and New Mexico, have their own legislation that mandates services for gifted students.

Jane Case Williams is now with the Program Development Branch of the U.S. Bureau for the Education of the Handicapped. She directed the 1971 study and report to the U.S. Congress on education for the gifted and talented and was deputy director of the Office for Gifted and Talented, U.S. Office of Education.

DETERMINATION OF NEEDS

Education for the gifted and talented became an initiative of the United States Office of Education with the passage of the 1969 Amendments of the Elementary and Secondary Education Act. A section of this act directed the U.S. Commissioner of Education to conduct a study of the existence of, and need for, gifted education generally and to review the activities of the Office of Education with recommendations for an appropriate federal role, if such was indicated.

The findings of this study were reported to Congress in 1971. Among the conclusions were these: (a) the gifted were among the most educationally neglected children in this country, particularly in disadvantaged populations; (b) nearly 60 percent of school administrators in the United States professed to have *no* gifted or talented students in their schools and thus made no special provisions for them; (c) the U.S. Office of Education administered no programs or activities that specifically benefited gifted and talented students.

As a result of this study the commissioner established the Office for Gifted and Talented, a small advocacy office, and directed the expenditure of some discretionary funds toward the initiation of a few catalytic national activities.

The funded activities included training of teams of leadership personnel at the state level, support of a clearinghouse to obtain and disseminate information nationally, and the establishment of three state leadership awards to consortia of states working to strengthen regional programs.

This small beginning was soon augmented through the passage of legislation by Congress in 1975 that authorized continuation of an office for the gifted within the U.S. Office of Education. The legislation specified a program of awards for the purposes of support to state and local education agencies for leadership training for graduate students, administrators, and others; for information development and dissemination; and for model demonstration projects. These program activities were augmented by the continuing role of advocacy of the Office for Gifted and Talented, which resulted in many cooperatively supported national conferences and an increased interest generally on the part of educators in recognizing and responding to the educational needs of gifted and talented children and youth.

The legislation authorizing the federal program was continued in 1978, with a shift of program funding emphasis to the states. This reflects the generally accepted idea that education is the responsibility of state departments of education and that the federal government should assume a role that is catalytic and enhancing rather than prescriptive.

There is no doubt that the increased federal role has greatly stimulated the growth of services to the gifted population in recent years. As an example, in 1970 only ten states employed the equivalent of a full-time person to handle responsibility for gifted education; by 1975 this number had doubled, and by 1979 every state had identified someone with at least part-time responsibility for education of the gifted and talented, of which nearly 80 percent were full-time staff at the state Department of Education.

The growth of services to gifted and talented children within the states has been commensurate with this increasing provision of administrative personnel by the states. A 1977 study done by the Council for Exceptional Children showed that states were combining other resources (state and local) with federal funds and indicated significant annual growth in expenditures for gifted education. For example, between the school years 1975–76 and 1976–77 there was an increase of 26.5 percent with a total expenditure of about $27.5 million of combined funds for gifted education in the school year 1976–77. Of this total, only $1.9 million could be identified as coming from federal sources; the remainder was clearly the result of increasing commitment by administrators and educators to meeting the needs of their gifted and talented students.

EDUCATION FOR THE GIFTED IS A TOP PRIORITY

Recent national studies, such as one that evaluated perceived needs by members of state boards of education, show that gifted education is among the top priorities of concerned educators. This finding, combined with the recognition among educators that services for the gifted and talented is the fastest-growing area of education today, indicates that education for the gifted, with the ultimate provision of specialized services to meet the needs of *all* gifted children, has a promising future. This future will continue to be encouraged and supported by the expressed commitment to gifted education by legislators and educators at the federal level. Annual appropriations for education for the gifted will increase, and as they do, states and localities will continue to increase their support. The result of this interaction will mean that federal leadership has been a significant factor in raising the national consciousness to the needs of gifted children and that, ultimately, appropriate educational provisions will be available to *all* gifted children.

23
The British National Association for Gifted Children

Henry Collis

The mail that reaches the headquarters in London of the National Association for Gifted Children is very varied and comes from all over Britain and, since the first World Conference, from many countries abroad. Here are two extracts from letters. The first mother was referred to us by the family doctor and writes, "With my four-year-old boy any answer to a question only leads to another question. My husband and I are both teachers but are completely worn out. We have tried tranquilizers on him, and the doctor has tried psychiatry. All to no avail. Today he has had the tantrum of all tantrums because I was not able to tell him why he could not see the wind. Do *please* help us to help him, instead of shouting and getting cross." The other mother was referred by a health visitor: "We have had thirteen years of worry over John, who is now thirteen. The last six months have been sheer hell. I know there must be an answer somewhere, and I pray that it is your association. Is it?"

A PLACE FOR PARENTS TO TURN

It is not for me to say whether our NAGC is the answer or not, but it certainly was partly for parents and children like this that the association was formed in 1966. Many parents join us when distraught

---

Henry Collis was director of the British National Association for Gifted Children from 1973 to 1979. He was coordinator of the First World Conference for Gifted and Talented Children (London, 1975) and was formerly a headmaster for twenty-eight years.

because of their exceptionally demanding and restless children and are very relieved to meet other parents and not to feel so alone. Our membership stays constant at between four thousand and five thousand families and other professionally interested persons (for example, doctors, teachers, educational psychologists, health visitors). Why, with a constant stream of new members, does the total not grow? Because when the children are about fifteen, our job is done, or unlikely to be done, and families drift away. The new intake of, say, fifteen hundred families a year brings new life and new problems and keeps us involved with some seven thousand gifted children.

Let me now tell you the main planks on which the NAGC stands. First, general organization. When there are enough adults in a town or rural area who are interested enough to pay a small annual subscription (£6) to join the association, a local branch is formed. At the moment there are forty-three branches in Britain run entirely by voluntary chairpeople, secretaries, treasurers, and committees. The English are said to be mad, and one of our national characteristics is that there are thousands and thousands of voluntary organizations looked after almost entirely by people so dedicated to the cause that they actually pay in order to serve as members. Their satisfaction lies in devoting leisure time to what they feel to be worthwhile. The NAGC is the only organization of its kind in Britain, and it is encouraging to see official departments gradually moving in to give support. Having gifted children is not always a welcome idea.

Most parents who join us are in the lower-, middle-, or very low income bracket, and for these we are always ready to waive the subscription. Many are recommended to come to us by an educational psychologist or head teacher. The more disadvantaged a family, the more resistant they are to accepting the idea that they have an exceptionally intelligent child. To be talented in music, the arts, manual dexterity, or sports is to be different, and that is prestigious for the parent and an asset to the school. But in the area of academic achievement many people thrive on conformity, and sometimes children are even urged by their parents to produce poor work at school.

We ask for no proof of giftedness in the child, because to do so would be to smack of elitism and might well exclude the *very* families who need our help most — those in very underprivileged areas where, for environmental reasons, children may test out moderately even though they have a latent potential well in the gifted category that is only waiting for the opportunity to show itself.

PARENTS EXCHANGE VIEWS

The principal object locally is for the parents and other members to meet and exchange views and to talk, perhaps for the first time, quite freely about their children. Hitherto it may well have been an embarrassing subject. Then we hope they will run weekend activities for the children (whom we call directly Explorers Unlimited). In London there are two centers that operate on Saturdays except during school holidays. Over two hundred children attend, and there is a waiting list of 150. Some children as young as three, but of course with a much higher mental age, are catered for. The main group, whose ages range from six to fourteen, are split up into small units and taught as wide a variety of skills as the expertise of the parents and adult volunteers make possible, for example, drama, computers, electronics, art, crafts — including candlemaking, basketmaking, balsa modeling, jewelry, woodworking, and pottery — mineralogy, chess, ecology, music making, science, astronomy, anatomy, ornithology, French, and Italian. Care is taken to avoid direct conflict with school curricula, or we should only exacerbate the situation by making them further ahead still. One branch includes Esperanto and another Chinese calligraphy — both rarely taught in school!

What is the object behind all this effort? Primarily it is so that like minds may challenge each other. This can mean that children unique in their school classes, perhaps even in their school (top 2 or 3 percent) come to realize that just to be very clever is not enough. They have to get motivated, or they will be overtaken in life by others more able than they are. In these activities and in their discussions with other Explorers they may encounter an experience quite new for them — that of not being on top and *not* winning every argument. How salutary this can be and what a valuable lesson for life, where we have to meet success *and* failure and still survive.

CHILDREN NEED OTHER CHILDREN

Frustration at school and mishandling at home may have made the children self-centered, withdrawn, or aggressive, but three hours with their intellectual or creative peers can begin to make them better adjusted and less antisocial. We are lucky here in that the great majority of our members' children are delightful, well balanced, enthusiastic, and blessed with that special sparkle that indicates giftedness. In their company the isolate makes friends, the manipulator finds that somehow *she* has been gently coerced into doing what she never intended to do, and the "center of attraction *wherever* he goes," as his fond mother says, rather enjoys being ordinary for a change. One thing we regard as very important: So as not to split families, the brothers and sisters are usually welcome, however ungifted, and can also become useful members of the Explorers Club, working together in their own groups. We are fortunate to be helped by the Inner London Education Authority with free premises and some teachers to supplement the instruction undertaken by members.

Residential courses are run during the summer on all sorts of subjects. A week is usually as long as the instructor can survive! One course for eleven- to fifteen-year olds was run by International Computers Limited, with their chief training instructor in charge and two assistants. I visited the course after two days and asked the instructor how he felt. "Dead beat," he gasped. "They keep me up till midnight."

IMPROVING TOLERANCE FOR GIFTED CHILDREN

Before I leave the subject of organization, I must say that we do our utmost, on very limited finances, to have a few professional field officers — five at present — covering different areas and giving practical help to hard-pressed volunteers. We also maintain a London headquarters of five staff persons so that we can in many ways be a kind of resource center for the branches. We issue newsletters and deal with many day-to-day enquiries from professionals and the general public, and plod on trying to improve the attitude of tolerance to gifted children. In this our media are the greatest help.

A most important aspect of our work is to run a voluntary counseling service, because parents of gifted children experience difficulties strangely similar to those experienced by parents of handicapped children — strains on family relationships, educational problems, and the dilemma of how much time, money, and resources to spend. Thanks to a grant from our Ministry of Health, members of standing who may have had *and* have overcome their own problems are selected to be trained by professional marriage guidance counselors. The object is that before long every branch will have this sympathetic ear to whom parents can turn when the perpetual motion and relentless questions of their gifted children begin to prove too much. In some cases marriages can founder because one parent is intellectually dim and is ignored by the son or daughter. The counselor's role is not to advise (except to refer the parents to professionals), but rather to help parents to reassess the situation and come to terms with it, in the hope that they will learn to understand why their child is friendless; in that case and that patient talking through of a problem with a dispassionate counselor can help enormously. Each counselor has the local backup of a marriage guidance tutor, with whom he or she will have discussions at least six times a year. Divorced, adoptive, or single-parent families particularly need support and reassurance. For instance, a girl with an illegitimate child by a foreign student may find she has a legacy far more intelligent than herself, with no one to turn to. Perhaps she had a guilt complex already and now finds that she has created what she cannot nurture.

SPECIAL NEEDS OF THE GIFTED

Surprisingly doctors and child health specialists often feel at a loss when dealing with families with gifted children. The low incidence of these children does not justify a full study of their characteristics during the training of these professionals. NAGC therefore has an official grant to enable us to hold seminars in different areas to help the medical profession and allied disciplines recognize and understand children with high intellect.

More germane to our real concern is of course the need for all teachers to become aware of the needs of the gifted and talented and to give them the special consideration they require, but we prefer this to be in their ordinary schools. NAGC is against special schools because of the risk of these children growing up thinking that they are normal and everybody else is very stupid. However, we fully appreciate that this is just a point of view and we respect those who feel differently. Clearly music and ballet must be taught at top levels in a specialist setting, for early professional training is essential. It should be stressed that the NAGC also works closely with the Ministry of Education, which makes us a small national grant, just as some local education authorities give our branches annual financial assistance. But most of our money has to come from fund raising.

We try to get home to teachers basic points such as the following: Never forget how vulnerable these parents can feel, especially those in deprived circumstances. Always be ready for "Yes *but*. . . ." Don't neglect the divergent thinker. He or she may be the visionary or philosopher of the future. You cannot bluff gifted children. Do not accelerate the child unless he or she is sufficiently mature emotionally. Gifted children need learning communities, not inflexible instruction. Be firm but understanding over the appalling handwriting that can be the result of brain outpacing hand. Try to develop an instinct in identifying gifted children. Then by intuition you can help those who are frustrated by being misunderstood. Above all have the patience of Job, create a warm rapport, and keep your sense of humor. These are the finest ingredients for motivation, and if you are new to teaching, they will prevent your being in awe of gifted children.

PHYSICALLY HANDICAPPED—INTELLECTUALLY SUPERIOR

We find it necessary to remind teachers that physically handicapped or deformed children can still be very bright. One of our Explorers is a five-year-old boy who weighed only 2 pounds 5 ounces at his premature birth. When he was six months old, he was found to be suffering from cerebral palsy. The parents would not give up hope, and imagine their amazement when just before his second birthday he started reading a few words. He has a high IQ, now feeds himself normally, and happily ferries himself around in a wheelchair. We got him a special child's electric typewriter two years before official quarters allow one free. Recently three normal five-year-old friends went to play with him. When they left, Dominic said how *sad* it was that they were handicapped. His mother asked in what way they were handicapped. He replied `` *They* can't read.''

CAUSE AND EFFECT

Gifted children do most things in extremes, and in advising both teachers and parents we stress that when a usually normal young child suddenly starts behaving strangely, the reason *must* be found. Why was the five-year-old boy biting people every day, including the ankles of the ladies serving dinner? Eventually it was discovered that he was becoming severely disturbed just because his parents would not let him teach himself to read. Once he was given books, he immediately shed his carnivorous habits. Again why did the eleven-year-old make himself sick in the mornings by violently pulling in his pajama cord far too tightly? Just because one teacher refused to let him ask any questions in class and had made him hate school.

Our resources are too small for us to reach the bulk of the teaching force directly, but we have some good allies in principals of colleges training students and in wardens of centers where teachers meet. Similarly we try to get at industry, commerce, and the professions so that they will not fail to attract some of the most intelligent, creative, and artistic young people in the land. Our members who have children talented in music are greatly helped by being able to spend half a day without charge at the house of our music counselor, Michal Hambourg, a well-known concert pianist herself. Brilliant children thrive on mentors, and she helps them to understand what it is like to live music.

CAREER CHOICES

Where the business world often goes wrong is in not realizing that gifted and talented children may well make up their minds on careers three years ahead of average schoolchildren and that they will often choose the professions they know most about. Being highly sensitive, they can be put right against industry by seeing on television a violent strike scene outside a factory. When a decision is taken, it can be extremely difficult to influence them in another direction.

SOME QUESTIONS

Research and an attempt to build up a storehouse of information feature large in our plans. With many thousands of family records to examine we have what must be a unique collection of personal data on families with gifted children. For example how commonly does hyperactivity mean giftedness? What effect do certain drugs like progesterone during pregnancy have? Is there any proof that a quick birth helps toward high intelligence? How significant are those somersaults in the womb?

I have tried to cover our main objectives — parental participation, Explorers' activities and courses, developing a professional staff to serve and work with the volunteers, training counselors (music counselors included), conducting seminars for child specialists, teaching the teachers, advising parents, using the media, helping firms to recruit brilliant employees, and gradually piecing together environmental and genetic data collected over twelve years.

But in addition to these aims there is another that is fundamental to the whole existence of the NAGC. It is the constant concern for the individual children who may be suffering socially by virtue of being brilliant, may be deliberately underachieving and wasting potential, or may be shrugging their shoulders at the world and redirecting their talents. If gifted children opt out of ordinary conventions, they can do extraordinary things. They could be some of the world's greatest and most eccentric inventors or visionaries. Equally they could turn into master criminals, planning misdeeds with superb precision behind the scenes. Let us never forget that whatever is happening outside to improve their lot, all that really matters to them is their own limited horizon. All children deserve to have their day in the sun and need to have fun and to know that we enjoy their company and are determined to see that they prosper. We believe this can best be accomplished by treating the gifted and talented as basically normal children who have very special endowments (not always to their benefit). We would not want to label them openly as a special category, since this seems to confer on them a kind of public qualification. It could make parents far too ready to use giftedness as a status symbol or as the realization of their own unfulfilled ambitions. I remember as a headmaster interviewing an eleven-year-old who answered my query as to how he was that morning, "Oh quite normal, sir, despite my parents." How perceptive these children are. Having met his parents, I knew he was absolutely right. He was a delightful boy who embellished school life wherever he touched it, and I only hope we did something to educate those parents. Our overriding aim is to help the many well-adjusted gifted children to fit in easily with their fellows and not to take themselves too seriously. The same goes for their families.

THE FIRST WORLD CONFERENCE ON GIFTED CHILDREN

In 1973 the British NAGC made a momentous decision — to think big, to look wide, to plan hard, and to hold the First World Conference on Gifted Children. For what was then a much smaller and less secure association this was quite a risk. Failure could have put us out of business. The conference was held in London in 1975 and was attended by over five hundred participants, from fifty-one countries, including a number of official delegations. As a result, the World Council for Gifted and Talented Children was formed. In 1977 the Second World Conference met in San Francisco, and the Third World Conference was held in Jerusalem in 1979.

There is an executive committee of the World Council consisting of seven members, each from a different country. The first members to be elected in 1977 came from Iran (chairperson of the World Council), America (vice-chairperson), Australia, Britain, Bulgaria, Israel, and Venezuela.

It will be many years before the impact of the World Council is really felt internationally. Meanwhile, gradually in more and more countries members will be beavering away to uphold its goals and purposes, which are the following:

- To focus world attention on gifted children and their valuable potential contribution to the benefit of mankind.

- To explore the nature of their talents and resultant problems in childhood and adolescence.

- To create a "climate" of acceptance of gifted children, not as a privileged elite but as a valuable global asset.

- To assemble, for an exchange of ideas and experiences, people from all over the world who are interested in the gifted and talented.

- To persuade the governments of the world to recognize gifted children as a category for special attention in normal educational programs.
- To establish a means for a continuing worldwide exchange of ideas, experiences, teaching, and teacher-training techniques in respect to gifted children.

Put more simply and in a more personal way, it is our earnest hope that as a result of the World Council more gifted children everywhere will develop naturally and not grow up to be like the tragic person in Stevie Smith's poem:

"I was too far out all my life,
And not waving but drowning."

4 GIFTED CHILDREN IN SCHOOL

The Prayer of the Lifelong Student*—Kyla Koehler

Lord
with Your guidance
and with the guidance of parents, teachers, counselors,
    friends, and books
I have learned to guide myself.

How much more important I am
than calculus, chemistry, and phys. ed.
I have learned much of these,
and I have enjoyed discoveries in these areas
    — they have helped to make me what I am.
But how much more wonderful it is
    to begin to discover myself.

I can learn by studying
but I can also learn by living.
Lord, thank you for life.
I will always be a student.

Age 17,
Moorestown, NJ
High School

*Reprinted with permission from *Voices of Youth,* edited by Dr. Charles R. Keller.

24
Parent Roles in Changing Schools

Sidney P. Marland, Jr.

Once upon a time, as a young superintendent of schools working nights and weekends on my further education, I conducted a modest survey on the subject of gifted children. My purpose (apart from a graduate study exercise) was to learn what a number of selected school systems were doing to serve these exceptional children. I addressed my sampling instrument to about one hundred school superintendents in representative communities across the country. While the responses I received were, as one might expect, mixed, I recall one in particular. Across the face of my questionnaire in large print was the response, "We do not have any gifted children in this school system."

Well, that was in the late forties, and we have come a long way. But the needs of gifted and talented children are still unattended in many communities.

School administrators today are well aware of the presence of gifted and talented young people in their schools. But they have many priorities to attend to, not least of which are the enormous needs of *other* exceptional children, notably the disadvantaged, the handicapped, the underserved minority youngsters. It is very clear that the thrust of our public policy over the past fifteen years has emphasized the needs of the have-nots. (I happen to concur with these priorities.) Only very recently, however, has formal public policy, as encouraged by Congress, elevated the gifted child to a significant level of concern.

National public policy or not, many school systems under enlightened leadership have for years dealt responsibly and creatively with the

Sidney P. Marland, Jr., Ph.D., is a former commissioner of education, U.S. Office of Education, Department of Health, Education and Welfare, and former president of the College Entrance Examination Board.

gifted. Large sums of additional money are not necessarily entailed. A *realignment* of existing faculty, community resources, and materials, including laboratory and library facilities, can be accomplished with modest funding.

The *parent*, to whom this volume is primarily addressed, can play an essential part in any change in school systems' policies that will introduce new services to the gifted and talented. If you are the parent of a gifted child, you have been told many times, I am sure, that you have an exceptional responsibility. You have been cautioned to treat your child as normally as possible while still affording him or her opportunities for the child's exceptional potential for growth. You are cautioned to be sensitive, loving, supportive, tolerant, resourceful, and patient.

If you are in a situation where you believe the schools are unresponsive to the needs of your child, *and if indeed you have firm evidence of your child's exceptional characteristics beyond your own subjective prejudice,* you can help the schools to make the necessary changes. The procedure least likely to succeed would be to assault the superintendent or the board of education with confrontation and demands. Their understandable preoccupation with the urgent traditional priorities of public policy mentioned above makes it easy for them to rationalize the familiar response that ''the gifted can take care of themselves.'' Not so. The gifted need just as much understanding and support as the handicapped. The new priority in support of the gifted is as worthy as the priorities serving the disadvantaged.

Setting aside the confrontation route, a quiet, constructive conversation with the appropriate school administrator is the first step. He or she will know of new and emerging resources and techniques for serving the gifted and will know that such children are present in the district, whether or not an adequate program is in place. Offer your services as a volunteer to help the *school leadership* do what it feels is best. Offer to assist in assembling other like-minded parents. Offer to further supportive state legislation if needed. Offer to gather talented adults in the community to establish systematic voluntary relationships with the schools. Offer to raise modest voluntary funds for special library or laboratory materials. In short, place yourself as an ally of the already heavily burdened school staff, to facilitate their program in behalf of your child.

Those qualities that you have been admonished to sustain in your relationship with your child will serve equally well in seeking constructive responses from recalcitrant school policy makers. While I cannot insist on ''loving'' your superintendent, I do counsel all the other qualities: Be sensitive, supportive, tolerant, resourceful, and patient. While your superintendent may not be gifted or talented, he or she will be far more likely to respond if you show yourself to be a companion in concern, as distinct from a combatant in controversy.

The time is past when any school administrator would consign a gifted child to his or her own devices without provocation. The higher priority for the gifted is established in the public policy statements of Congress and many states. There remains the implementation of systematic programs. The gifted do not have a substantial political constituency for the furtherance of that public policy except in their parents. School leaders and teachers need your help and companionship in serving the needs of your child.

25

Elementary and High School Education of the Gifted

Joseph Mas

With few exceptions, the public schools have only recently considered gifted and talented children as a group in need of special help. The prevailing thought has generally been that because of their exceptional capabilities gifted children will somehow succeed on their own. Fortunately more and more parents and educators are realizing that these children not only need special attention but, more importantly, society needs their potential.

It is undeniable that the growing literature on education for the gifted and talented is just beginning to be put to use. For example, while the proceedings of the First World Conference for Gifted Children, held in London in September 1975, consisted of twenty-five papers by visiting speakers, only two were related to school programs. As at other conferences on the gifted and in many publications, topics such as the philosophy of education for the gifted, the need for programs for these students, and the identification of gifted students are usually adequately covered. However, there is a scarcity of materials on the topic of program development.

As reported in the winter 1975 issue of *The Administrator Quarterly,* few New Jersey school districts have adopted policies coordinating their district's efforts in this direction.[1] However, the study did reveal considerable hope for the state's gifted and talented children. For example, 96 percent of the responding superintendents stated that children are grouped with emphasis on individual achievement and ability.

Joseph Mas, Ph.D., has served as superintendent of the Glassboro, N.J., Public Schools and is currently superintendent of the public schools in Waldwick, N.J. Dr. Mas is president emeritus of the Gifted Child Society of New Jersey.

The data also revealed that the precepts of continuous progress instruction and honors classes have been accepted and incorporated into the curriculum of approximately half of the responding school districts. While patterns of this type are important, programs for the gifted in the public schools should transcend continuous progress and honors classes. Many of the programs described in this article build on a school's existing curriculum, incorporate the philosophy of facilitating the optimum growth of every child, and establish a curricular framework that peaks with the gifted. As described in the *Study of Gifted in England,* "Gifted children are like other children in one important respect: they are individuals and should not be thought of as a group, with common characteristics. In order to meet their needs, it is more useful to think of provisions for particular aspects of giftedness, than to attempt to provide for general giftedness."[2] Ideally, the school curriculum, if developed on a foundation that facilitates the optimum growth of every child, should offer specialized programs for the gifted and talented in all of the disciplines and their related activities.

Excellent programs that have evolved from this philosophy may not in fact be called programs for the gifted. Conversely, programs with intriguing titles may, upon close scrutiny, be only a superficial response to either a state mandate or local parental pressure. What is crucial are the procedures for organizing instruction, the instructional objectives, and, most important, the motivational and challenging aspects of the daily classroom events.

ELEMENTARY SCHOOLS (K–8)

Possibly the easiest form of acceleration to contemplate, but the most difficult to achieve, is the early admission into kindergarten of children exhibiting advanced physical, mental, social, and psychological maturity. If children are to be viewed as individuals, a single cutoff date for admission into kindergarten is antagonistic to this concept. Since many school systems provide prekindergarten screening in the spring for the identification of perceptual handicaps, it need not be a fiscal or a conceptual burden to include academic indices in the process.

While some school systems limit this screening of intellectual readiness to children who miss the established kindergarten cutoff date by two or three months, others accommodate larger groups. In any case parental permission is essential. (An interesting aside has evolved from this preschool screening of children; if some children are ready for kindergarten earlier than their peers, are there not some who will benefit from delayed admission to kindergarten?)

CONTINUOUS PROGRESS INSTRUCTION

Continuous progress instruction, especially in reading and math, would appear to be an essential foundation for the development of programs for the gifted. Permitting each child to progress at her or his own learning rate and not be locked into what has normally been considered first-grade reading or third-grade math provides a basis for both acceleration and enrichment in a context that minimizes social and emotional complications.

Along with continuous progress instruction, which relates more to how children are scheduled for instruction rather than to instruction itself, a number of other organizational patterns should be considered. Starting as early as the mid elementary grades, a number of districts have developed honors classes that correlate with the kind of program found in the primary grades that enables children to learn at their own rates. This does not in itself mean that a homogeneous group of gifted children is enrolled together for all purposes. Honors sections can exist in a variety of areas and with varying student populations. The composition of an honors art section could differ markedly from an honors science section; a student eligible to take honors reading need not be eligible for honors math.

Once organizational patterns are achieved (for example, placing gifted children together with interested and hopefully capable teachers), consideration should turn to instructional strategies. In this context, labwork, research, and independent study in all disciplines are worthy areas of investigation. Supporting these extensions of existing curricula, a number of "pull out" programs have been well received in a number of schools. While labels differ, these programs provide gifted children with the opportunity to investigate highly specialized themes that transcend the typical classroom. Differing from the in-school and after-school club programs, cognitive areas as varied as creative writing, aerodynamics, computers, philosophy, and opera are pursued in an atmosphere that stimulates student interest.

However, the positive impact of the more routinized in-school and after-school activities and clubs should not be minimized. For years our best programs for talented children were in this area. The excellent results of choral groups, drama productions, art shows, and school newspapers cannot be denied. A logical extension of this success would place equal emphasis on chess and math teams, debating, ecology, and computer clubs.

Organizational patterns, while differing, should provide elementary school gifted children with varying degrees of contact with others in their age group. Gifted children should have the opportunity to work together on a daily basis and also with children of other abilities, in both formal as well as informal educational settings. And, of course, they should be also given the opportunity to work independently.

HIGH SCHOOLS (9-12)

Many of the programming concerns relative to gifted younsters in the elementary grades continue to be of importance at the high school level. Gifted students still need the opportunity to work with other gifted children as well as to relate to the larger social setting of the high school. However, at this stage the opportunity for independent study becomes a means for in-depth development of the student. There are various strategies for arranging instructional programs for gifted children in grades nine through twelve that may operate within the existing structure of the school and yet at the same time provide for a qualitative differentiation for these able students.

One of the most common procedures that has been in operation in many high schools is to have honors sections in subject areas. Participation in honors sections has usually been based on past achievement, although in some schools a student may nominate himself or herself to join an honors section. Subject areas may be in any phase of the school's curricula, including music, art, and business. Honors sections should stress more in-depth study of the subject, may go at an accelerated pace, and may in fact be an impetus for independent study on the part of some students. Teachers of honors sections will wish to focus on the higher levels of thinking as identified in Bloom's *Taxonomy of Educational Objectives*.[3] Research shows that most school learning is centered on the first level of thinking, knowledge, and that the highest level, evaluation, which includes the notion of decision making, is too infrequently reached even in classes for gifted students.

Another strategy similar to having an honors section is to offer students a full program of advanced electives. Such courses as advanced drama workship, astronomy, or anthropology might be included in a school's course of study. If, because of limited funds, enrollment, or human resources, this is difficult for a school to achieve, the idea of a consortium of schools pooling their resources and working out cooperative scheduling arrangements is a realistic possibility.

Work-study programs that involve part of the day in classes and part in supervised on-the-job training have been a feature of many high school programs but have generally been geared to those children who were planning to enter the work world directly upon graduation. An extension of this idea for gifted and talented youngsters would be to make the same provisions possible for those students planning to go on to study the arts and professions. For example, a student might take a morning program of English, science, history, and math and in the afternoon work with a physician to learn examination and diagnostic procedures. Another extension of a work-study program is the executive high school internship program whereby, for a specific period of the school year, the student works in an appropriate business organization. Within this setting, the gifted student is provided with opportunities for decision making. A student might work with a curator of a museum, and responsibilities may include setting up an exhibit and publicizing it.

College courses and seminars are available to the gifted student in some communities. If a youngster wishes to pursue an advanced computer course, for example, the school administration and that of the higher institution in the area can work out procedures to make the course accessible and grant college credits.

Schools with sufficient numbers of gifted children may wish to become involved in formal programs, such as the Advanced Placement Program and the International Baccalaureate Program. The Advanced Placement Program is sponsored by the College Entrance Examination Board in New York City. Content is on a college level, and successful completion of a final examination prepared by school and college instructors generally enables the student to receive college credit for the course.

The International Baccalaureate Program, which originates in Geneva, Switzerland, also demands a high level of subject mastery. Although the two-year program is outlined by the parent organization, it is flexible, and a school is permitted to write its own program capitalizing on the strengths and interests of the students involved. A diploma, which is recognized by the major European universities, is issued to the participating students. For students with the International Baccalaureate a full year of college credit is offered by many United States universities.

Many of the strategies and programs that have already been described may be used within a program of independent study. Independent study allows the individual to do in-depth research at an appropriate pace. Thus the elements of enrichment, continuous progress education, and acceleration may all be features of a student's independent exploration of a topic. The school can facilitate a student's progress in this area in many ways. It may appoint a teacher or a team of teachers to act as mentors and/or suppliers of resources; it may provide personnel to help the student get to a resource area; it may help in finding relevant opportunities in the community. The mentor(s) can also arrange for the student to present his or her work and get interaction and criticism from classmates.

Opportunities for independent study abound. A student who is gifted physically may study modern dance with a mentor and become involved in a community production. If the same student is also gifted in working with others, he or she may initiate a dance group in the school. An academically gifted student with a particular interest in science could select from a variety of self-directed projects. A mentor would aid the student in locating resources, developing procedures, and providing facilties. The student may be able to publish the results of this work or enter it in a national science project contest. The data acquired might provide a welcome contribution to the local library.

As a student in an independent study program, the gifted and talented individual is offered the opportunity to explore interests while realizing his or her personal contribution in a world outside the confines of the classroom.

Having a school program for gifted children does not guarantee that children so identified are adequately instructed. But it does show that the school is aware of the possibilities and is seeking a solution.

Notes

[1] Joseph Mas, and Gina G. Ginsburg, "What Are We Doing for Our Brightest Students?" *The Administrator Quarterly* 4, no. 3 (Winter 1975).

[2] Department of Education and Science, "Gifted Children in Middle and Comprehensive Secondary Schools," HMI Series, (London, 1977).

[3] Benjamin Bloom, Ed., *Taxonomy of Educational Objectives, Handbook I, Cognitive Domain.* New York: David McKay Company, 1956.

26
Complementary Options for Gifted Students

Jerry Foster and Marie Shaffer

One certain fact about gifted and talented children is their scarcity. Studies tell us that only 3 to 5 percent of our children are gifted. Such small numbers present schools with a real dilemma. Classes, curricula, even lunch menus are geared toward the majority of students. There is good reason for this: Designing and implementing programs for small groups of students, gifted or not, is costly. To design and implement a new program, school personnel need to show that "enough" students who need or want that program are enrolled in school. "Enough" usually means one class group; depending on the student-teacher ratio at the school, between twenty and thirty students. If, for instance, twenty-five students need a special program, it may be possible to provide them a teacher and instruction. But if only three students need a special program, school administrators face a conflict: either provide the three children the special program at high cost and explain that action to budget-conscious constituents or fail to provide the program and hope that the three children get by. The path of least resistance is often chosen.

Thus, even though they are a minority group, gifted children receive the same education as the majority in most of our schools. Even a secondary school that offers advanced courses cannot serve all the needs of its gifted children. The advanced course must still be designed for a full class of twenty-five students, a design that does not necessarily take into account the special needs of two or three gifted children. Given

Jerry Foster is founder and former director of the National Network of Complementary Schools, located in Boston, Mass., and former vice president of Elderhostel, Boston, Mass. He is presently national director of SAGA International Holidays, Ltd.

Marie Shaffer is presently director of the National Network of Complementary Schools.

the variety of gifts and talents children have, advanced classes may or may not serve them. What of the gifted art student whose school offers advanced math or the gifted science student whose school offers advanced writing?

The case of one student illustrates our point. A senior in a small independent high school, Lisa had great interest and ability in science. She came from a science-oriented household. Her father taught physics at the local university, and her mother worked as a chemist for a local industrial corporation. Lisa completed her diploma requirement in science by sophomore year and by junior year had completed *all* the science electives in the school catalog. She wished to study more science as a senior but had literally run out of courses to take. As it happened, Lisa's school offered an excellent art curriculum with several advanced-level courses, but these courses were irrelevant to her needs.

As we see, Lisa's problem is really a numbers problem. There are not enough gifted science students at her school to make a special science program cost-effective. But if Lisa's school could cooperate with several other schools to offer specialized programs, Lisa's opportunities would increase. Each school could concentrate on perhaps one or two subject areas, offering a special program for gifted students in only these areas. Each school could open its specialized program to qualified students from all the other schools, thereby increasing the pool of students it draws from. Lisa's school could develop a specialized art program, and another school in the "consortium" might provide the in-depth science program Lisa is looking for.

The concept behind this consortium of schools is called complementary schools, that is, several institutions working together to provide a wider range of educational opportunities for their students. Education is a process of personal development that occurs not in a specific moment but over a long period of time. If we take a sophisticated view of an individual's education, we see that varying educational experiences, some intentional and some incidental, complement each other to make up the whole of his or her development. All of us can think of examples of these experiences — music camps, drama lessons, summer enrichment programs. But perhaps even more logical as complementary learning sites are several schools, each offering students one or more specialties. Students can choose programs that fit individual needs at specific times during their school career.

There are many ways to structure complementary schools. Schools already work together for a variety of reasons: to develop an overseas campus, to enlarge an applicant pool, or to offer a district-wide program. Complementary schools can also provide a group of institutions with more programs for gifted and talented students. Suppose that five schools join together and that each has an enrollment of 1,500 students. Suddenly, each school's "student body" grows from 1,500 to 7,500! If 5 percent of the collective student body is gifted, each school suddenly "enrolls" 375 gifted students rather than 75. Suddenly, too, each school has access to the resources of five faculties and the facilities of five campuses. Any school can offer more when it has increased resources and a larger student body from which to draw.

One group of schools that has reaped the rewards of complementary schools is the National Network of Complementary Schools. Formed in 1974, the Network is a national group of diverse schools and districts that have joined together to share their specialized programs. By pooling their offerings, these schools have provided all their students with a wider range of quality programs. Students may elect any Network school program; once arrangements are made, they exchange, usually for periods of a few weeks. The exchange student studies just one subject or works at one community internship while attending the "host" school. Hence the exchange student has an opportunity to focus on an area of special interest, thereby complementing the education received in the "home" school. Network programs generally exploit a specific geographic or programmatic resource of the school. For example, a Network school in Florida might offer an oceanography program, whereas a Philadelphia school could offer colonial history or Quaker studies.

The host school arranges a home stay in the local community or housing in a school dormitory (if it is a residential school). The excitement of a special program is thus enhanced by the opportunity to experience a new community, new friends, and a new host family. Because exchanges last only a few weeks, students tend to pack a great deal of learning into a very short period of time. They return to the home school revitalized, with a different outlook. One Network principal who has personally debriefed each of his Network exchange students notes that most return with increased self-confidence. Students are far more aware of what they can accomplish when they have ventured into a new school and community, studied with new people in a new way, and lived with a new family.

Of course, even an in-depth program for two or three weeks does not constitute a complete course in any discipline. But these mini-programs of concentration are able to introduce students to areas of knowledge beyond what is possible in the regular curriculum. Once exposed to the new study area, the students can set future goals that will include their new learning. Without this special introduction most young people would never know that such options exist.

Complementary schools fit many descriptions. A consortium for gifted and talented students might contain both public and nonpublic schools — local independent schools, church schools, and public schools. It might be regional or national, depending upon the kinds of programs the schools would like to offer. Rural schools, city schools, and suburban schools create considerable diversity in a consortium; even schools of varying size add variety. We've found that choosing schools that are quite different from one another adds to the excitement of complementary schools. Even within a local area, the differences between schools can be remarkable. Schools can have many resources that make them unique — a special facility, a teacher or parent with a special interest or talent, a connection to an agency or institution in the local community. Programs for the gifted can be designed around any of these resources. The key is knowing where to look for them and how to develop something ordinary into something unique. A darkroom is only a darkroom until someone changes it into a photography program for gifted art students. Often the consortium provides just the prod needed to bring that change about. Schools in a consortium tend to reinforce the spirit of self-improvement: "If they can offer something that good, so can we." The possibilities are endless.

In these days of shrinking education dollars, a consortium of schools makes good sense. We don't know of a better way to provide so broad a range of options for so little cost to the school and the student. Instead of duplicating programs and services, schools can share their resources and better serve individual students at the same time. Gifted children, with their wide range of individual needs, are sure to be better served if they have more options at school, or, at several schools.

27

Horizons Unlimited

Tara N. Stuart

Horizons Unlimited, presently a six-week summer program, offers an innovative model of teacher training for those who are preparing to work with gifted children. Horizons is a program for gifted adolescents fourteen to seventeen years of age, as well as for teachers. Its special approach is in the integration of students, teachers, and faculty, who jointly participate in workshops and in Horizons' activities. The dynamics of learning through the examination of ideas, and through informal relationships that are formed enhance knowledge and understanding. The interwoven themes of self and service form the basis for the educational venture. These themes are explored through the study of art, dance, writing, drama, cross-cultural studies, physical sciences, American Indian studies, and music. The experience of the themes is intensified through living as a community during the summer on the Keene State College campus in Keene, New Hampshire, and actively reflecting on the experience.

The five years of planning and implementing Horizons Unlimited have led some of us on the faculty to ponder the question What lies behind the manifestation of giftedness? What is the inner quality that is present in the outer expression and characteristics of giftedness so thoroughly explored and categorized by experts in the field? From our studies and observations we believe that the inner cause is closely related to consciousness. According to Webster's dictionary *consciousness* is "the

Tara N. Stuart is an associate professor of English at Keene State College, University of New Hampshire. She was cofounder and codirector of Horizons Unlimited, an integrated program for gifted adolescents and teachers interested in working with the gifted.

awareness of something within oneself." This awareness is caught first by the few, perhaps the more highly gifted. It is historically true that such people, who were and are responsible for some of the greatest changes in humanity's growth, were persecuted and rejected and laughed at, as are many of the gifted and highly gifted who carry a higher degree of consciousness. They are the spearhead toward the future of ever greater expansions of consciousness and of increased sensitivity and perceptive awareness. Giftedness, as I see it at Horizons Unlimited, is a matter of consciousness.

In Horizons, faculty, teachers, and students experience this feeling in a variety of ways. Some of the students' comments reveal this:

> Jim: "Before, I was a writing person, now I am not limited to paper and pen. I'll try anything — dance and art. I was put in a position to meet new people, people who weren't my type. I found that everyone has something inside you can touch. If you hide yourself from other people, you hide from yourself."

> Ginny: "I'm a lot more open with people. I feel more trusting with people than I do at school due to the kids themselves and living together. I've learned to accept people for what they are. I was clustering people too. You can be different here without being laughed at. I can be myself."

> Mary: "I feel like I'm coming home to myself. At school I feel put down for being different."

> Shelly: I've grown up. I'm taking responsibility for myself. I've learned to share. It was easy, I was used to it the second day. This is the best thing that ever happened to me. I've found myself. A lot of fears about people and dreams have changed. I understand what is going on inside myself better through art and writing. I feel closer to myself."

LEARNING FOR SERVICE

If they are self-aware to a high degree and searching for their own path or already pursuing it, service is often a characteristic of the gifted. Service may be defined as the spontaneous outflow of a loving heart and an intelligent mind. One of the responsibilities of teachers of the gifted is to guide them toward service by helping them find themselves. To accomplish this, it is important that the teachers themselves look within, exploring their own self-awareness and self-acceptance. We can only teach with wisdom out of our own knowing and understanding, not only of our own educational disciplines but also of ourselves. If we as teachers mask and deny our own searching and unknowing, the gifted quickly know the counterfeit. This past summer during an informal discussion on values, three-quarters of the Horizons students said that they most valued integrity in others, particularly their families and teachers. In pondering the purposes for living, over half of the group said that life, to have meaning, has to involve sharing with or servicing others in some way.

It would seem, as teachers, that we must explore our own gifts first and go through our own process of becoming self-aware before we can help others see and develop their creativity, their giftedness. Therefore, the teacher-training dimension of Horizons Unlimited guides teachers first to look inward and make contact with their own creative potential and then turn outward in order to understand Who are the gifted? What do they need? How may their needs be met? Herein lies the serving aspect of teaching the gifted. To selfishly possess one's own gifts is to see them atrophy and become useless. To use one's gifts responsibly is to see them wax strong and grow. Only by continually emptying the cup can it be refilled and in the process quench the thirst of many. To have gifts and talents beyond the ordinary implies personal as well as social responsibility.

Horizons Unlimited offers teachers, counselors, and administrators of elementary and secondary schools an opportunity to participate in either of two three-week accredited graduate-level seminars at Keene State College on understanding gifted children. The program is directed toward the in-service training of educators in order to more fully meet the needs of gifted children in their own schools and communities. Seminars for educators focus on identification and needs of the gifted, the psychology of giftedness, and an investigation into the nature of creativity. Educators participate in workshops with gifted students during the program and have the opportunity for an enriching experience of sharing ideas and different points of view. A major purpose of Horizons Unlimited is to encourage and guide educators in developing programs for their own classrooms, school, and communities.

Each year, six to eight months before the beginning of the program, the Horizons faculty gathers as a group to develop and plan the program for the following summer. The faculty members are selected on the basis of their having had successful experience in teaching gifted adolescents, their willingness to commit themselves to a very demanding and intensive program, and their being experts in their own fields of study. The various academic disciplines, though they have separate workshop times, integrate their approaches to the creative process so as to best meet the needs of the students and teachers in each workshop.

INTEGRATING SUBJECT AREAS

For example, one boy was having extreme difficulty with syntax and grammar in creative writing. It was discovered in the physical science class that besides being brilliant in mathematics he had an affinity with computers. The science faculty member noted that if we encouraged him to explore the possibilities of programming computers, his writing problems might be resolved, since the computer is a most exacting machine that allows no error in syntax or grammar. With some minor changes in scheduling, George enjoyed a fascinating time with the computer, while his increased competence in basic writing skills reflected his improved self-concept and resulting flow of creative ideas.

There is a natural interrelationship of creative study. The art class may sketch students in the dance and movement group, or someone in music will use another's poetry as an inspiration for an original composition. Since exploring the creative process is the basis for all the courses offered, the wholeness of learning and thinking is implicit in all the various parts of the program.

Students applying for the Horizons Unlimited program are asked to complete an application form and a written autobiographical questionnaire; submit three written recommendations, one of which must be from a peer; provide a high school transcript; and draw a self-portrait. Whenever possible, prospective students are asked to have an interview with a member of the Horizons faculty. The autobiographical questionnaire is as follows:

1. What occuption do you have or do you envisage? For what reasons did you choose the work you are doing or planning?

2. Have any particular cultural works held deep meaning for you (for example, books, films, music, theater, painting) and how were you affected by them?

3. How would you describe the quality of your relationships with other people, including strong and weak points? How would these affect your participation in a living/learning situation with twenty other people for four weeks?

4. What significance and value has friendship for you?

5. What events, activities, and inner conditions have given you the most satisfaction and joy? Which have made you suffer most? Which have had most meaning and significance for you?

6. Are there any values and ideals that you hold firmly as a result of your own experience? How do you express these in your life? How do you fail to express them?

7. What is your perception of education? How do you think you learn best?

8. What is your opinion about the present epoch in human history and consciousness? In what ways do you think we are making progress or losing ground? What do you see as the major challenges facing human beings today?

The directions for the "self-portrait" are as follows:

Self-expression has many forms and holds a significant place in each of our lives. We encourage you to ponder and share the exploration of yourself with us through a self-portrait. Rather then showing how you appear to others, express yourself as you feel yourself to be. Your self-portrait may be a symbol or image of any combination of line, shape, and color that stands for you.

After you have completed your self-portrait on a separate piece of paper, write a brief interpretation of it in the space below.

Horizons Unlimited seems to have a lasting influence upon many who take part in the intensive weeks of study, sharing, and growing. Letters come back from students and teachers, and we then know that the effort and the energy have been well invested. A teacher from Denver, Colorado, wrote,

It seems to me that in order to experience working effectively with the gifted, we must see the process in operation, experience it, take part in it. What a rare opportunity you have given us! Horizons Unlimited methods are so different, so superior, I'd compare it to the difference between being tolds truths and experiencing truths. You helped me to be aware of my responsibility to gifted children's academic and intellectual needs in a unique way, as well as to their emotional, social, and physical needs.

A parent wrote very briefly, "Thanks for giving my son a part of his life he'll never forget." A teacher from Keene, New Hampshire, wrote,

Thanks for providing this unique and invaluable opportunity to learn about educating gifted and talented children. I feel that in those few weeks I grew personally and professionally. The presence of teenagers in the workshops enabled us to observe the results of the teaching methods. As a teacher whose experience has been with elementary school children, it was enlightening to listen to the teenagers talk about their experiences in elementary school and how they were affected by those experiences.

During the Horizons weeks, original prose and poetry, creative drama, paintings, musical compositions, experiments in relativity, and new dances flowed with the renewing energy of young adults who found themselves trusted and accepted, and with the joyous surprise of adults who renewed their own creativity. Together as a group of human beings, we have explored the "looks" of our own longing and thus have unblocked the vision of our own unlimited horizons.

28

The Gifted Handicapped or the Handicapped Gifted: A Matter of Focus

Gladys Pack

WHO ARE THE GIFTED?

While traveling about New York State, working with parents and teachers in an effort to bring about increased awareness of the needs of the gifted and talented, I began to explore perceptions of giftedness, using a brainstorming technique in which each group was asked to name gifted people. Upon examination, the list of names generated in these sessions yielded some interesting observations. Albert Einstein is the first name associated with giftedness in 99 percent of the groups polled. Thomas Edison falls within the top ten names in 90 percent. Hellen Keller, Stevie Wonder, and Vincent van Gogh are consistently and frequently found on these lists. These are lists of gifted people as perceived by parents, teachers, and school administrators. When the list in a given session is completed, a discussion follows. Often the group members are unaware of the difficulties that both Einstein and Edison had in schooling and of the possible handicaps of these eminent men. This brings up the question of focus. When we are looking at eminent gifted people who happen to be handicapped, we are focused on giftedness. We honor these people for their gifts, not the many compensations they had to make.

There have always been people who have been both gifted and handicapped. Goertzel and Goertzel (1962) and Baker (1970) have delved into the lives of these people to give us more insight into the development of talent when handicaps exist. Among them, these authors have identified over 454 gifted handicapped people, thus dispelling the myth that the percentage of handicapped is too small to consider in either category.

Throughout the history of education for the gifted we have been dealing with perceptions. At one time the gifted child was thought to be physically weak and a social misfit. As we moved from earlier perceptions to more enlightened ones, we drew a picture of a gifted child that combined the best features of Adonis and Robert Redford. Somewhere we lost sight of the real child, who has both strengths and weaknesses and has needs with regard to both.

WHO ARE THE GIFTED HANDICAPPED?

When we attempt to identify or to work with students who are both gifted and handicapped, we have a problem of semantics and law. In our language adjectives precede nouns. Thus, it becomes important to determine whether we are talking about a "gifted handicapped" child or a "handicapped gifted" child. As a parent, if you are seeking an appropriate educational program for your child, the law may dictate your focus and your choice of phrase. However, you must exercise your own best judgment in accepting what is offered.

WHO ARE THE HANDICAPPED?

Public Law 94-142 has been hailed as one of the greatest parent-advocacy gains in education. The Education for All Handicapped Children Act of 1975, P.L. 94-142 ensures the right of all handicapped children to an appropriate education in the least restrictive environment. This federal law defines the term *handicapped children* as mentally retarded, hard of hearing, deaf, speech impaired, visually handicapped, seriously emotionally disturbed, orthopedically impaired or other health impaired, or children with specific learning disabilities, who by reason thereof require special education and related services. This law specifies procedures for identification of such children and mandates appropriate programming within rigid time lines. The law also mandates that each handicapped child receive an Individual Educational Plan, specifying both long-term and short-term educational objectives. In addition, the law provides for parent input to all phases of the Individual Educational Plan. The law recognizes that you, as a parent, know your child's needs.

WHO IS GIFTED?

In 1978 Congress enacted the Gifted and Talented Children's Education Act under Title IX of the Elementary and Secondary Education Act. Although there are funds allocated for state programs and for model projects for the gifted, this law does not provide specifically for gifted children with handicaps. Thus any child who has a handicapping condition as defined in P.L. 94-142 and demonstrates achievement of designated potential in one of the five areas in the Gifted Act may be classified as a gifted handicapped child.

CHARACTERISTICS OF THE GIFTED HANDICAPPED AND THEIR PARENTS

Most articles on the gifted proceed from a "who are" section to a "characteristics" section. This section always amazes me, for every characteristic I find in such a section is based on large groups, and individual students always defy such descriptions.

Children who are both gifted and handicapped display a variety of characteristics associated with both aspects of their functioning. Often these students display self-doubt and confusion and often they seek explanations for both their heightened awareness and their specific areas of weakness. Young gifted children with specific physical handicaps may seek answers to their problems from others and may create ingenious medical explanations.

One eight-year-old neurologically impaired gifted boy developed his own explanation of brain damage. He believed that at birth he had one damaged brain cell and that with each succeeding year one more cell became damaged. This faulty explanation was created by a child who had the ability to recall and explain historical facts of wars from the Crusades on and who could explain the workings of any empire, but could not read or pass a simple spelling test. The explanation enabled him to understand his failures but on the other hand depressed him as he saw only further deterioration in his future.

One small six-year-old gifted boy with cerebral palsy entered a first-grade class for physically handicapped students and gave his teacher a full and true explanation of his handicap and of his medical needs, describing the working of a shunt. He had been given facts and he understood his own needs.

Learning-disabled gifted students are often confused, as are their parents. Bright, verbal, and precocious children may enter school and begin to evidence failure for the first time. The student may have specific problems with the receiving and processing of information or with expression in either verbal or written material. These students, too, seek explanations for what is happening. Some are able to articulate their experiences. Recently I came across a poem written by my daughter, which described such feelings:

Confused thoughts caught within a maze
Trapped inside like a big blob of never-ending wire.
Years of stored knowledge behind lock and key.
But always more seeping through as endless days pass.
Traveling through this maze step by step absorbing
    all of life even its toughest obstacles.
Like traveling through all the links of the maze of life.

This poem speaks of the feelings behind the awareness that there is more coming in than the individual can process or cope with. This came from a child who has never been viewed as learning-disabled gifted.

The child who is learning disabled and not articulate may evidence other characteristics. He or she may act the clown or withdraw from the group. The feelings of being different may result in many different behaviors, which may appear as characteristics but may be a reaction to a setting that cannot answer the questions of the child.

The gifted handicapped child characteristically seeks to compensate for handicaps. Often more subtle handicaps are hidden. The gifted hearing-impaired child may use other clues for quite some time before the true nature of the problem is discovered. The learning-disabled or physically disabled child may find willing helpers to aid with writing or note taking or even buttoning. Compensation may be ingenious! It sometimes slows down our discovery that the gifted child is also handicapped.

Parents of gifted handicapped children also evidence confusion and a need to find answers. Parents often find themselves in a state of constantly shifting perceptions. They are often confused as to where to seek answers and about the different messages they are given. I once told a parent that his son was gifted. He looked quite startled and asked, "How can he be gifted when he can't get above a 50 in school?"

The parent may constantly shift the focus from the handicap to the talent, finding it hard to address both needs and not knowing where to go to help this child.

HOW CAN WE HELP?

In order to aid handicapped gifted children, we must first identify them. Under P.L. 94-142 for the Handicapped, the school must provide an assessment of the child and then use the information to find an appropriate program. Be aware, however, that none may exist.

In order to define a child's needs educationally, we first have to assess the child's strengths and weaknesses. This is often difficult to do with a handicapped child. Many of our evaluation tools involve pencil-and-paper tasks, and many require adequate auditory or visual perception in order to hear directions or see printed material. For children who are blind, visually or hearing impaired, deaf, or neurologically impaired, these tools are often inadequate, and we must look for better ways of assessing the child's abilities. There have been methods developed for optimally evaluating students who are blind or deaf. The importance of using appropriate methods must be stressed.

The assessment of the handicapped child culminates in a meeting of professionals involved in evaluation, a parent advocate, and the child's parent, to determine optimal programming. This is the place, I feel, for a shift in view. Your child is being serviced under the handicapped law, but at the same time your child is gifted. It is as important to stress the strengths in an assessment as to pick up on the weak areas. The program must address the strengths and continue the child in these areas while providing compensation and development for those areas weakened by the handicapping condition.

PROGRAMS FOR HANDICAPPED GIFTED STUDENTS

There is no one program for all handicapped gifted students. The beauty of the Education for All Handicapped Children's Act is the concept of the Individual Educational Plan. Those professionals involved with the student as well as the parent must work together to develop this plan.

The handicapped gifted student may need those tools developed by modern technology to aid in his or her growth. Often the use of tape recorders, calculators, typewriters, large-print material, and/or talking books can bridge some of the gaps between the physical problems and the talents of the child. Nothing, however, can take the place of the insightful teacher who can work with children and allow them to move on at a pace appropriate to their area of strength or talent, while at the same time handling remediation. The understanding of the teacher as well as of the group is crucial.

Within a program for handicapped children the handicapped gifted child may be quite alone. This is a child who functions on two levels at once. If we accept the premise that 2 to 5 percent of the population is gifted and that out of this population approximately 2 percent is handicapped, we realize that we are working with a small, select minority. P.L. 94-142 speaks of the "least restrictive environment." For this child, the least restrictive environment may involve spending part of the day in the school's program for the gifted, or it may mean involvement in a program for the handicapped gifted if one exists.

Your school's gifted-child program has its own screening process. This may involve the use of standardized paper-and-pencil tests. The handicapped gifted child may do poorly in these tests and may not be selected for the program. Your child study committee or committee on the handicapped can help effect this placement if it is appropriate. As a parent of a handicapped gifted child you should find out what programs are available in your school district and in surrounding areas. Start with societies interested in your child's area of weakness or strength, or call your school administration and local university. If your committee is not aware of programs, you may have to alert them by forming an advocacy group or by becoming an advocacy group of one. Often the professionals in one of these areas are not fully aware of programs in the other.

Throughout the country today there are a number of model projects for gifted handicapped students. June Maker (1977) describes twenty of these pilot projects throughout the United States. These projects have been designed to reach gifted handicapped students by focusing on areas of strength or talent rather than deficit. Whether it is best to work with gifted handicapped students in a class for the gifted handicapped or with different classes to meet specific needs remains an unresolved question. Programs of this sort are new and can only be evaluated in terms of how they meet the needs of the individual child. The concept of least restrictive environment is important. In order to feel like a whole, integrated person who is gifted and happens to have a handicapping condition, the handicapped gifted child needs assistance and counseling in whatever program he or she is in.

For the handicapped gifted child the parent may be the best resource. No school program can offer the added hours spent reading, sharing, exploring, and encouraging that an involved parent can provide. No program, whether in school or out, can know as well as you, the parent, how to provide that mixture of support and appreciation that is due to every child.

You have a rare opportunity to nurture your child's gifts. Your child will benefit, society will benefit, but the greatest reward will be yours.

Selected References

Baker, Harry J. *Biographical Sagas of Willpower.* (New York: Vantage Press, 1970).

Education for All Handicapped Children Act. P.L. 94-142, 1975.

Gerken, K. C. ''An Unseen Minority: Handicapped Individuals Who Are Gifted and Talented.'' In *New Voices in Counseling the Gifted.* Edited by N. Colangelo and R. T. Zaffrann. (Dubuque, Iowa: Kendall/Hunt, 1979).

Gifted and Talented Children's Education Act. Title IX. *Elementary and Secondary Education Act,* 1978.

Goertzel, Victor, and Goertzel, Mildred G. *Cradles of Eminence.* (Boston: Little, Brown, 1962).

Maker, June. *Providing Programs for the Gifted Handicapped* (Reston, Va.: Council for Exceptional Children, 1977).

Terman, Lewis M. and Oden, Melita H. *Genetic Studies of Genius.* Vol. 4 *The Gifted Child Grows Up.* (Stanford, Calif.: Stanford University Press, 1947).

29
College Is Not for Everyone

Betty Cottin Miller

He threw his bottle out of the crib as an infant — no more milk, thank you. He was an avid Boy Scout in grade school, but no merit badges for him, no earning higher rank. He went and learned and fully enjoyed, but didn't want measurements attesting to how much or how well he did.

In high school he organized an underground newspaper that flourished first in his own school, then countywide. He wore jeans to school before most other kids did, certainly before they were acceptable or even fashionable. And he argued interminably against school regulations and requirements, although his marks stayed high and his scores superior.

Now that he's close to thirty, it is easy to look back and understand the pattern of rebellion and individuality, of challenge and impatience with procedures that didn't make sense to him, of curiosity about new ideas and determination to try different things.

But when living through each crisis, as his parents, we certainly didn't laud his desire to forge new paths and deny our conventional ones. Naturally, we had taught our children to question and challenge and think for themselves. But . . . in moderation!

The heaviest blow came when he was eighteen, six months a college freshman.

"Not go to college! You, with your brains! What will you do? Where can you go, without an education?" His father and I said those words feelingly, desperately. To us, education was the ladder to achievement, college the avenue to intellectual fulfillment. Especially to us, both

Betty Cottin Miller is an English teacher in a Westchester County, N.Y., public high school. She is associated with Mercy College, Dobbs Ferry, N.Y., in a humanities program and has been a consultant for the National Endowment for the Humanities and has also worked for the John Hay Fellows Program in the Humanities. She and her husband have four children.

school teachers, learning was a goal, a challenge, a joy. Not to use one's intellectual capacities — meaning not to go to college, we thought — was an unforgivable sin.

"Of course one must go to college." No, not everyone. It is easy, now, to look back and accept it, to understand that structured learning need not be the only way. For some bright youngsters, intellectually as adept as their peers who choose the college road, the world must be their university. It has been so for our second son.

Don did begin college. The college he chose, and that accepted him, was known for its flexible, seemingly unorthodox format. We felt it was a good match. The world was just emerging from the awful 1960s, and everyone was so hopeful that the next decade would be less harrowing. We all were very unaware of the depth of unease and defiance in the class of '69. Years later Don described his "catastrophic outlook." He and his friends felt bitterly that the world was heading toward absolute ruin: the atomic arms race, the assassinations, the FBI scrutiny of dissenters, the radicals' rhetoric could only end in destruction.

College for Don and so many of his classmates was an intense letdown. He loved the excitement of new ideas, the sharp joy of intellectual challenge. To find, as so many bright students did, that the professors of freshman courses were dull was a reenforcement of their general disappointment in the established way.

"Why go to that class? I can read the textbook he's lecturing on in four hours and understand it all. Why pay four thousand dollars for that!"

But Don stayed through the first college quarter. Second quarter was a work period, and he headed toward New England. Unfortunately, bright young people are too often overestimated. Because they are so verbally adept, it is frequently assumed that they are more self--sufficient than they really are. His work group was left to fend for itself—to get employment and accommodations, to master appropriate skills, all without guidance of any kind.

"I needed a lack of restrictions," he says, reflecting on those years, "not a lack of structure."

Floundering together they managed to cope. As the time approached to return to campus, the prospect was less and less welcome.

Don, like many gifted young people, wanted to construct and create. His college program was neither challenging him intellectually nor allowing him scope to expand artistically. He refused to return.

"Learning by doing" is a tired cliché. Yet for our son — who has made the whole world his classroom — that phrase has crackling reality. As soon as he abandoned college (over our tearful, fearful protestations), he apprenticed himself to a carpenter and learned the pleasure of craftsmanship. This carpenter was a perfect mentor — a former research scientist who had left that career to become an intellectual workman. Don learned not only a craft but an attitude and a respect in this experience.

Next course — U.S. geography, with the nation his classroom: California to Texas to New Hampshire to Ohio and back to California. Fruit-picking, handyman, and farm jobs provided sustenance. Steinbeck and Dos Passos move over; another pilgrim was meeting America. His grade for this course? Pass with honors.

On to advanced geography, for which language training was an essential corollary. Off Don went to Asia and a stay in Japan. Tuition (fare) was provided, for the only time, by his parents. In Japan, Don learned Japanese in return for English lessons. As a follow-up to his U.S. lessons in Beginners Carpentry 1, he studied Japanese construction techniques.

Easily now, he finished his "sophomore year" of his education. One course naturally led to another, so he completed his world geography study by heading home overland, picking up a sitar in India (another subject: world music), writing poetry in a hut high in the Himalayan clouds of Nepal, and farming in France before returning to the United States.

In his "senior year" he returned to California to use his Japanese language ability and his carpentry skills from both cultures, working with Japanese carpenters who were reconstructing an important Buddhist temple. His newest skill was learning to cook for a crowd, members of the commune who were building the temple.

When that activity ended, Don returned to New England to "settle down," a graduate now. He has since worked in several natural food restaurants, managed coffeehouse musical programs, been in charge of the dining services at a summer camp, and studied fine cabinet making, all building on the skills and knowledge acquired in his "learning years."

He is still absorbing new expertise, along with refining old talents, as any educated person should. The summer camp was a music camp, so, while planning and cooking, Don listened and learned about classical music. When he was working in one restaurant, someone was needed to do bookkeeping. Don pored over library books, consulted people who knew how, and taught himself the necessary bookkeeping procedures.

This is the crucial truth we have learned from Don's education. For intellectually alert, motivated persons, each experience is a learning challenge. Our other children, equally intelligent, chose college for their education. It served each of them admirably.

But our second-born had different needs and a different temperament. With our support, albeit most reluctantly given at first, his educational pattern was distinctly his own — to serve him as his needs demanded.

He has no degree to certify his learning; that is true. But he knows what he knows, and so far this knowledge and the experiences themselves have been credentials enough for his work. Today he is content with his life, self-supporting, and creatively satisfied. Occasionally he talks about getting a degree, but then he wonders why. For his work and his life, it has not been needed. Knowledge was needed, and that he has acquired.

If we sincerely believe in the educational maxim of individualizing instruction to each student's requirements, this is as it should be. College is the right goal for many, indeed for most, intellectually able young people. But there are some for whom it is not the right answer. Ten years ago I wouldn't have said so with any conviction. Now I do. Our son has taught me that.

5 THE GIFTED CHILD — POTENTIAL AND REALITY

The Future and My Contribution—Paul R. Wetzel

The future spreads before me over the horizon,
Waiting to be explored and tested in all directions,
   The sky spreads before a young bird.

I am so optimistic that I may be unrealistic
Holding down the surging feeling of idealism,
   Stopping
     just short of
becoming quixotic.

My contribution of the future will be
the meeting of the challenge.
I am willing to contribute my talents, and purpose
To this certain destiny of man.

My contribution may be small, unknown;
Fleeting in the immensity of the world.
It may be commendable; benefiting the community.
It may be eminent; valuable to the entire nation.
It may be profound.

Whatever my contribution is,
If the future is better for at least one person
With the simpleness of smile
Or the brilliance of ideal.

Then my challenge is met,
My goal achieved,
My life fulfilled.

Age 17
Gull Lake High School
Richland, Michigan

30

Children and the Arts

An Interview with Mark Schubart

Stephen W. Gray-Lewis

SG: Let us begin with your career as educator, administrator, music critic, and author. As a youngster you were trained as a musician. Would you tell us how the playing and composing of music became a part of your life? What got you interested and kept you going?

MS: Music was my first love, and like a lot of other kids who have a particular bent, I had a high degree of interest in it. I took piano lessons, flute lessons, and then I studied composition quite seriously into my twenties. I pursued musical studies privately while I finished high school here in Westchester County.

SG: Did you ever intend to become a professional musician?

MS: No, I never thought of it as a vocation; I always assumed that music would be my avocation and that I would have to earn a living some other way. Another interest of mine was writing, journalistic writing. So I got various jobs on publications, mostly not in the arts field, and then, through a series of circumstances, I finally got a job as a music critic, which led eventually to a position as music editor of *The New York Times,* which I occupied for four or five years.

Mark Schubart is director of the Lincoln Center Institute, New York City, which coordinates a large-scale program for elementary and secondary schools. Formerly, he was director of public activities, dean, and vice-president at Juilliard School of Music.

Stephen W. Gray-Lewis, Ph.D., is currently an associate professor of English at Saint Bonaventure University, Saint Bonaventure, N.Y. He is also director of the university theater group, where he has had the opportunity to work closely with many gifted students.

My interest in music and my interest in writing had become joined, so to speak.

In 1946 I moved on to Juilliard as director of public activities, which meant public relations for the school and all the concert and public events of the school, which are considerable. I then became dean of the school in 1949, continuing there as dean and vice-president until I came to Lincoln Center in 1963.

Obviously, I did write some music and I had a few pieces played, but I am not really talented in this field. Nor have I ever had any desire to be a performer. I just don't have that interest. But these experiences, and a lot of others, opened up the whole world of the arts to me, and it has always been central to my life. At Juilliard I was concerned entirely with professional education. When I came to Lincoln Center, I experienced a total career change, because I am now doing the exact opposite of what I did formerly. Instead of training the musicians, I am in a sense training the public to realize how the arts relate to the general public and especially to young people in elementary and secondary schools. It has been a fascinating experience.

SG: As I understand it, you are presently overseeing a new Lincoln Center program in teaching aesthetics to teachers. What is the purpose of the program?

MS: We are training teachers in order to get to the kids. The purpose of our project is to reach young people. What we are trying to do is to find ways of putting into the hands of general classroom teachers skills not to teach the art, but to serve as someone who poses questions, who moderates, who leads kids into discussions, calling their attention to what there is in a work of art that is there to be mined, so to speak, to be explored. Most of the teachers involved are English teachers, and a lot are in social studies.

SG: Not art teachers?

MS: In a funny way, the music and art teachers are not always the best people to deal with such a situation, because of their expertise. The regular classroom teacher is, in a sense, in the same position as the student; both are exploring something. The teachers are going to say, "I really love music. Now we're going to have a string quartet. Let's find out what's in this piece. Let's get a violinist in to talk about it, and let's divide our class into four and learn a little choral piece to see how four voices go together." So the teacher is sharing with the students the exploration of various kinds of artistic experiences, and it's a very natural, very easy role. It takes some doing because first the teachers themselves have to learn to go through this process. It's very important — and this is the point – for teachers rather than artists to be used in such a program, because then the artist can continue to work in the schools as an artist and not as a teacher. The artist is there as the artist, and the teacher as the teacher. I think that's a critical difference. This is why we are training the teachers. We are not trying to make art teachers out of English teachers.

SG: And you find that English teachers, and so forth, work well in these circumstances?

MS: It is very interesting with English teachers. For example, we did a workshop and spent a couple of days on Shakespeare's *Romeo and Juliet*. There were many, many English teachers who had been teaching that play all their professional lives who had never approached it as a living, breathing work of art on the stage. They'd always approached it as a piece of literature, period. A very exciting thing happened. Their heads were turned around as to how they might deal with the play, which in turn made it more real for the kids. The upshot was that the kids were not looking at it as something dead and gone in the past, but as something very much alive in the present.

SG: To return to your own experiences, do they suggest what other people should do to help children who have particular talents – to spot them and to offer them things to do to encourage them to pursue their interests? Did your family, for example, encourage your interest in music?

MS: My family, especially my mother and my grandparents, were extremely supportive. Music was in the home, and I grew up in what is unattractively referred to as a "cultured" setting. There was a lot of art around. My mother was interested in painting, and my grandmother was a good amateur pianist, so the arts were always there. They were an integral part of my life, which is a great plus. I was very fortunate in that way.

SG: But isn't this kind of upbringing relatively rare?

MS: If you look at the world realistically, which I must, most people are *not* interested in the arts, despite a lot of publicity that's going around now. Progress has been made, but even now, I imagine, for 95 percent of the families in this country, and consequently for 95 percent of their children, the arts really don't figure in life at all. So the thing that interests me is, in what ways can the schools intervene in changing that direction as it has historically changed so many other directions?

SG: Do you really think schools can accomplish this?

MS: I have sometimes made an analogy with literacy. There is a school of thought that says this is not something you teach; either you've got it or you haven't got it. I disagree strongly with that. One could have taken exactly the same position 150 years ago regarding literacy, at a time when a lot of very sincere people believed that being a literate person was something you were born to by heritage and tradition and that, therefore, it could not be taught. Well, American education has proved conclusively that this is not so. It was largely through the intervention of education in general and public education specifically that the effort was made, and the effort succeeded. Exactly the same is true in a number of other areas, including what I sometimes call aesthetic literacy, which is an awareness of this human potential and the ability to find it. It's there if you want to have it.

SG: If schools are to promote "aesthetic literacy," it would seem equally important if not more so that they come to grips with the problems of training the artistically gifted at the same time. Not nearly enough seems to be happening in this field.

MS: One of the greatest problems for kids who are gifted in the arts — in other words, the potential professional — is that we teach the wrong thing at the wrong age. The tradition of education is that you finish your elementary, secondary, and undergraduate schooling, and then you go on and study the arts. The assumption is that you don't train as a professional until the college level. In some disciplines this is probably true. But in the case of the performing arts, particularly music and dance, it is much too late. This is no discovery of mine; everybody recognizes it. Any good violin teacher will tell you that if you cannot give a professional recital at eighteen, you will never be able to. And the same thing is true of dance. On the other hand, while dancers really have to begin when they are little kids, a singer doesn't even know he's got a voice until he's seventeen or eighteen. Actors very often develop around that age, too.

What I really feel strongly about is that the educational institutions have to be more professional in their attitudes toward the realities of the world of the arts if they, in fact, want to get involved with that world by making sure that the child has the right kind of training at the right age. It is not important for a little kid to study the history of music at the age of eight or nine, but it is very important for her to begin forming and making her fingers or her legs or her body work the right way. In other words, the physical parts of performance in the arts or facility in the arts is something that has to happen right away. In a funny way it may be analogous to teaching a foreign language, which is so easy for little kids and so terribly difficult for older children, because it calls for a physical and oral aptitude rather than an intellectual or cognitive kind of achievement.

SG: So you feel that, in many cases, practical training in the arts comes too late.

MS: I do indeed. So I think that one of the things that has to happen is that our schools and colleges have to be more realistic about the arts. At present, there is an attempt to force them into the same chronological track as "advanced" studies. It doesn't work that way. It has to go at its own time and rate of development. For example, I remember from my years at Juilliard one of the most baffling things was — and still is, I guess — that a lot of the most gifted children with the most artistic talent are teenagers, and somehow the thing that they do best in the life — that the good Lord seems to have equipped them to do most naturally — is systematically excluded from their education because it conflicts with the assumption that everybody has to do certain things at a certain age. And this poses some real problems. There have been some fairly good attempts made to resolve the conflict in art high schools — the High School of Music and Art here, the North Carolina School of Arts, and so forth — but even their kids have a lot of trouble finding time to make room in their lives for the thing they want to do most. I don't know if you have heard this mentioned, but there have even been some criticisms leveled against the idea of the High School of Music and Art on the grounds that it is elitist. But that's not true.

SG: I guess it's one of the problems with a democratic society that anything special is elitist, in some sense or other. There seems to be a feeling among many people that anybody involved in the arts is involved in a highly specialized activity that excludes everyone else. I imagine most people in the arts come face to face with this attitude sooner or later.

MS: But you certainly can't destroy the art just to be democratic, because then you have nothing left. It's like throwing the baby out with the bathwater.

SG: Then it comes back to the question of what is basic to education and when it needs to be taught.

MS: The thing I would really like to stress the most, if I may repeat myself a little bit, is the need for educational institutions to have a greater understanding of where the arts belong in terms of the age of the child and somehow to find a way to make them available in the structure of education. I am talking about the gifted child, the artistically talented child. I think it's very important.

SG: Have you observed any instances where this is in fact done?

MS: In Moscow — I was in Russia a number of years ago — they have something called the Children's Music School, which is, in effect, an elementary and secondary school for gifted children. I am sure it still exists. But in this country, even in New York, even the High School of Music and Art, for example, which is a very good school in the public school system, is an academic school. It's not an art school; it's a school for academically gifted kids who have a real interest in the arts. That's fine for the kid who is motivated toward the arts. But for the really gifted child, the potential professional, most of the Music and Art kids have to supplement their schooling with professional training on Saturdays. The Juilliard Preparatory Division has a couple of hundred children who are exceptional, but those kids have to go to school five days a week. There are some academic schools, such as the Professional Children's School and a couple of others, that are specifically designed for artistically gifted kids and try to be accommodating in their schedules and so forth. But it's ridiculous that all that cannot take place within one educational pattern. If you can do it at the college level, why can't you do it at the high school level? Why can't a kid go to his high school and spend two or three hours a day on his academic studies and spend three or four hours a day on his principal interest in life, which may be music?

SG: You think, then, that the Russians are more responsive to the practical needs of beginning artists than we are?

MS: In some respects, yes. Certainly in terms of the need for early training in the arts with professional potential. I think they are ahead of us. But we are ahead of them in terms of the state of the art. Musical life in this country, for example, is far richer and more interesting than it is in the Soviet Union, at least in my observation.

SG: Do you find that many people tend to feel that training in the arts is something somehow removed from "education"?

MS: Very much so. Let me describe it this way: I remember at Juilliard parents would come and say, "I am delighted that my child is here at Juilliard and that he is playing the piano so well and he is getting his degree from Juilliard, but is he going to be an educated person?" The assumption is that even though somebody studies hard, that process is not in itself educating, which strikes me as ridiculous. To study a sonata of Beethoven is just as much an intellectual pursuit as taking a course in philosophy. It is a very profound kind of experience, and it educates the person regardless of whether or not that person goes on to be a pianist, which is immaterial. It's difficult for parents to perceive the difference between what I call professional education and the commercial freaks of professional education. The assumption is, if you are studying an art intensively and if you have a strong gift for it, that immediately means that if you don't go on to become Arthur Rubinstein, you are a failure. And that, of course, is not true. After all, how many kids graduate from college as English majors whose parents moan and groan when they don't become famous writers? An intensive study of the English language and developing skills in literary composition is assumed to be educational, whereas developing skills in music is not. Now, this attitude has always struck me as totally absurd, and it has had a very bad effect, particularly on the minds of young kids, whose natural instincts gradually lead them toward music or painting or the theater, but who somehow feel they are not being educated because all they're doing is learning an art. Some of the professional schools have tried to counteract this bias, but I must say that the educational establishment in general is not sympathetic to the idea that the arts are, in themselves, educational.

At the same time, the professional schools have a very heavy responsibility to educate their students not to feel that their lives are a waste if they don't wind up as a major soloist with orchestras or a leading dancer in a ballet company. They, too, have to understand and look at their training in some reasonable proportion.

SG: I imagine that in the arts, especially, success is the yardstick by which all things are measured.

MS: That is true, and yet, having been away now from Juilliard for fifteen years, it's very interesting to look at the generations that were actually there when I was there and to see what's happened to them, to see some of the very gifted ones who really did not do anything particularly distinguished and others who were perhaps not so brilliant in some respects but who have made very substantial careers, albeit different kinds of careers.

SG: Not necessarily in the art they had studied?

MS: Often in the art they had studied, but different careers within that art. For example, I can think of one person whom, on a scale of one to ten, with 1 being the most talented, I would rank as perhaps three or four as compared with a John Browning or a Van Cliburn or a Leontyne Price. He was obviously a good musician, enormously intelligent, very energetic, who happened to be a pianist. Today, he is one of the leading accompanists in the country. He has a major career as an accompanist and is in demand all over the world and plays with all the great artists. He has made a really astonishing career.

Another kind of mentality with, say, a grade three in terms of virtuoso talent, might have said, "To hell with this; I'm not number

· one so I'm not going to do it!" But this man has done it and has become an artist in a truly extraordinary way and has made a marvelous career out of it. There are some others who at age twenty or twenty-one were clearly number one in the sense of their ability to handle the instrument, but somehow did not find their way in the world, did not become real artists.

SG: Do you have any idea of how many arts students ultimately find themselves doing something other than what they were trained for?

MS: A lot of them don't go into their fields. Many years ago we did a study and found that about 20 percent made their full-time existence as performers or composers or conductors. About 60 percent combined that with teaching. Interestingly enough, there were only about 20 percent who were not somehow making a living, directly or indirectly, through the art that they studied.

SG: While you were at Juilliard, how did you distinguish between those applicants who were basically dilettantes and those who were truly gifted and committed?

MS: The way the curriculum at Juilliard was structured made it almost impossible for anybody to survive as a dilettante, because the amount of energy and concentration required was so enormous that anyone who really did not have the ability and perseverance could not have survived and, in fact, did not. A lot of weeding out took place before the students came into the school. The entrance examinations and the admissions procedures were quite rigorous and assumed a lot of previous experience on the part of the students, because the program was and still is basically a college-age program, so the kids were seventeen or eighteen when they came to the school as undergraduates. A musician or dancer at seventeen or eighteen has already had a considerable amount of training. We knew, for example, when we had an application from a student who had taken piano for one year, that it was almost inevitable that he would not be admitted, because he first had to perform a Bach fugue, a Beethoven sonata, a romantic work, a contemporary work, and so forth. There were, as you can see, certain requirements for entering auditions that weeded out the less prepared and the less talented.

SG: How do universities compare with professional schools in this respect?

MS: Like most good conservatories in the country, Juilliard has always tried to be very clear about what it was it proposed to do or what its purposes were. In this respect the so-called professional schools have been much better about this than the colleges. I know any number of colleges that, if you read their catalogs and the descriptions of their programs in the arts, always use words like "professional-level training" when in fact they do not offer it because they cannot for one reason or another structure their admissions procedures for the course of study to conform to that goal. Kids have been made very unhappy because they came out of college with a degree in music or in dance or whatever and simply did not have the capacity to function in the professional world of the arts. Now student expectations might be a good deal more realistic if colleges came right out and said, "Look, we are not training you for the profession; we are training you to explore your own life interest." That would be fine. But many schools make claims and talk about training people for the profession of the arts and in fact do not have either the curriculum or the admissions procedures to support those claims. That makes a lot of problems for kids.

SG: Would you say that the same problems exist for creative as opposed to performing artists?

MS: Now, we haven't talked about creative artists. We've talked about the violinist, the pianist, the dancer, but what about the playwright, the choreographer, the composer, and so forth? I am not sure that these are fields that can really be taught. You can teach the craft. I think the more craft and the more discipline a person has in the craft, the better. But I don't think you can teach the art. That usually develops somewhat later in life. There are very few Mozarts who write symphonies when they are eight years old.

SG: There seems to be a different pattern of development from that of the performing artist, who generally has to get started very young. The creative artist most often gets started when he has had enough experience to have something to say.

MS: Yes, it's not a physical thing; it's a mind thing. It's a question of his imagination, his whole cultural background, and his observation of life. I tend not to worry about creative artists except when somebody says, "I want to be a composer." I say, "Okay, great, go and study the piano; study the violin, get as much training as you can get. Go through the exercises, and get all of the craft." It's like developing handwriting. A kind of apprenticeship is good.

SG: Then going to college can provide a pretty good background in the "craft" of writing, painting, and so on?

MS: In some cases, perhaps, but I worry a lot about the relationship of the universities to the arts. I realize that universities differ widely. One shouldn't really generalize, but I think a lot of our finest universities have a very negative effect on the artistic life of our country. This is a strong statement, but I think they often tend to insulate young people from the world, and in a sense the atmosphere is almost too sympathetic, too understanding, and not demanding enough. It can develop a kind of cocoonlike existence within the university situation that is not good for the artist. This is a bad generalization because it obviously isn't totally true, but would-be artists must be very careful about where they go, to what university. Whenever possible they should go where there are artists of real stature in their discipline.

SG: It would seem also that universities are sometimes given to a certain amount of trendiness. What's new must be good, so let's follow that for this year. Back in the fifties, for example, everyone in acting was into the Method, and now they're into self-expression and "finding" themselves.

MS: Around here we call it the "rolling around on the floor syndrome," a sort of touchy-feely approach.

SG: Well, it certainly seems to make some people feel very creative.

MS: It's funny that the word *creativity* is thrown around so very loosely, but in the arts it has a very specific meaning. Creativity in the arts means writing poems, writing plays, designing, choreography, and so on. But when we talk about the "creativity" of children, it means something totally different. The two often get confused. Someone says, "Oh, my child is creative," because he or she makes charming little children's drawings or something. That's very nice, but that's not art.

SG: What about the commonly held opinion that art is, by and large, an expression of feeling?

MS: Most people don't understand that art is not an emotional thing nor is it entirely, to use the educational jargon, an affective experience. It is a mixture of the affective and the cognitive, and the two cannot be separated. Misunderstandings about this lead to the rolling-around-the-floor and the touchy-feely kind of exercise and the perception of art as not being something very serious. But actually, as you well know, the arts are not only a matter of creativity; they also demand a great deal of discipline and thought and rigor. In the work we do in the schools we stress this. It's not just fun and games and being creative and expressing your own feelings about everything under the sun. It, too, makes its demands and is in fact a discipline.

SG: There are many gifted and talented children who pursue their interest in art with passion until they become teenagers. Then, with the demands of academics, sports, schedules, and so on, most of them abandon the arts. Can you think of any positive things that can be done to sustain that interest and to nurture it instead of stifling it?

MS: Some kids naturally lose interest, and I don't see anything wrong with that. Sometimes they find it again later in life, and sometimes they don't. It will always be there; it's a life experience. But I think with others it is squeezed out. Sometimes it is squeezed out by peer-group pressures, sometimes by parental disapproval. If a young person really has a strong feeling and a strong aptitude, however, he or she is not going to give up so easily. The person is going to stick with it.

SG: So you don't feel we are losing many major artists through this process?

MS: No, that really doesn't worry me. People make choices about their lives at different times in their lives. Kids get passionate about baseball when they are ten, and then they go to college and start reading poetry, and suddenly baseball is no longer important. It works both ways, of course. This is part of the natural evolution of the human animal. I am not really sure that anything can or should be done about it.

However, having said that, I think that the way the arts are handled in the educational structure tends to militate against their continued study. Because, as you well know, the arts in elementary school are a cinch. All children are creative, and the teachers are creative, and it's all very flexible, and there is that wonderful world out there. Then you get to junior high school and finally to senior high and are faced with the specter of college entrance exams. Finally, you get to the university, where you begin professional studies or you pursue some established academic discipline, and the arts get squeezed out of the system altogether. Of course, the colleges are largely responding to pressures from parents and to the economic necessities of earning a living. I think the only remedy for this situation is to develop, over the next couple of decades, a clearer notion of what is basic to education and to sort out what is really important in life. It has to be possible for a child who has an interest in an art to be able to pursue that interest through college, even if he or she is going to medical school. One should be able to have that aspect of one's training considered a valued asset to one's life as a doctor.

SG: What recommendations in the education of gifted and talented people would you give teachers and administrators who work in general areas rather than in specialized schools like Juilliard?

MS: To begin with, the talent must be identified. To the general administrator I would say, first, be aware that you yourself are not a professional in the field of the particular art and that you should not be making the judgments, so draw upon the cultural resources of your community to evaluate the ability of the kids. Parenthetically, it is astonishing to me — here we are in New York City with thousands of musicians of high quality running around who have a real interest in the needs of kids — how seldom the administrators of schools reach out to their musical community for guidance in the design of their musical programs or for help in identifying exceptionally talented children and so forth. So I would say that rule number one for administrators should be: Get to know the artists in your own community and use them. Don't try to make those judgments yourselves.

The second thing, ideally, would be that once those kids are identified, they should be helped as much as possible by placing them in situations where they can develop their talents. Also, be as flexible as you can in making room for those talents within the children's lives at school. That's a very, very difficult thing to do, for there again you run up against the elitist argument and a number of other things. But there are ways of doing it.

SG: You seem to be asking a lot of administrators, among whose main functions is decision making.

MS: It's very tempting for administrators to make judgments about their kids, because they are used to making them in so many areas in which they are competent, such as their ability to write and spell and master history and so forth. To call upon the same kind of expertise in the evaluation of an artistic talent is not so easy. But I think this is a role that art institutions can play increasingly in working with school systems. There is an increasing interest in the arts in schools. This is a growing movement that is going to spawn a lot of talents, it's going to discover a lot of kids, it's going to turn a lot of kids on to the arts. It's going to get a lot of kids excited about this whole world. So administrators are going to have to learn how to deal with this. To do that they are going to have to rely heavily on the artistic resources in their communities, which fortunately are growing, for there are more and more art groups around the country. There has been a remarkable development in this respect. We are becoming gradually more sophisticated about the arts.

SG: Is there anything you might say to teachers, that is, teachers who are not themselves involved in teaching the arts? Let's assume they should be able to recognize talent in children, but where do they go from there?

MS: Well, again, I think establishing some kind of a link between the arts resources and the people who are teaching at that school. Reaching out and getting help to deal with talent is the way to foster it.

SG: In terms of percentages, the gifted and talented must make up a very small part of the population. Wouldn't it be a problem, just on the instructional level, to find teachers qualified to handle children who are gifted and talented in the arts? How many really good music teachers are there?

MS: I think there are quite a few. Certainly in New York there is no dearth. Around the country there are a lot of good musicians, and many of them are out there teaching in colleges and sometimes in schools in very frustrating circumstances. I think there are some very good ones. There are certainly enough to take care of the needs of the small number of kids who have exceptional talent.

SG: What about the obvious problem of the expense of such training?

MS: The money thing is a very important consideration. Professional-level education in the arts is terribly expensive, and there is no way around that, particularly in music, where you have that one-to-one piano lesson. It's also expensive because the group activities with the professional and performing arts are costly to run in many cases. And they need high-priced people. But the expense is justifiable, because if you don't give those gifted children what they need when they are young, thirty years from now we aren't going to have any artists left. So, you see, it's really essential. You can even justify it on the basis of there being no one else to take the lead in presenting the arts experience to the broad base of the population of the country.

SG: This must be a real problem when the talent to be discovered and encouraged comes from lower-income groups.

MS: Yes, this is particularly true in socioeconomic groups outside the white middle class. For example, one of the greatest concerns is the lack of minority representation in instrumental music. I am absolutely persuaded that this has nothing to do with talent or ability. I know it's out there. What it does have to do with is the unavailability of training facilities at a very early age. A *very* early age. I am talking about little kids. There are marvelously talented people out there whose parents can't say, "Okay, Sonny, go to school Monday through Friday, and Saturday and Sunday you get music lessons." The possibility isn't there. I think there is an economic factor that is terribly important, but I certainly don't have an answer that would solve the problem. It would certainly be a good investment. That I do know.

SG: You spoke a moment ago about a quickening interest in the arts across the country. Yet at the same time there seems to be an almost nationwide movement toward tight budgets for schools. In my experience, at any rate, at such times the first things to be trimmed are the allotments for the arts. It would be nice if you could tell me I am wrong about this.

MS: Unfortunately, there is a curious situation going on right now, for example, in the New York City school system. The number of music teachers in the last six years has gone down from something like 3,000 to 600. There are, to cite one example, no more music specialists in elementary schools in the city. They just aren't there anymore, with one or perhaps two exceptions. And the same thing is true of art teachers. Now, the number of art and music teachers in the schools was woefully inadequate to begin with. You can imagine 3,000 teachers for 1 million kids. And the number of teachers is diminishing constantly because communities, educators, and parent groups perceive that kind of traditional arts instruction as peripheral. It's a frill, and any time there is a budget crunch, that is still the first thing to go.

Oddly enough, at the same time that this is happening, and I am at a loss to explain this, there is a greater interest in providing a broader range of students with their first contact with the arts. In other words, at the same time that the school band and the school orchestra are disappearing and at the same time that it's becoming more difficult for a kid to take piano lessons or to get someone to coach a woodwind or brass quintet or to direct the school play or to form a dance group, there is a greater receptivity to programs such as the ones we are doing here at Lincoln Center, which are really designed for the kid who has never thought about whether he or she wants to play in the band or the orchestra. Eventually this is going to catch up with itself, because the more the kind of thing we are doing continues and expands — and other groups are getting into this kind of activity — the more that happens, the more you are going to get kids interested in the arts as an important part of their lives, and there is going to be an increasing demand for music teachers and drama coaches. I don't know where that's going to come out, but it's a very peculiar thing that's going on now.

SG: Well, then, what's basic for the artistically talented child is in some ways the same as for children who are not. This seems to be a concept that has not been generally accepted. For most people, the arts are a "frill," as you say, a Saturday-morning lesson.

MS: This isn't dealing only with the gifted and talented but with children as a whole. And it is something that should be said. We who are in the arts must face up to our responsibilities, because if we say that the arts are basic to the education of the child, we have to say why, and the arts community has failed to do this. You can't talk about culture and enrichment and you can't talk about the use of leisure time and you can't talk about the finer things in life. That's not an answer; that's not basic. The things basic about the arts experience have to do with cultivating the human ability to perceive. That is very basic, and it has implications in every area of learning. That is the rationale for everything we do in the arts, ranging from the initial-exposure kind of program to the highly specialized training for gifted kids. The one, you see, feeds the other. The gifted artist is the one who presumably perceives the most intensely and should be in a leadership position.

SG: I'm afraid our time is up. Thank you for your interesting and informative comments. I'm sure they will provide a challenge not only to parents but to many others who are trying to guide young people and to develop their interests or their talents in the arts.

31

Ability and Access to Advanced Training in Selected Countries

Harold F. Clark and Joe C. Davis

Only in recent decades have the knowledge and skills acquired by persons, or "human capital," as it has been accurately, if inelegantly, termed, been generally acknowledged as a key factor in explaining why the economies of some countries grow faster than others. Of course, training alone does not make individuals more productive; ability is also extremely important. Thus, maximizing the human contribution to economic growth and efficiency requires more than enlarging training opportunities; it also requires the identification, selection, and schooling of talented persons for occupations in which they are most needed. By able persons, we mean those with above-average mental powers, not necessarily the top 1 or 2 percent who are "gifted."

In this paper the performances of a number of countries in using their able persons are compared, with emphasis on the crucial point at which candidates are chosen for the higher education that prepares them for top administrative and professional jobs. We will also touch briefly on the types of training offered and on special programs for the talented. Before beginning our case studies, we analyze demand factors that help explain why, around the world, a significant number of talented young

Harold F. Clark, Ph.D., LL.D., is professor of economics at Trinity University, San Antonio, Tex. Formerly professor of economics in education at Teachers College, Columbia University, New York City, Dr. Clark has been a consultant with many governments and industries on education and the training of high-level manpower.

Joe C. Davis, Ph.D., is associate professor of economics at Trinity University., San Antonio, Tex.

people do not receive the advanced training necessary to prepare them for the better jobs. We then discuss supply problems: why some young people with high ability do not acquire the elementary and secondary schooling necessary for selection and why some talented persons do not choose higher education even though they possess the necessary prerequisites.

SELECTION

The selection decision is important everywhere, even in affluent countries such as the United States, where there are more places available in higher education than applicants for them. In the United States the number of places in the more prestigious institutions is limited, and there are ceilings in all institutions on the number of persons who can be trained for professions such as medicine. In poorer countries the restrictions are more basic. Other needs are more pressing than the desire to provide higher education for all who want it. Consequently, selection is necessary.

The selection of persons for higher education is politically motivated in all countries, some more than others. Because economic growth and efficiency are only two of the many goals that countries pursue, it follows that these conflicting objectives may lead to selection on grounds other than ability. Egalitarianism, for example, often leads countries to give more weight to social background than to ability. China and the Soviet Union reserve places in higher education for the children of peasants and workers, and the United States for minorities.

Another factor that may lead to the exclusion of able persons grows out of the uncertainty as to what constitutes "ability" and how to measure it. Clearly the person with the best academic record or examination scores will not necessarily make the best manager, physician, or teacher. When other attributes such as creativity, adaptability, and leadership must be gauged, selection is more difficult. Those making the selections face the possibility of two types of mistakes: They may misjudge ability to the extent that they prevent abler persons from entering, or they may admit less able persons. The probability of making both types of mistakes can be reduced by acquiring more information about candidates. But acquiring information is costly, and these costs must be compared with the costs of not seeking the information, that is, the cost of training some of the wrong persons. Where differences in ability are small, the costs of not training the more able students could be less than the cost of obtaining sufficient information to ensure that they were admitted. It is quite likely, therefore, that consideration of the relevant costs and benefits will result in some able persons not receiving advanced training and that, unless the cost of information can be reduced, such an outcome will represent the most efficient use of the limited funds available for training the able.

Another characteristic of the selection process that often works against abler students is the incentive system for those making the choices. Passing over the less able child of a Party official in the Soviet Union or of a politician or benefactor in the United States will likely lead to a complaint. The information problem just discussed can be used by the selectors to rationalize their behavior. Children from families who have displayed ability in the past may be chosen over persons from less well-known backgrounds. Background, then, becomes an inexpensive screening device, as do grades and diplomas from recognized preparatory schools. Given the framework in which selections are made, it is idealistic to expect that abler students will always be chosen over less able ones.

PREPARATION

For the able to be selected for higher training, they must qualify at the primary and secondary levels. Some talented children do not complete secondary schooling, or they opt for vocational rather than academic secondary schools. According to economists, one important reason why households do not push their children into academic preparations is that they believe that the present costs, including tuition and foregone earnings (what they could earn if employed instead of at school), are not sufficiently exceeded by the potential higher earnings associated with the schooling. In all countries, even in command economies such as the Soviet Union, household decisions about the amount and type of schooling are key factors in determining who eventually will obtain higher education and have access to the top jobs. Part of the problem is informational; some families may not possess adequate information about the benefits of investment in human capital. Because the benefits to society of additional schooling often exceed the private benefits as estimated by the individual household, the cost of schooling is subsidized by the state in all countries. Still, the indirect costs of forgone earnings are sufficient to ensure that many able persons do not complete the secondary school necessary for entrance into college.

TRAINING OF THE ABLE IN SELECTED COUNTRIES

How has the performance of other countries in marshaling their talented people compared with that of the United States? Is selection based on ability or on other factors? Which occupations are able persons trained for? Are there special programs for the able?

Soviet Union Before the Revolution, the children of the aristocracy and the wealthy commanded the places in Russian universities. The Bolsheviks reserved this privilege for "their people" and kept the descendants of the old elites out. Despite crash courses designed to prepare workers and peasants for higher education, the results of the program for the economy were so disappointing that in the 1930s the "exploiting classes" were once again admitted. Since then offspring of urban intellectuals have claimed a large share of university places, although the Soviets continue to maintain special preparatory schools for soldiers and rural children. The latter are permitted to enter higher educational institutes without facing competitive examinations. It appears that some of the children of Party and government officials also follow this expedited nonexamination route into college.[1]

The Soviet Union has been a world leader in its efforts to identify the highly talented students at an early age and to place them in special schools. Beginning in the 1920s the government set up elaborate testing programs called olympiads, which seek to find the ablest mathematics students in the country. In Siberia, for instance, in three rounds of testing, some one hundred students survive from over ten thousand who begin the tests. The winners are sent to special boarding schools for intensive schooling in mathematics and physics, from which they go on to higher education and research.[2] Such programs are especially interesting in view of the fact that Soviet educational philosophy rejects the possibility of innate ability.

For most applicants, however, examinations are only one of the factors considered in determining who gets higher education. Some 80 percent of places are reserved for distinguished veterans and workers with two or more years' experience, especially those recommended by plant managers. Political screening and pressures by influential parents are also factors.[3] The result of this selection process is that some young Russians of high ability are not given access to advanced training. There have been complaints about the quality of students entering higher education.[4]

The type of training that is offered Soviet students is determined by the government in line with the estimated requirements of its planned economy. Just as their industrial planning leads to considerable misallocation of resources, there is good reason to believe that their educational planning does the same. Higher education is oriented toward engineering; the liberal arts and business administration are played down. While engineering may be the best form of training for the top jobs when the task is to build steel mills and dams, it does not necessarily develop the skills needed in a dynamic world economy.

Should a talented young person not undertake higher education, the harmful consequences for the economy are probably greater for the Soviet Union than they would be for the United States. Higher education is a mandatory credential for entrance to high-level jobs in Russia, whereas it is still possible for a talented person without higher education to advance in the United States by starting his or her own business enterprise.

The high cost of higher education precludes some talented Soviet youth from advanced training. Although tuition is free and stipends are provided, the cost of forgone earnings is an important barrier to children from low-income families.

China The People's Republic of China has also placed the goal of uplifting peasants and workers into higher-level jobs above that of getting the talented into these positions. During the Great Leap Forward in the late 1950s research centers were opened up to ''peasant scientists'' and ''worker engineers.'' These persons, some of whom were illiterate, were thrust into these positions because ''it gives the masses the impression that anyone could become a scientist if faithful to the party line.''[5] After a brief cooling, egalitarian zeal broke out anew in the late 1960s during the Cultural Revolution. The Chinese leaders who were later called the Gang of Four argued that Chinese education was too theoretical and that the majority of students and teachers were ''bourgeois intellectuals.'' Under such criticism, the universities began to select new students from among workers, peasants, and soldiers who had done two or more years of practical work and who had demonstrated ''ideological fervor.'' Examinations and grades were denounced as capitalistic relics. One student was made a national hero for turning in a blank examination paper. Lectures were often given by workers, and revolutionary theory took up a great deal of class time. The result was, of course, a serious decline in the quality of college training.[6]

The Gang of Four and their ideas of education lost out in the power struggle after Mao's death. In 1977 entrance exams were reinstated. Intellectual ability was again an important factor in college admission. However, class background and ''political awareness'' remained important considerations.[7]

Japan Prior to World War II, able students from poor families were underrepresented in higher education, in part because of the high tuition charges in secondary schools. During the Occupation, tuition was reduced, enabling greater participation by all income groups in higher education. Examinations determine admission to the relatively few places available each year, and competition is fierce. Those fortunate enough to get in, especially into prestigious institutions, are recruited by the government and corporations for leadership positions. The Japanese believe that their system identifies persons who are highly talented and motivated and is fair to all social groups.[8] On the surface, it does appear that talented persons have fewer barriers placed in their paths in Japan than in many other countries.

Some doubt has been cast on this belief, however. The entrance examinations, some argue, do not test cognitive ability, because they primarily deal with esoteric details. Success comes from long hours of cramming and attendance at special preparatory schools, often for two years after secondary school graduation. The cost of time and tuition for the preparation apparently deters able young people from lower-income homes from pursuing admission to universities.[9]

Unlike some other countries, Japan does not separate students on the basis of ability in elementary and secondary school. This single-track approach, which was imposed during the Occupation, has the benefit of permitting a larger number of persons to become qualified for higher education; it has the disadvantage of not pushing the abler students to their potential.

West Germany The Federal Republic of Germany had an open-admission policy for higher education until 1972. All secondary school graduates were guaranteed admission by law. As the demand for places began to outpace the supply, a quota scheme was employed. Only 45 percent of places are assigned on the basis of secondary school grades; the remainder are reserved for social-hardship cases, foreign students, students committed to careers in public health and the military, and those students who have been on waiting lists from earlier years.[10]

Latin America The education programs of Spain and Portugal have had a great effect upon the world, especially in Latin America. At one time in the thirteenth and fourteenth centuries the Spanish educational system might well have been the most advanced in Europe. Along with the programs of education in Italy and France, they affected many other countries. The students who went to college came almost entirely from the aristocracy and wealthy families. They went to work largely for the government, the military, or the church. Trade and business stood much lower in the scale, and few with education went into them. This would ultimately have a great effect on the economy of these countries.

In the intervening centuries these educational systems were transferred to Latin America. They provided superb training for certain types of activities. But for many occupations in the modern world they provided almost no training. This brought about weaknesses in many technical and professional sections of the economy.

Most students of economic development in Latin America are convinced that one of the most important things they will have to do is to find methods of selecting the ablest people at all levels of the population and training them for a wide range of activities.

Up until recently there were extremely limited facilities to train people in agriculture. This needs to be expanded both at the secondary and the higher levels. The same thing is true with training in business, scientific, and technical fields.

In some ways the problem is even worse at the secondary school level. The training is inadequate for the highly skilled trades. Facilities for identifying and training able young people at the college level or for highly skilled training are hard to find.

Brazil is an example of a country that made great improvements in developing its human potential. Academically talented children of the middle class now find university training within their grasp, although those from lower-income families do not. Science and mathematics training are being expanded in secondary schools to prepare for advanced university training conducive to development.[11]

Great Britain The percentage of the college-age group going to institutions of higher learning in Great Britain is low as compared with a few of the very highly industrialized countries, but compared with the percentage in the entire world it is high. Great Britain was slow in expanding its higher education into many of the technical and professional fields. This has been a factor in the relative decline of Great Britain as an industrial power.

Historically, most of the students who went on to higher education in Great Britain were from families who were in the upper social or economic groups. That is not an adequate basis of selection for an industrial society. Great Britain has very recently substantially expanded the base on which children are accepted for advanced training. Scholarships and other assistance have been fairly widespread. Nevertheless, many able young Britons outside the private preparatory schools do not get advanced training, in part because they are not taught how to take examiniations. Their teachers "are not prepared to neglect the many to cram the few."[12]

The British system has had an enormous effect upon the world. In the last part of the nineteenth and early twentieth centuries the British Empire included approximately one-fourth of the world, in terms of both population and land area. The net result was that the British system had a great effect on India, Australia, Canada, South Africa and other British colonies in Africa, and many other places in the world. In all of these places the selection of students to go to college was profoundly affected by the British model. They more recently have been trying to expand the selection over wider ranges of the population.

In most of these countries this expansion has been based primarily on ability as measured by school records or tests. In some of the former British colonies in Africa the tribal influence has become important. The tribal group that has control of the government sometimes favors its own tribal members to a large extent. Of course, this happens somewhat in most countries where tribal or racial influence is very great. An outstanding example is Malaysia, where recently an extremely high number of places have been reserved for the Malays, who live largely in rural areas and who have not participated in higher education in proportion to their share of the population in the past. The Chinese in Malaysia, who rate higher on tests and academic records, are given a relatively smaller proportion of higher-education openings. Examination scores have been disregarded. In addition, more and more instruction is being done exclusively in the Malay language, which discriminates against non-Malay groups.[13]

United States The number of colleges and universities in the United States has grown to the point where any applicant can find a place. Still, a large proportion of the young do not attend college, including some of the very able. Of a group of high school graduates studied in the 1950s, only 60 percent of the most promising completed college.[14] In the United States many highly paid jobs do not require college training. This fact, together with the substantial costs of college, make college a poor investment in the minds of many.

Ability is the primary criterion guiding selection in institutions that restrict the number of admissions. National tests of intellectual ability are widely used. Such tests have been attacked by critics, who charge that they are culturally biased.

The U.S. government has moved fairly slowly in making any special effort to see that able children, at all economic levels, have opportunities to advance to their full capacity. During the 1950s and 1960s the United States started many large and expensive programs to aid children in very low income areas and, in many cases, children who have low ability. Several varieties of programs were established for children who scored low on tests or who had difficulty in learning.

All through that period a few voices were raised saying it was necessary to provide some special assistance to potentially able students wherever they were to be found. Little attention was paid to this suggestion at first. Many billions of dollars were spent to help the slow learners. This was a wise expenditure, but it was not wise to neglect the other end of the ability spectrum. Finally in 1978 Congress appropriated $25 million to begin to study what specific effort should be made to find and educate as many of the extremely able students as possible, wherever they were in the population. The appropriation was to rise slowly to a somewhat larger figure.

At last the United States seems to be ready to start on a program that will offer and make available to students the most difficult programs they can handle. The widespread custom has grown up in high school and college for students to take the easy courses and for instructors not to expect hard work from students. This, of course, is a very bad environment for a student of very high ability. This student can do an acceptable level of work without any real effort. It is going to be difficult to devise an educational program that will be optimal for these able students in such an atmosphere.

CURRENT WORLD VIEW

More and more countries are discovering that their economic and social progress depend to a large extent upon getting the largest possible number of able students into institutions of higher learning and into research, management, and all fields requiring high ability. This has forced a great expansion of the range of instruction offered in institutions of higher learning.

Agriculture, for example, has been neglected in most countries of the world, and some types of engineering activities have been slighted. These defects are being corrected. One would be justified in saying that practically all countries in the world now understand the extreme importance of getting people of high ability in science, research, arts, management, and such fields. As a result we are seeing a healthy reassessment of the procedures for finding and educating people of very high ability.

Notes

1. Dimitri Pospielovsky, "Education and Ideology in the USSR," *Survey,* Autumn 1975.

2. Seymour Rosen, *Education in the USSR: Research and Innovation* (Washington, D.C.: U.S. Dept. of Health, Education and Welfare, 1978), pp. 20–22.

3. Nicholas DeWitt, *Educational and Professional Employment in the USSR* (Washington, D.C.: National Science Foundation, 1961).

4. David W. Carey, "Developments in Soviet Education," in *Soviet Economic Prospects for the Seventies* (Washington, D.C.: Joint Economic Committee, 1973).

5. Chy-Yuan Cheng, *Scientific and Engineering Manpower in Communist China* (Washington, D.C.: National Science Foundation, 1965), pp. 12, 63.

6. Nai-Ruenn Chen, "Economic Modernization in Post-Mao China: Policies, Problems and Prospects," in *Chinese Economy Post-Mao: A Compen-*

dium of Papers (Washington, D.C.: Joint Economic Committee, 1978); Yong Hung, "Education in China Today," *China Reconstructs,* May 1975.

7. Jan Sigurdson, "Technology and Science: Some Issues in China's Modernization," in *Chinese Economy Post-Mao: A Compendium of Papers* (Washington, D.C.: Joint Economic Committee, 1978).

8. Donald F. Wheeler, *The Structure of Academic Governance in Japan* (New Haven: Yale University Press, 1976), p. 14.

9. William K. Cummings, *The Secret of Japanese Education* (Washington, D.C.: National Institute of Education, 1977), p. 229.

10. Barbara R. Burn, "Access to Higher Education in the Federal Republic of Germany and the United States," *International Review of Education,* 1976.

11. Deborah L. Truhon, *Focus on Brazil: A Case Study of Development* (Madison, N.J.: Global Studies Institute, 1977), pp. 110–115.

12. "Why You Won't Get to Oxbridge in a Comprehensive Car," *Economist,* June 10, 1978.

13. Rodney Tasker, "The Politics of Education," *Far Eastern Economic Review,* June 23, 1978.

14. U.S. Commissioner of Education *Educated of the Gifted and Talented,* vol. 2 (Washington, D.C.: 1971), pp. A21–22.

32
New Opportunities for Talented Women

Letty Cottin Pogrebin

When I was graduated from Brandeis University in 1959, Pierre Mendès-France, a French statesman, and Edward R. Murrow, a news commentator, spoke of lofty goals and remote global problems. They were addressing the young men in our class, who were expected to go forth and do the world's work.

Even if we women had been affirmatively included in their remarks, we would have exempted ourselves. The price of high aspirations and accomplishment for a woman was the threatened loss of "femininity." As Matina Horner, now president of Radcliffe, demonstrated in her study "Why Bright Women Fail," the fear of success has a chilling effect on female achievement.[1] We would rather be popular than powerful; we preferred to marry success rather than to possess it.

In those days, if a woman was smart or strong, if she was a scholar, a math wizard, or a business genius, she underplayed her talents. The more clever she was, the better she had learned from childhood that smart girls scare away the boys. To assure her elusive "femininity," she molded herself to fit the diminutive female ideal. She had to be smaller, weaker, and less intelligent than he — whoever he might be. Male standards and the requirements of the male ego coerced her into pretended inferiority. Thus, thousands of bright women allowed themselves to be trivialized in return for being loved. The optimum status for a woman — any woman, all women — was wife and mother. Individual dreams, personal autonomy, and each woman's unique potential were subsumed in a single "feminine" goal: to be claimed and cared for by a man.

Letty Cottin Pogrebin, editor/writer for *Ms.* magazine, is the author of two books on women and employment. She is also a columnist for the *Ladies Home Journal.* Her latest book, *Growing Up Free: Nonsexist Childrearing in a Sexist Society,* has just been published.

As Cynthia Ozick has written in her essay "Women and Creativity," "Female infantilism is a kind of pleasurable slavishness. Dependency, the absence of decisions and responsibility, the avoidance of risk, the shutting out of the gigantic toil of art – all these are the comforts of the condoning contented subject."[2]

Until recently women were condoning, contented subjects. We wore our derivative identities with pride. We were our father's daughter, then our husband's wife, then our children's mother and our grandchildren's granny. We never noticed that when we were pronounced man and wife, he was pronounced a person and we a role. We tried not to think about the research we once wanted to do or the doctorate moldering in a desk drawer or the poems we ached to write. A "real" woman was supposed to find fulfillment in domesticity and motherhood, so we poured our energies into "creative homemaking," into volunteerism, and into everyone in the family but ourselves.

George Bernard Shaw described that self-perpetuating cycle of female commitment to *Kinder, Kuche, Kirche* in his famous parrot analogy: "If we have come to think that the nursery and the kitchen are the natural spheres of woman, we have done so exactly as English children come to think that a cage is the natural sphere of a parrot – because they have never seen one anywhere else."[3]

But in the United States today things are different. Talented women are out of the parrot cage, soaring, excelling, and flourishing in a wide variety of fields. While the nursery and the kitchen have not been abandoned, they are no longer labeled the female's "natural spheres," but simply two possible options among many, such as:

- **The Professions.** Since the start of the 1970s women's enrollment in schools of law and medicine has almost tripled. Nearly 20 percent of the 1977 law and medical degrees went to women graduates as compared with only 5 percent in 1970, and the number of practicing female dentists has nearly doubled since 1960. More than twice as many women are engineers now than was the case twenty years ago, and today's beginning female engineers often command a higher starting salary than their male counterparts.[4]

- **Business and Finance.** Since 1960 female bank officials and financial managers have increased their representation from 18 percent to 25 percent of the total. In June 1978, the Harvard Business School awarded M.B.A.'s to 116 women out of a class of 729.[5]

- **Nontraditional Fields.** As the barriers of sex discrimination and sex-role stereotyping are being broken down, jobs in the construction trades, skilled crafts, and scientific and technical fields are increasingly being filled by qualified women. Two examples of nontraditional occupations (that is, jobs formerly labeled For Men Only) are aviation and sports.

One aviation association paid $1 million for a three-year promotion campaign to get 300,000 new pilots into the air by 1980. In the next decade one-third of the pilots now flying will be retiring, and the carriers will require 1,700 new pilots annually. Industry observers say that a large proportion of them will be women.[6] Thanks to recent legislation, women athletes have been guaranteed greater opportunities in sports, from the Little League to the Olympics to the equalized purses in professional golf and tennis to the plum coaching jobs in schools and colleges.[7]

- **Organized Labor.** Although the last twenty years have seen a decline in the proportion of American workers who are organized, there has been a marked increase in the proportion of union members who are women. (In 1976 one union member in five was female.) As their membership ranks swell, talented women unionists are expected to assume union leadership positions — and the money and power that go with them.[8]

- **Government and Political Office.** In the November 1978 elections, women won six lieutenant governor spots and ten secretaries of state. Legislatures throughout the nation boosted their representation to more than 10 percent for the first time in history. Nancy Landon Kassebaum (R.-Kansas) was the only woman senator seated in the Ninety-sixth Congress and the first female not preceded in her seat by a husband. While the number of women in the House of Representatives dropped from eighteen to sixteen, a groundswell of female candidates is predicted in future years because of new delegate selection procedures mandated for the party conventions in 1980. As a result talented women, more than ever before, can aspire to positions with important political influence.[9]

- **Adventure.** The astronaut training program has chosen six women to participate in the space shuttle; Navy women are now permitted to choose active sea duty; the Army and Air Force have opened many military occupational specialties to women; and females can be found climbing the Himalayas, exploring the ocean floor, studying the behavior of apes in the wild, and making scientific discoveries dramatic enough to win the Nobel Prize.[10]

Today we call all these breakthrough women our role models. Rather than the isolated token woman, there are now dozens, hundreds, even thousands of brilliant talented women using their minds, contributing their skills, and clearing a path for all the bright women to come. And for each of these talented women, marriage and motherhood are becoming voluntary options in a full, rich life, rather than a totally consuming manifest destiny. If marriage is no better than institutionalized male supremacy in a home setting, then today's talented woman will either avoid it or reform it. She knows that more than one marriage out of three ends in divorce, that husbands die an average of eight years earlier than their wives, and that marriage is an inadequate economic security blanket if it puts a woman only one man away from welfare.

With the help of the women's movement, many of us have been able to replace myths and false expectations with realistic plans and personal goals based on facts. We know that nine out of ten women work outside the home at some time during their lives[11] and that unless we pursue an education and develop viable skills and a serious career commitment, we will end up at the bottom of the heap. We know that women make up 41 percent of the labor force but average only fifty-seven cents for every dollar earned by their male counterparts and that the earnings gap has actually widened since 1960.[12]

While celebrating all the breakthroughs and role models, we are not blind to the remaining inequities. We know, for example, that:

- On the average, talented women earned five thousand dollars less per year in the professions and seven thousand dollars less per year in management jobs than do comparable men.[13]

- Although the employment of women increased impressively during the last ten years, women workers remain concentrated in a few low-paid occupations. Over half of all women hold clerical, operative, and service jobs.[14]

- Despite the inroads of women into nontraditional fields, except for beginning engineers and industrial chemists, women's salaries are lower than those of men with equal training and experience, at every age, every degree level, in every field, and with every type of employer.[15]

Today's well-informed woman also knows that if she chooses full-time motherhood, she will work a ninety-nine-hour week at no pay, with no sick leave, fringe benefits, or vacations. And the only time anyone will even approximate her true worth is after her death, when the surviving father has to pay about ten thousand dollars a year to try to replace the irreplaceable services she performed for love.[16]

The average woman has sent her last child to school by the time she is thirty-five. With women's greater life expectancy, she is still faced with forty more years of living.[17] She may as well decide now whether she will live those years as Portnoy's mother – vulnerable, desolate, and useless in her "empty nest" – or as her own person – vital and self-sufficient to the end.

Such choices have been enlarged and facilitated by the second wave of feminism that has swept across America during the 1970s. Despite all the ridicule and distortions and with all the setbacks and reactionary hysteria, the years of struggle, street demonstrations, organizing, and lawsuits have borne fruit. We have come a long way? Maybe. Equality for women has been termed a national priority. Tokenism has been roundly condemned. Sexist injustices have been named and catalogued. Statistics abound. Legislation is passed, and more is pending. The courts respond to the call for justice. Women's networks are forming. Affirmative action is opening closed doors. The collective consciousness has been raised. And in all these areas of struggle, gifted and talented women have been in the forefront to speak up for all women.

All that is left to do is the hardest work of all: changing attitudes, changing behavior, and changing values.

Take, for example, "equal pay for equal work." It is a concept that no one argues with, yet few live up to. How can talented women ever receive equal pay with men, even of average ability, if they are only competing with other women in occupations these men shun and demean, such as nursing or typing or housework? How can talented women obtain equal pay for equal work if sex discrimination laws are flouted, preventing these qualified, talented women from gaining access to the work that would make them more equal? The way things are now, equal pay for equal work is a cruel oversimplification and an impossible goal. As long as woman is the "second sex"[18] everything an individual woman does will remain second rate in the marketplace. Talented women will always be worth less if whatever they do is devalued ("Aw, that's just women's work!") while whatever men of lesser ability do is rendered primary. In primitive societies where men are responsible for the weaving and women for the food gathering, it is weaving that is considered the prestigious labor.[19] And in our "advanced" society, where women type and men drive trucks, it is the driver, not the highly skilled typist, who gets top pay and Teamster power. In a patriarchal culture, value is assigned according to the sex of the jobholder rather than according to the inherent worth of the job, and only deep attitudinal change will alter that basic inequity.

What must change, after all, is the very meaning of *woman*. The assumptions that precede every woman into a room. The generalizations that categorize women before they can differentiate themselves. The fact that the prefix *woman* is a pejorative: "Women's logic" is irrational, idiosyncratic: "women's intuition" is quirky guesswork, rather than the sharp insight it would be termed coming from a man; a "woman's prerogative" is to change her mind, a testimony to her supposedly lightheaded, indecisive ways.

If the very meaning of *woman* were free of these cultural impediments, no talented, educated woman would beam proudly when told that she "thinks like a man." There would be no virtue in disavowing one's gender, because there would be dignity and positive associations attached to both sexes. Men and women alike would acknowledge the ill effects of sexist conditioning.

If talented women are to work changes in society, we must be visible, vocal, and strong, strong enough not to crumble when the first man calls us "aggressive" or "strident," strong enough to unlearn the habit of *asking* for justice or waiting passively for equality. Today's talented women understand that freedom and power are never given — they must be sought.

When I graduated from college under the paternal eyes of Pierre Mendès-France and Edward R. Murrow, I had a B.A. in English and American Literature — and a set of sterling silver. With both possessions I and my sister graduates could dream of winning husbands who were doctors, scholars, artists, or revolutionaries. It is my hope that the talented young women today are dreaming of *becoming* the kinds of people that my generation of women wanted to marry.

Notes

1. Matina S. Horner, "Toward an Understanding of Achievement Related Conflicts in Women," *The Journal of Social Issues* 28, no. 2.

2. Cynthia Ozick, "Women and Creativity: The Demise of the Dancing Dog," *Motive* 29 (March–April 1969): 7–16.

3. Quoted in Ruth Rosen, "Sexism in History or, Writing Women's History Is Tricky Business," *Journal of Marriage and the Family,* August 1971, pp. 541–44.

4. *1975 Handbook on Women Workers,* U.S. Department of Labor Bulletin 297, Employment Standards Administration, pp. 92 ff. Also see "Report of the Scientific Manpower Commission," cited in *The New York Times,* November 20, 1978; and "A Perspective on Working Women," *Cunningham and Walsh Corporate Communications* (260 Madison Avenue, New York, N.Y. 10016), September 1978.

5. "A Perspective on Working Women" Also see, *1975 Handbook on*

Women Workers; U.S. Working Women: A Databook, Bureau of Labor Statistics, 1977.

6. Karen Coye, General Aviation Manufacturer's Association, quoted in the *Miami News,* March 27, 1978. Also see, "Women in Nontraditional Jobs: A Conference Guide — Increasing Job Options for Women," Women's Bureau, U.S. Department of Labor.

7. The Amateur Sports Act of 1978; Title IX of the Educational Amendments Act of 1972.

8. Linda H. LeGrande, "Women in Labor Organizations: Their Ranks Are Increasing," *Monthly Labor Review* (U.S. Department of Labor), August 1978.

9. *Women Today* 8, no. 24 (December 11, 1978): 137–39.

10. Ibid.

11. National Commission on Working Women, Center for Women and Work, 1211 Connecticut Avenue, N.W., Washington, D.C. 20036.

12. Ibid.

13. "A Statistical Portrait of Women in the U.S. during the Twentieth Century," Bureau of the Census, U.S. Department of Commerce. p. 49.

14. Ibid.

15. Scientific Manpower Commission report. *Op. Cit.*

16. The Women's Bureau, U.S. Department of Labor. Also, Chase Manhattan Bank study of net worth of housewife/mother services, 1972.

17. The Women's Bureau, U.S. Department of Labor.

18. Simone de Beauvoir, *The Second Sex* (New York: Knopf, 1953).

19. Margaret Mead, *Male and Female* (New York: Morrow, 1975).

33
Business Perspectives for the Gifted

Richard J. Campbell

Successful business organizations must maintain a steady flow of talented individuals into the organization if they are to remain successful. Two key resource needs for many organizations are talented scientists and managers. A prime task for the business organization is to identify and recruit individuals with the potential for leadership in technology and management and to provide an environment that enables the individual to develop and achieve.

Universities provide a substantial portion of today's industrial managers as well as scientists. The experience of the Bell System, the nation's largest private employer, with over 1 percent of the civilian labor force, provides an illustrative case. Each year the Bell System recruits several thousand people for entry management positions. The new recruits fill a wide variety of jobs. Some begin as supervisors of business offices, others supervise construction crews or telephone installers, still others may enter research and development or engineering positions. The new recruits run the gamut from B.A.'s in the liberal arts to Ph.D.'s in the sciences. As their careers unfold, they are expected to provide leadership in their function — the managers eventually may become middle- and upper-level managers; the scientists strive to reach the leading edge of technological development. A recent outstanding example of the latter was the award of the 1978 Nobel Prize in physics to Arno A. Penzias and Robert W. Wilson of Bell Telephone Laboratories, who were cited for their discovery of the background radiation remaining from the "big bang" explosion that gave birth to the universe some 18 billion years ago.

Richard J. Campbell is director of management staffing and development at the American Telephone and Telegraph Company.

COLLEGE SUCCESS AND BUSINESS SUCCESS

Since scientific achievement has been given considerable attention, the remainder of this section will focus on the perhaps less-well-understood nature of the high-achieving general manager. How does one identify managerial talent? How is it nurtured? How does success in management affect other aspects of a person's development? The Bell System has conducted intensive research on these issues for a number of years. While the summary of findings that follows is restricted to studies of managers in *one* large organization, it is based on intensive longitudinal research.

The earliest known research in this area conducted by the Bell System goes back fifty years. This pioneering study examined the relationship between scholarship (academic success in college), campus achievement (class office, editorial board, and so on), and several other factors, and later success in management.[1] The findings showed that both scholarship and campus achievement were clearly related to later success as a Bell System manager.

A similar but expanded study was made of seventeen thousand college graduates in the 1950s. The study confirmed the earlier findings that scholarship was predictive of managerial success. The importance of campus achievement was only partially confirmed. The data showed that only a high level of nonacademic achievement was indicative of success. Those who were campus leaders fared better as managers; mere participation in extracurricular activities bore no relationship to success.

These findings have had an impact on the Bell System's recruiting and selection practices. Recruiters seek out those who graduated in the top half of their class and have demonstrated leadership on or off the campus. Many of these individuals will rise to significant positions of leadership. Since the Bell System relies heavily on promotion from within, it is essential that new people hired into management possess considerable potential for advancement.

MANAGEMENT PROGRESS STUDY

These studies and practices have proven very useful, yet they provide very limited answers to our questions on the nurture of talent. Which leads to a third study. The mystery or ignorance surrounding the nurture of managers prompted a longitudinal study of 274 college graduates who entered the Bell System during 1956–60 shortly after graduation. The study is still underway some twenty years later, and these individuals will be followed until retirement from a managerial career.

This study, called the Management Progress Study, was conceived as a study of development. It began in 1956, when relatively little data were available on the development of adults once they reached their early twenties and departed the halls of academe. The focus was on the characteristics of the men (yes, all 274 were males) when they were hired, changes and stabilities in these characteristics over time, and a search for the causes of these changes or stabilities. Obviously the impact of company policies, practices, and climate on the individual was of particular interest. Although developmental issues were the core of the study, attention was given to how the characteristics of the newly hired men were related to later progress in the organization.

A wealth of information has been collected on each person in the ensuing years. The study design involved measurement of an individual's characteristics by means of attendance at an assessment center shortly after hire, annual interviews with the individual, and periodic interviews with either the individual's supervisor or someone else in the company knowledgeable about the individual's career and experiences. Eight years after hire, the individual attended a second assessment center, where a parallel set of measurements of individual characteristics were obtained. This basic design permitted an evaluation of changes over the eight-year period, plus changes that could be related to experiences and progress in the organization. It should be noted that the study attempted to evaluate developmental changes beyond the work sphere, for example, involvement and satisfaction in the familial and community spheres of life.

SUCCESS IN MANAGEMENT

Let us now take a more comprehensive look at the characteristics that bode well for success in management. The earlier studies indicated that scholarship and demonstrated leadership predicted eventual success, but the focus now shifts to personal characteristics of the individuals.

The assessment center was devised to measure as accurately as possible the abilities, motivation, attitudes, and personality dimensions of the persons involved. They attended the center in groups of twelve and participated in a number of activities. These included ability tests, personality inventories and projective techniques, and individual and group simulations. The simulations confronted the individuals with situations and tasks similar to those they would eventually encounter in the organization. For example, in an individual exercise, they had to handle administrative tasks that normally appear in the in-baskets of managers. They formulated plans, made decisions, wrote memos, and so on.

Another simulation involved groups of six newly hired men taking part in business games. While participating in these exercises, they were observed by the assessment center staff. The staff wrote reports of their observations, then met as a group to rate the men on a number of characteristics based on all of the information available. Finally, judgments were made about each one's potential for advancement.

All of the data concerning individuals in the study has been kept confidential, which avoids the problem of the "self-fulfilling prophecy" or use of the researcher's findings to influence the careers of individuals. Hence, it was possible to relate the measures of personal characteristics to later progress without concern that the study had influenced the natural unfolding of the individual's progress through the organization.

One of the judgments made at the assessment center concerned the individual's potential to advance to middle management within ten years, the target of the recruiting effort. The assessment staff ratings indicated that approximately half of the recruits had good potential for middle management. These judgments were compared with actual progress eight years later. Approximately two-thirds of those judged to have middle-management potential had progressed to middle management; in contrast, only one-third of those judged not to have this potential achieved middle management. In other words, it was possible to predict with considerable accuracy who would be successful based on measures of potential obtained shortly after hire (eight years earlier). A person's characteristics at the time of hire exert a strong influence on his success.

We began with the question of how to identify managerial talent, or which individual characteristics are important for success. The study showed that the following seven factors each had a role to play:

- **Administrative Skills.** A high-potential manager plans and organizes his work effectively, makes decisions willingly, and makes high-quality decisions.
- **Interpersonal Skills.** A high-potential manager makes a forceful and likable impression on others, has good oral presentation skills, leads others to perform, and modifies his behavior when necessary to reach a goal.
- **Intellectual Ability.** A high-potential manager learns readily and has a wide range of interests.
- **Stability of Performance.** A high-potential manager maintains effective work performance under uncertain or unstructured conditions and in the face of stress.
- **Work Motivation.** A high-potential manager finds that satisfac-

tion from work is more important than from other areas of life and wants to do a good job for its own sake.

- **Career Orientation.** A high-potential manager wants to advance significantly more rapidly than his peers, is *not* as concerned as others about having a secure job, and is *unwilling* to delay rewards too long.

- **Dependence on Others.** A high-potential manager is *not* greatly concerned with gaining approval from superiors or peers and is *unwilling* to change life goals in accordance with reality opportunities.

The men who were being studied varied considerably on these dimensions when they joined the company. The study, of course, cannot tell us how these individuals got that way. But it was possible to look at how experiences in the organization affected them and their careers. The situational characteristic that appeared to have the greatest impact on success was job challenge. The measurement of job challenge was based on information contained in the interviews with company representatives. Each individual was assigned a rating for job challenge based on the situations he encountered over the entire eight-year period. The ratings considered such things as the variety and difficulty of tasks, amount of learning required to perform well, and so on. A comparison between the degree of job challenge provided and eventual success showed that 59 percent of those rated high in job challenge reached middle-management positions, whereas only 8 percent of those in the low-job-challenge group made middle management. These findings clearly suggest that the organization can foster development of talent by providing the proper job situation. Recall that one-third of those rated high in potential at the time of hire had not progressed to middle management in eight years. What happened? The concept of job challenge offers a partial explanation. Considering those with good potential, 76 percent of the high-job-challenge group made middle management, whereas only one-third of the low-job-challenge group reached middle management. The message seems clear. Even those with good potential need stimulating job situations to maximize their development and achievement. The Bell System has instituted programs designed to ensure that stimulating jobs will be given to new recruits as a result of these findings.

Success in a business organization is but one way in which talent can be manifested. It is not the individual's whole life. What was occurring in other areas of the individual's life? The interviews with the men yielded rich information. It was possible to make annual ratings of each person's involvement and satisfaction in nine major areas, among them marital-familial, recreational-social, service, and religious-humanism. Perhaps the best way to summarize these extensive data briefly is to present the two hypothetical life-styles that emerged — that of the "enlarger" and that of the "enfolder." These were formulated by J. Rychlak and were described as follows:

> The enlarging life style is oriented toward the goals of innovation, change, and growth. The Enlarger moves away from tradition and places his emphasis on adaptation, self-development, and the extension of influence outward, into the work and community spheres. The Enlarger looks for responsibility on the job and is likely also to seek and achieve a position of influence in service organizations. Self-development activities are stressed; thus Enlargers are likely not only to read, attend the theatre, and keep up with current events, but they take night courses and even respond to the promptings of physical fitness and health food buffs. At the same time, their earlier ties to parents and formal religious practices begin to weaken. The Enlarger finds that his values have changed so dramatically that he no longer enjoys the company of old friends in the neighborhoods of his childhood. Except for a certain nostalgia when he visits parents and relatives, he is not satisfied with the ties of yesteryear. A complete commitment to one religion is similarly less meaningful, particularly since he makes every effort to see alternative points of view and to lend himself to new experiences of all varieties. This does not mean that he breaks off from his church entirely, of course, but that also happens.

> The enfolding life style is oriented to the goals of tradition, stability, and inward strength. Rather than pitching his influence outward, the Enfolder seeks to cultivate and solidify that which invites attention within his more familiar sphere. He is not a "joiner" of social or community organizations, and when he does enter into such activities he rarely seeks an active role. On the other hand, he may be quite active in his church, or in Boy Scout troops or Little League teams that have their origins in the church community. His "good works" are usually tied to his church affiliation. He values parental ties and seeks to keep a relationship active with boyhood chums, if this is at all possible. He may find it quite upsetting to leave the home town area, even if the move portends job advancement. In a new locale he is likely to have considerable difficulty feeling "at home." He is not likely to attend night college or to study on his own time unless he feels assured that his effort will bring direct job rewards. He may begin a self-improvement program, but his heart is seldom in it, or he begins it later than the next man and usually stops it sooner. He likes to settle into a job and see it through to a full conclusion, getting great satisfaction from a job well done. He is not awed by fads and usually senses that not enough people today "count their blessings." He forms close attachments to a small circle of friends, and most of his socializing is done with relatives. Status considerations sometime embarrass him, and he

> values informality, sincerity, and genuineness in human affairs.
> The enlarging and enfolding life styles are only hypothetical types, but they serve to sum up many of the observations encompassed in the numerous interviews.[2]

The findings of the Management Progress Study indicate that development continues well beyond an individual's twentieth year of life. Equally important is the finding that the personal characteristics an individual brings at the time of entry into a business organization strongly influence his subsequent career and life.

Do the findings have implications for development of talent in the earlier years of life? The results are very suggestive, at least. The amount that can be accomplished in the critical task of fostering talent by a significant other, be it paent or mentor, is a challenge to the involvement and ingenuity of the significant other.

One final comment is necessary. All of the data presented were derived from studies of men. More recent studies of women in the Bell System indicate that the same characteristics are predictive of success for men and women. Studies of college-graduate women indicate levels of potential comparable to those of men. The similarities are more striking than the differences. Managerial talent appears to be pan-sexual; fostering of talent must be equally so.

Notes

1. D. S. Bridgman; "Success in College and Business," *Personnel Journal* 9, no. 1 (June 1930).
2. Douglas Bray, Richard Campbell and Donald Grant, *Formative Years in Business: A Long Term AT&T Study of Managerial Lives* (New York: Wiley-Interscience, 1974), pp. 103–104.

Afterword
About the Association

Anne E. Impellizzeri and Marjorie L. Craig

The American Association for Gifted Children was founded in 1946 by two friends, Miss Pauline Brooks Williamson and Dr. Ruth Strang, who had long worked together in the field of education and felt that the gifted were the most neglected group in our society. Miss Williamson had always been interested in helping children and young people grow to their fullest potential. She had taught in all grades of elementary and high school and in college and had been a rural supervisor for health, employed jointly by the State Department of Education and the State Department of Health in Virginia. She recognized only too well the plight and unhappiness of gifted and talented children. Later, as chief of the School Health Bureau of the Metropolitan Life Insurance Company, she directed studies on practicable school health programs and teacher education, emphasizing children's individual differences, their needs and abilities.

Dr. Ruth Strang was a professor of education at Teachers College, Columbia University, for many years and was well known as a great friend of children. She was a prolific writer. Her many books and articles are widely read by teachers and parents all over the world. Her thoughtful studies of individual children opened many doors to unexpected pleasures and skills in reading and writing for them. She was especially sensitive to the needs of gifted children as she worked with them, their families, and their teachers.

Anne E. Impellizzeri is president of the American Association for Gifted Children and Vice President, Corporate Social Responsibility, Metropolitan Life Insurance Company.

Marjorie L. Craig is vice-president and executive director of the American Association for Gifted Children.

It was inevitable that these two friends would come together to help the gifted. They were long-time believers in working "two by two" and in "teams," and they felt that people who were friends and who complemented each other could accomplish the most in working for children. The American Association for Gifted Children was established, and Miss Williamson and Dr. Strang found enthusiastic support among their associates and friends who were interested in the gifted. They represented a variety of professions, including university professors, businesspeople, lawyers, physicians, parents, writers, actors, economists, authors, and many others.

Dr. Harold Clark, a well-known professor of education at Teachers College, Columbia University, noted economist and author, was elected the association's first president and served in this capacity until he was elected chairman of the board in 1975. Other founders of the association included Dr. Carson Ryan, head of the Department of Education at the University of North Carolina and long a leader in the mental health field; Sally Lucas Jean, a giant in the area of public health education; Dr. George Wheatley, former president of the Academy of Pediatrics and well-known public health expert; Joseph Collins, Esq., and Churchill Rogers, Esq., both lawyers of national renown; and Charles Coburn, never-to-be-forgotten actor and lecturer. We pay homage to the thoughtful dedication of these and many other of the initial members.

A special tribute is made to Dr. Paul Witty, professor of education at Northwestern University in Evanston, Illinois, who served the association for many years as vice-president and editor. In the words of Dr. Walter Barbe,* his long-time friend and associate,

> Dr. Paul Witty added appreciably to our understanding of children with varying intellectual levels from different social and racial backgrounds. His research and publications in the area of gifted children began in Kansas in the 1920s and spanned the next half century. As Editor of *The Gifted Child*, the first book published by the American Association for Gifted Children, Dr. Witty contributed to the awakening of a long dormant interest in gifted children and provided insight and direction to assure that our nation did not neglect what has been referred to as its "greatest natural resource."

The American Association for Gifted Children has encouraged parents, teachers, community leaders, and the children themselves to reach out and provide the best for young gifted people. It continues its efforts through such activities as the preparation and distribution of books, pamphlets, and other literature. The most recent book, *On Being Gifted,* is the first book written by gifted students on the topic of what it is like to be gifted.

*Editor, *Highlights,* Honesdale, Pennsylvania.

The association receives thousands of inquiries from a great variety of people concerned with the growth and development of the gifted. Staff members assist through correspondence and conferences and by referrals to other educational resources. Scholarships are available to qualified students planning to pursue a career in business, mathematics, or science.

The American Association for Gifted Children works with other groups and organizations in the development of special activities for the gifted. For many years a joint committee with the American Library Association has developed information to help librarians work with young people and their families. Cooperation continues with various organizations in the arts and sciences and on special projects such as career education, delinquency, health, and the Friend to Friend program.

The association's administrative consultant is Mrs. Gail Robinson, who is ably assisted by Mrs. Stacey Riddell in coordinating the work of the organization. The board of directors and members of the association contribute to the development of the program through committee activities and special meetings.

The American Association for Gifted Children recognizes the great need for widespread awareness of the importance of teamwork among the family, the school, and the community on behalf of the gifted. It also encourages individuals to accept more responsibility for educating themselves through independent study.

The association welcomes assistance from those who nurture the gifted and wish to contribute their knowledge and support.

Appendix
Summer Challenges

Gail B. Robinson

The summer season is an ideal time for gifted children to become involved with new challenges. The list that follows is only a sample of the kinds of experiences available:

CAMPS AND TRAVEL/TOURING

In some areas, there are day camps as well as sleepaway camps available for gifted children. These camps frequently specialize in music, art, dance, or science. For more information, consult the office of the American Camping Association in your area. Several teen tours are available for travel here in the United States and also abroad. The experience of traveling with one's peers can be exciting and challenging. In addition, work camps are available. Contact the American Field Service for more information.

STUDY

Many colleges and universities offer summer courses to high school students. Some institutions include room and board, while others accommodate only commuting students. This can be a wonderful experience both educationally and socially for many young people. Contact individual institutions or your school guidance counselor for more information.

VOLUNTEER WORK

In every community there is a need for the services of volunteers. Hospitals, nursing homes, senior citizens' groups, churches, synagogues, community organizations, day camps, and summer school programs usually welcome help from volunteers. Contact these institutions in your local area to find out where your services will be most welcome. Other possibilities include offering music or art lessons to young children in your neighborhood or planning and supervising children's parties.

APPRENTICESHIPS/MENTORSHIPS

If your child is fortunate enough to be able to focus in on one particular area, find someone who has some expertise in that same area. Perhaps your child can be a summer apprentice. Perhaps your child has an area of expertise that he or she can share with others. Can your child tutor a younger child in reading or math? Is your child fluent in a foreign language? Does he or she play an instrument well or possess proficiency in chess or bridge? If so, how about helping the child share that knowledge with others? If your home is not suitable for instruction, check with your local library to see if space is available for mini-courses.

EMPLOYMENT

Not every young person need look for a job in the local variety store. Search your community carefully for employment opportunities. For example, one high school student interested in art and design got a summer job doing window displays for local shops. Opportunities exist for young people to work on farms also (4-H organizations, for example). Other opportunities include working in a newspaper office or at a local television or radio station. There are also many camps looking for art, music, dance, and science specialists as well as general counselors. Self-employment is a wonderful experience for some young people. One enterprising student designed, made, and sold silver jewelry, while several others formed a business providing services such as dog walking, house sitting, house painting, and so on.

EARTHWATCH

EARTHWATCH is a clearinghouse that matches people's interests with projects that need interested people. Scientists and research scholars need funds and volunteers to mobilize their expeditions. EARTH-WATCH meets these needs by offering the opportunity to join in research projects all over the world. Sponsors include the U.S. Department of Education and State Consultants for the Gifted and Talented. For more information, contact EARTHWATCH, 10 Juniper Road, Box 127, Belmont, Massachusetts 02178.

JUNIOR ACHIEVEMENT

Junior Achievement is the nation's oldest economic program. It teaches high school students the principles of the American free enterprise system by helping them run their own small businesses. For additional information, contact Junior Achievement, Inc., 500 Summer, Stamford, Connecticut 06901.

INTERNSHIPS

For the older adolescent, internships may be available in the office of local legislators. The student who is interested in government or politics will find this a challenging and worthwhile opportunity. However, few are available.

SERVICE CLUBS

All service clubs sponsor special programs based on their special interests. Some programs include helping senior citizens in convalescent homes, camps or local offices. Contact service clubs such as the Lions, Kiwanis, and so forth in your hometown.

SCOUTING MOVEMENT

Frequently the Boy Scouts and the Girl Scouts have special summer programs that may include service work, travel, or paid employment. To find out just what is available, contact the scouting office responsible in your area.

An Annotated Listing of Selected References on the Gifted and Talented

Prepared by Gail B. Robinson

This reference list has been compiled with the needs of parents in mind. Additional books and articles for all those concerned with the development and education of the gifted and talented can be found at the conclusion of individual essays.

American Association of Gifted Children. *On Being Gifted*. New York: Walker and Company, 1978.
The result of the National Student Symposium on the Education of the Gifted and Talented. It is written by gifted and talented high school students from all parts of the United States and is recommended for parents, teachers, and gifted and talented young people.

Aschner, Mary Jane, and Bish, Charles E., eds. *Productive Thinking in Education*. Washington, D.C.: National Education Association, 1968.
This book is the result of papers presented at two conferences on productive thinking. It is divided into four sections: (1) Intelligence and Its Development; (2) Motivation, Personality, and Productive Thinking; (3) Assessment of Productive Thinking; and (4) Education for Productive Thinking.

Barbe, Walter B., and Renzulli, Joseph S. eds., *Psychology and Education of the Gifted*. New York: Halsted Press, 1975.
A collection of papers and articles by outstanding leaders in the education of the gifted. Authors include Terman, Witty, Gallagher, Hollingsworth, Barbe, Torrance, and many others.

Bloom, Benjamin, ed. *Taxonomy of Educational Objectives, Handbook I: Cognitive Domain*. New York: D. McKay, 1956.
This handbook presents and describes six intellectual processes: knowledge, comprehension, application, analysis, synthesis, and evaluation. It is helpful to those responsible for curriculum planning for the gifted.

Coffey, Kay, et al. *Parentspeak on Gifted and Talented Children*. Ventura, Calif.: National/State Leadership Training Institute on the Gifted and Talented, 1976.

A handbook, written by six parents, that discusses their involvement with the gifted. It includes ways to establish parents' groups with samples of forms, guidelines, and so on.

Delp, Jeanne L., and Martinson, Ruth A. *The Gifted and Talented: A Handbook for Parents*. Ventura, Calif.: National/State Leadership Training Institute on the Gifted and Talented, 1975.

This handbook discusses identification, the role of parent organizations, and several other topics.

Durr, William K. *The Gifted Student*. New York: Oxford University Press, 1964.

A book that emphasizes educational techniques and school programs to help gifted students develop their abilities. Suggestions are also made for parents, administrators, and guidance personnel to help them carry out their own responsibilities for the education of the gifted.

Fortna, Richard O., and Boston, Bruce O. *Testing the Gifted Child: An Interpretation in Lay Language*. Reston, Va.: The Council for Exceptional Children, 1976.

A description of tests frequently used to identify children for gifted and talented programs. Included, among others, are the Wechsler Intelligence Scale for Children—Revised, the Stanford Achievement Test: Intermediate Level II Battery and the Torrance Tests of Creative Thinking.

Freeman, Darlene, and Stuart, Virginia. *Resources for Gifted Children in the New York Area*. New York: Trillium Press, 1979.

This is an excellent book describing resources in the New York, New Jersey, and Connecticut area. It includes sections on selected activities; recommended reading; games, puzzles, and projects; curriculum materials and books for teachers; schools and school programs; and programs and courses in the education of the gifted and talented. Parents and teachers will find this book extremely useful.

French, Joseph L. *Educating the Gifted: A Book of Readings*. New York: Holt, Rinehart & Winston, 1964.

A thorough discussion of such topics as identification, acceleration, enrichment, guidance, underachievement, and creativity of the gifted.

Gallagher, James J. *Teaching the Gifted Child*. Boston: Allyn & Bacon, 1975.

The author covers many aspects of gifted education. Subjects are under five major headings: (1) The Gifted Child and His School; (2) Content Modification for the Gifted; (3) Stimulation of Productive Thinking; (4) Administration and Training for the Gifted; and (5) Special Problem Areas.

Getzels, Jacob W., and Jackson, Phillip W. *Creativity and Intelligence*. New York: John Wiley, 1962.

Explores the relationship between creativity and intelligence. Many case studies are given.

Gibson, Joy, and Chennells, Prue. *Gifted Children: Looking to Their Future*. London: Latimer New Dimensions, Ltd., 1976.

A collection of the papers given at the first World Conference for Gifted Children, held in London in 1975. Included is a section called "What My Country Does for Gifted Children," containing contributions from twenty-four countries.

Ginsberg, Gina, and Harrison, Charles H. *How to Help Your Gifted Child — A Handbook for Parents and Teachers.* New York: Monarch Press, 1977.
A "how-to" book for parents of gifted children covering such topics as how to understand their children and how to organize parent groups in order to provide enrichment for these children.

Goertzel, Victor, and Goertzel, Mildred. *Cradles of Eminence.* Boston: Little, Brown, 1962.
A study of the parenting, environment, and education of several hundred successful men and women. Topics discussed are their environments, where they came from, and how they react to teachers and school.

Gowan, John C., and Torrance, E. Paul. *Educating the Ablest.* Itaska, Ill.: Peacock Press, 1971.
A book of readings by various contributors dealing with general aspects of the gifted child. Some topics included are characteristics, programming, curriculum, guidance, parents, creativity, and mental health.

Grost, Audrey. *Genius in Residence.* Englewood Cliffs, N.J.: Prentice-Hall, 1970.
The mother of Mike Grost, who has been identified as highly gifted, discusses his life from birth until his graduation from college.

Guilford, J. P. *Intelligence, Creativity and Their Educational Implications.* San Diego: Robert R. Knapp, 1968.
Guilford discusses his theory of intellect and the qualities of creativity as they pertain to education.

Hildreth, Gertrude H. *Introduction to the Gifted.* New York: McGraw-Hill, 1976.
This book contains a discussion of gifted children and their traits, the historical setting, and educational provisions for gifted children. There are chapters on the gifted student through college and also a chapter on the teachers of the gifted.

Hoyt, Kenneth B., and Hebeler, Jean R., eds. *Career Education for Gifted and Talented Students.* Salt Lake City: Olympus Publishing Company, 1974.
The product of the National Seminars on Career Education for Gifted and Talented Students held in Maryland in 1972 and 1973. It is divided into five general discussion areas: (1) Introduction to Career Education and to the Gifted and Talented; (2) Basic Background Papers; (3) Value Considerations in Career Education for the Gifted and Talented Students; (4) Exemplary Programs in Career Education for the Gifted and Talented; and (5) Implications for Curriculum Guidelines in Career Education for Gifted and Talented Students.

Kaplan, Sandra. *Providing Programs for the Gifted and Talented: A Handbook.* Ventura, Calif.: National/State Leadership Training Institute on the Gifted and Talented, 1973.
A complete handbook, invaluable for designing and implementing a program for the gifted, that includes a section on curriculum development.

Kaufmann, Felice. *Your Gifted Child and You.* Reston, Va.: The Council for Exceptional Children, 1976.

Primarily for parents, this book describes the identification, creativity, and social problems of the gifted. Included is information about parent groups, lists of resources, and a bibliography.

Martinson, Ruth A. *The Identification of the Gifted and Talented.* Ventura, Calif.: National/State Leadership Training Institute on the Gifted and Talented, 1973.

A discussion of screening and identification of the gifted, with special emphasis on the need for early identification. Included are instruments helpful in screening and identification.

Meeker, Mary N. *The Structure of Intellect: Its Interpretation and Uses.* Columbus, Ohio: Chas. E. Merrill, 1969.

This book interprets an intricate psychological model of intelligence to be used within the existing framework of curriculum.

Passow, A. Harry, ed. *The Gifted and the Talented: Their Education and Development.* Chicago: The National Society for the Study of Education, 1979.

A practical and important book on education, identification, development, and programs for the gifted and talented. The chapters in this book are articles written by distinguished people in gifted education.

Renzulli, Joseph S. *A Guidebook for Evaluating Programs for the Gifted and Talented.* Ventura, Calif.: National/State Leadership Training Institute on the Gifted and Talented, 1976.

A guidebook that discusses the role of evaluation as well as the basic design of an evaluation program. Sample evaluations are included.

Rice, Joseph P. *The Gifted: Developing Total Talent.* Springfield, Ill.: Chas. C. Thomas, 1970.

The emphasis is on identification of the gifted student, but the book also includes information on the staff and teacher qualifications necessary for a good program for the gifted.

Stanley, Julian C.; George, William C.; and Solano, Cecilia H., eds. *The Gifted and the Creative: A Fifty Year Perspective.* Baltimore: John Hopkins University Press, 1977.

Discussions on the history of gifted-child education, several approaches to creativity, and a longitudinal study of mathematically precocious youth.

Strang, Ruth. *Helping Your Gifted Child.* New York: Dutton, 1960.

The author discusses the subject of the gifted child from early childhood through adolescence. She also discusses the role of the parent in the education of the gifted child.

Strang, Ruth. *Guideposts.* New York: American Assocation for Gifted Children.

A collection of four guideposts written for parents, teachers, administrators, and gifted children. They give sound advice and are helpful to anyone interested in gifted education.

Torrance, E. Paul. *Guiding Creative Talent.* Englewood Cliffs, N.J.: Prentice-Hall, 1962.

A discussion of several ways of meeting the needs of the gifted. It covers such topics as development, characteristics, and repression of creativity, among others.

Vail, Priscilla. *The World of the Gifted Child.* New York: Walker and Company, 1979.

General information concerning the gifted child. It deals with recognizing gifted children and meeting their needs. A number of enriching activities are included.

Wallach, M. A., and Wing, Cliff W. II. *The Talented Student.* New York: Holt, Rinehart & Winston, 1969.

A short work that presents two basic themes on talented students and gives background on accomplishments outside of the classroom. Some good case studies are included.

Williams, Frank E. *Classroom Ideas for Encouraging Thinking and Feeling.* Buffalo: D.O.K. Publishers, 1970.

Hundreds of ideas and activities to be used with all grade levels.

Witty, Paul A., ed. *The Gifted Child.* New York: Heath, 1951.

Although written more than twenty-five years ago, much of what is discussed in this book is as pertinent today as it was in 1951, such as the problem of educating the gifted child. Included are discussions of major research in identifying and caring for these children.

Witty, Paul A., ed. *Reading for the Gifted and the Creative Student.* Newark: International Reading Association, 1971.

Program suggestions applicable to the reading characteristics of gifted children. A chapter is included on family practices that may bring about an early interest in reading.

Resources

American Association for Gifted Children
15 Gramercy Park
New York, New York 10003

Council for Exceptional Children
TAG Division
1920 Association Drive
Reston, Virginia 22091

National Association for Gifted Children
217 Gregory Drive
Hot Springs, Arkansas 71901

National/State Leadership Training Institute
Ventura County Superintendent of Schools
County Office Building
535 East Main Street
Ventura, California 93001

U.S. Department of Education
Office for Gifted and Talented
400 Maryland Avenue, S.W.
Washington, D.C. 20202

World Council for Gifted and Talented Children
Box 218, Teachers College, Columbia University
New York, New York 10027

Each state has an individual who is responsible for working with gifted
and talented programs. For information relating to your state activities,
write your state department of education in your state capitol.

Index